"A mesmerizing, disorienting journey into the afterlife."

—*The A.V. Club*

"A life-after-death mystery with a *Sandman*-esque edge. EUTHANAUTS is the type of comic that makes you jealous you didn't do it first."

—*Rob Williams (Unfollow, Judge Dredd)*

"Tini Howard's ear for dialogue and personal connection give the story depth. Nick Robles' beautiful art truly completes the book."

—*AiPT*

"A perfect blend of the pathos and the fanciful... expertly rendered."

—*Comic Crusaders*

"Exhilarating debut of one of the year's finest."

—*DoomRocket*

"Something extraordinary..."

—*The Brazen Bull*

"A gorgeous comic..."

—*Multiversity Comics*

"A beautiful and haunting look at the dead and the dying. EUTHANAUTS is the complete package."

—*CBR*

Eutha

Written by **Tini Howard**
Art & Cover by **Nick Robles**
Color by **Eva de la Cruz**
and **Nick Robles** (issue #1, issue #5 pages 16-21)
Letters by **Aditya Bidikar** (issues 1 & 2) and **Neil Uyetake**

Editorial Assistance by **Chase Marotz** and **Megan Brown**
Edited by **Shelly Bond**
Logo and Publication Design by **Philip Bond**

EUTHANAUTS is created by Howard & Robles

BLACK CROWN HQ
Shelly Bond, Editor • **Chase Marotz and Megan Brown,** Editorial Assistants • **Arlene Lo,** Proofreader
Philip Bond, logo, publication design and general dogsbody • **Greg Goldstein, President** & Publisher

BLACK CROWN is a fully functioning curation operation based in Los Angeles by way of IDW Publishing.
Accept No Substitutes!

For international rights, contact **licensing@idwpublishing.com**

Greg Goldstein, President & Publisher • **John Barber**, Editor-in-Chief • **Robbie Robbins**, EVP/Sr. Art Director • **Cara Morrison**, Chief Financial Officer •
Matthew Ruzicka, Chief Accounting Officer • **Anita Frazier**, SVP of Sales and Marketing • **David Hedgecock**, Associate Publisher • **Jerry Bennington**, VP of
New Product Development • **Lorelei Bunjes**, VP of Digital Services • **Justin Eisinger**, Editorial Director, Graphic Novels and Collections • **Eric Moss**, Sr. Director,
Licensing & Business Development
Ted Adams, IDW Founder

www.IDWPUBLISHING.com

Facebook: **facebook.com/idwpublishing** • Twitter: **@idwpublishing** • YouTube: **youtube.com/idwpublishing**
Tumblr: **tumblr.idwpublishing.com** • Instagram: **instagram.com/idwpublishing**

Introduction by Scott Snyder

blackcrown.pub

INTRODUCTION
BY SCOTT SNYDER

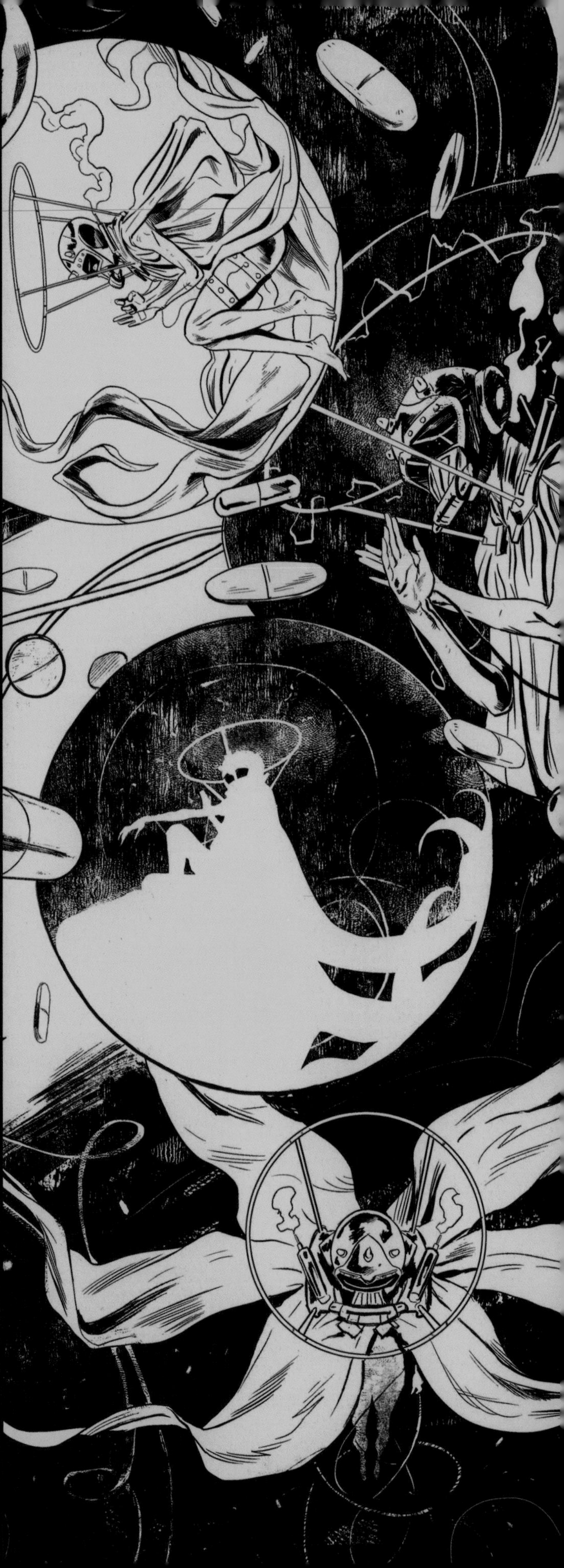

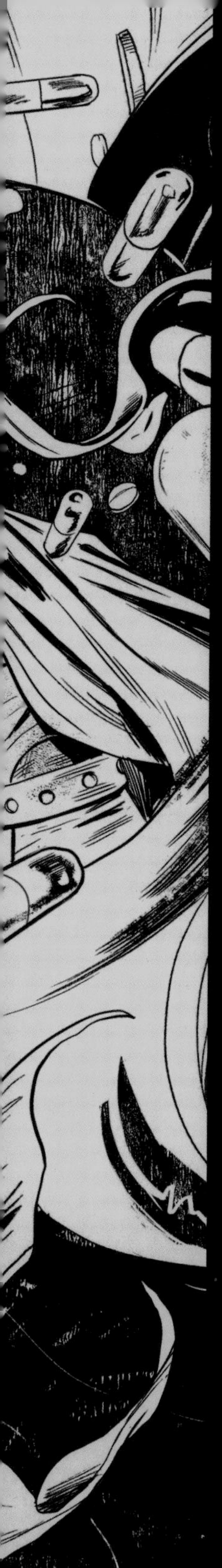

A confession: I have always been obsessed with death. It started early, but it really took off when I was 'round ten or eleven. We had a video store on the Lower East Side where I grew up that wouldn't rent R-rated movies to kids but would deliver them if you called. It was a neighborhood secret shared among kids, and together, we watched nearly every '80s slasher flick way too young. One day I rented *Night of the Living Dead*. When the movie arrived I was deeply disappointed that it was black and white. So old! No way it'd be scary. But as the film progressed, and hero after hero died, a novel kind of dread crept over me — a bone-deep dread. Because what the movie suggested, with its zombies marching slowly, inevitably in wave after wave toward your house — zombies who might have been your brother, your daughter, now merciless, mindless — was that death was inescapable and relentless and terrifyingly physical. Death wasn't heaven or ghosts. It was meat and bone and decay and leaves in your eyes. Dirt in your teeth. I understood it. It was plain and unstoppable and from then on, I couldn't stop thinking about it. I saw therapists, I tried all sorts of things. For a long time after — years — I had trouble staving off thoughts about death, dying, even in the happiest moments of my own life. Thoughts like, but how long will these people be around? All this will end soon... and so on. I started writing horror as a way of dealing with this obsession, and yet... as violent or morbid as my stories sometimes were, I never directly addressed death itself, or my fear of it — at least not for many years.

The turning point came when my wife and I had our first child. It was days after he was born and I was holding him in the hospital — that striped blanket and knit hat... The doctor was explaining to me that my son couldn't see very far yet, if at all. And I remember absorbing this, and nodding, and then its hitting me how little he'd be able to understand for weeks, months, years...? And silly as it sounds, it set off a direction of thought that just kept on... for actual years, he won't be able to understand time, or geography; he won't understand that there are other planets... his mind will literally be incapable of understanding these things. Out the window was a pigeon. This bird had no idea it was on the windowsill of a room in which my son was born, or who I was, or the fact that we were in New York, or that New York was a state in a country on planet Earth... And if I looked at every animal, every creature and acknowledged the limitations of its comprehension, physical and intellectual, then why did I never acknowledge my own? Not in a prosaic way, but in the grandest, most humbling way? Why did I not see that any understanding I had of death — the most unknowable of phenomena — must be limited? I can understand dirt-in-the-teeth dead. But I can understand heaven and ghosts, so it must be something more. So WHAT then? What? And from then on, I started writing about death, reading about it, not out of terror (though the terror will always be there) but out of wonder.

What I'm getting at with all this — and apologies for the long lead-in — is that books about death are very, very personal for me. I take them to heart, and don't judge them lightly. For me, any book about death has to address both sides: the terror of what we expect it to be, and the wonder of the way in which it resists that expectation. And this book, EUTHANAUTS, the one you're holding in your hands, does that in spades.

What Tini and Nick have done here is truly something special: they've created a series that embraces all the terrors and wonders of death as the great unknown, the great mystery, in a way that makes death a frontier you want to explore. I could talk about the characters, and how relatable and compellingly complicated they are, Thalia Rosewood in her obsession with death, her inability to look away. Or the mysterious Dr. Mercy Wolfe in her tragic and pathological determination to understand and map the afterlife. I could talk about the plot, how Tini yanks you in by page 11 — with twists that made me gasp and smile — and doesn't stop. How scene after scene pulled me forward, not unlike one of Dr. Wolfe's tethers. I could talk about the art, how Nick has outdone himself here; how he manages to create two distinct worlds that slowly, intrinsically bleed together... How the art is generous, intimate and yet wildly dreamy and expressive... so real and unreal. I could talk about the ideas contained here, which are huge and rich and twisted, or the story design, which feels vast and mythological...

But what I'll talk about — what I'll end on — is just to applaud the book for what it is in spirit: a story that will make you WANT to look at death, want to explore it for what it truly is — the most terrifying, wondrous frontier of all.

"WE'RE TIED TOGETHER
ACROSS THE LIVING
AND THE DEAD,
YOU AND ME."

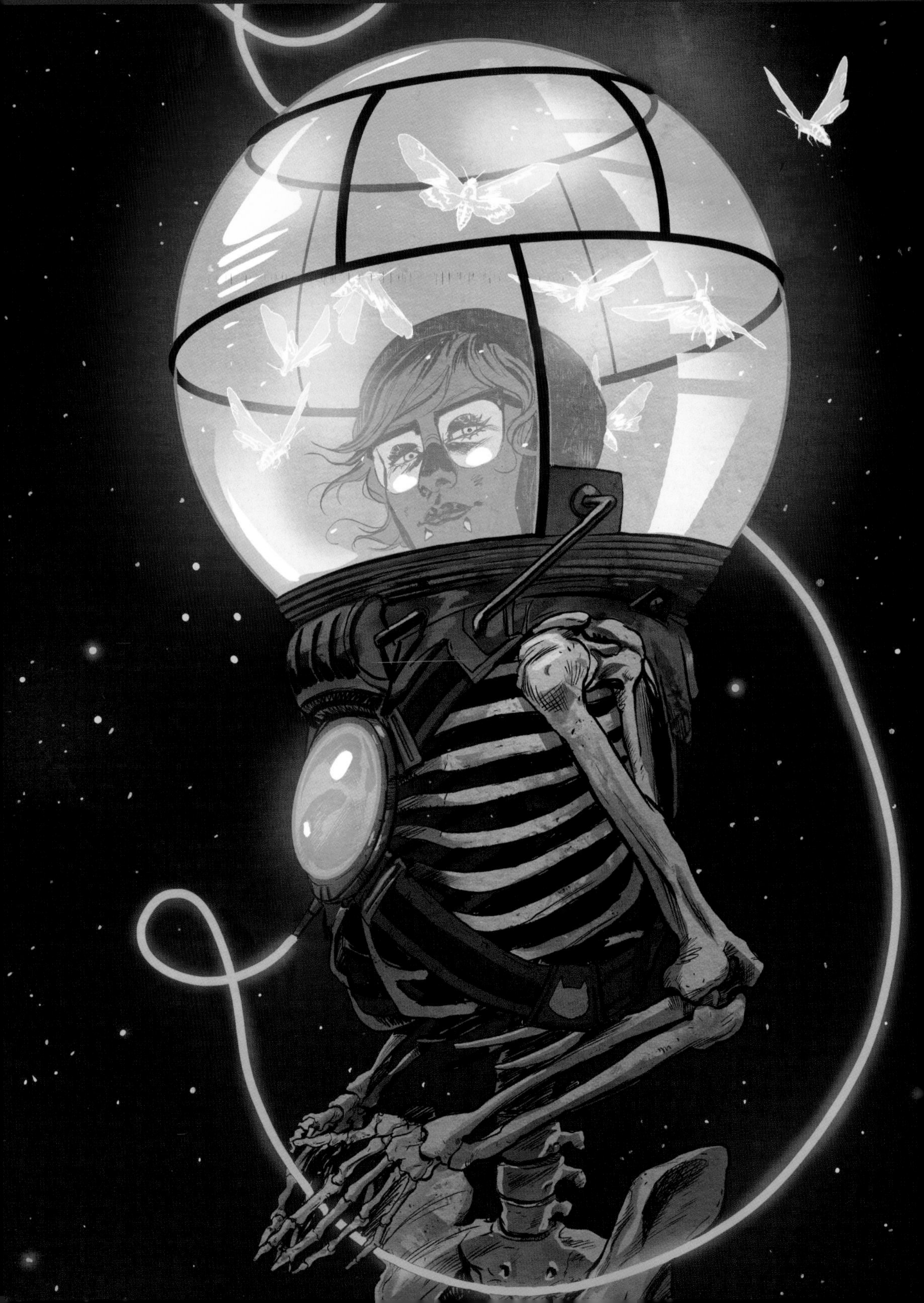

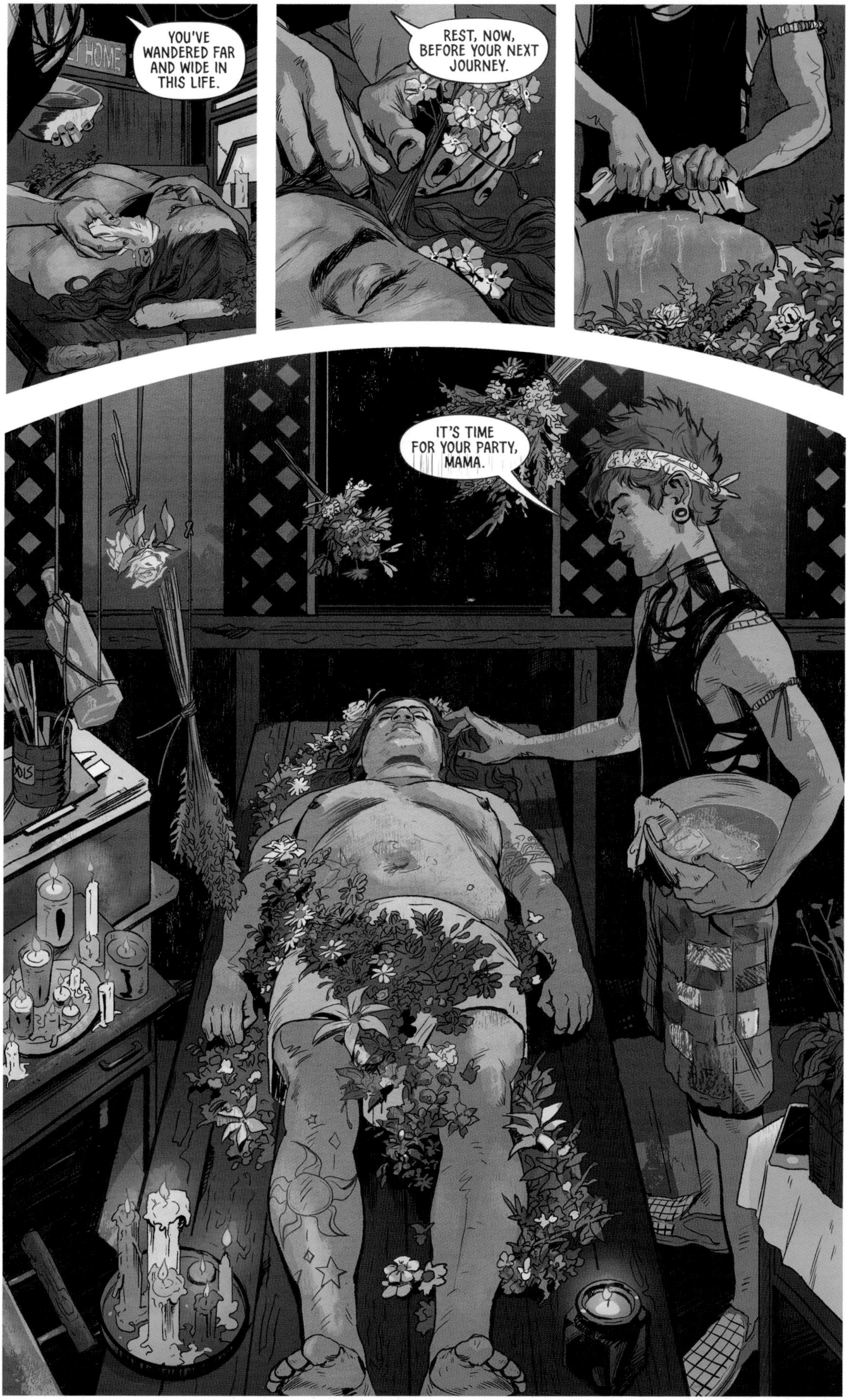

YOU'VE WANDERED FAR AND WIDE IN THIS LIFE.
REST, NOW, BEFORE YOUR NEXT JOURNEY.
IT'S TIME FOR YOUR PARTY, MAMA.

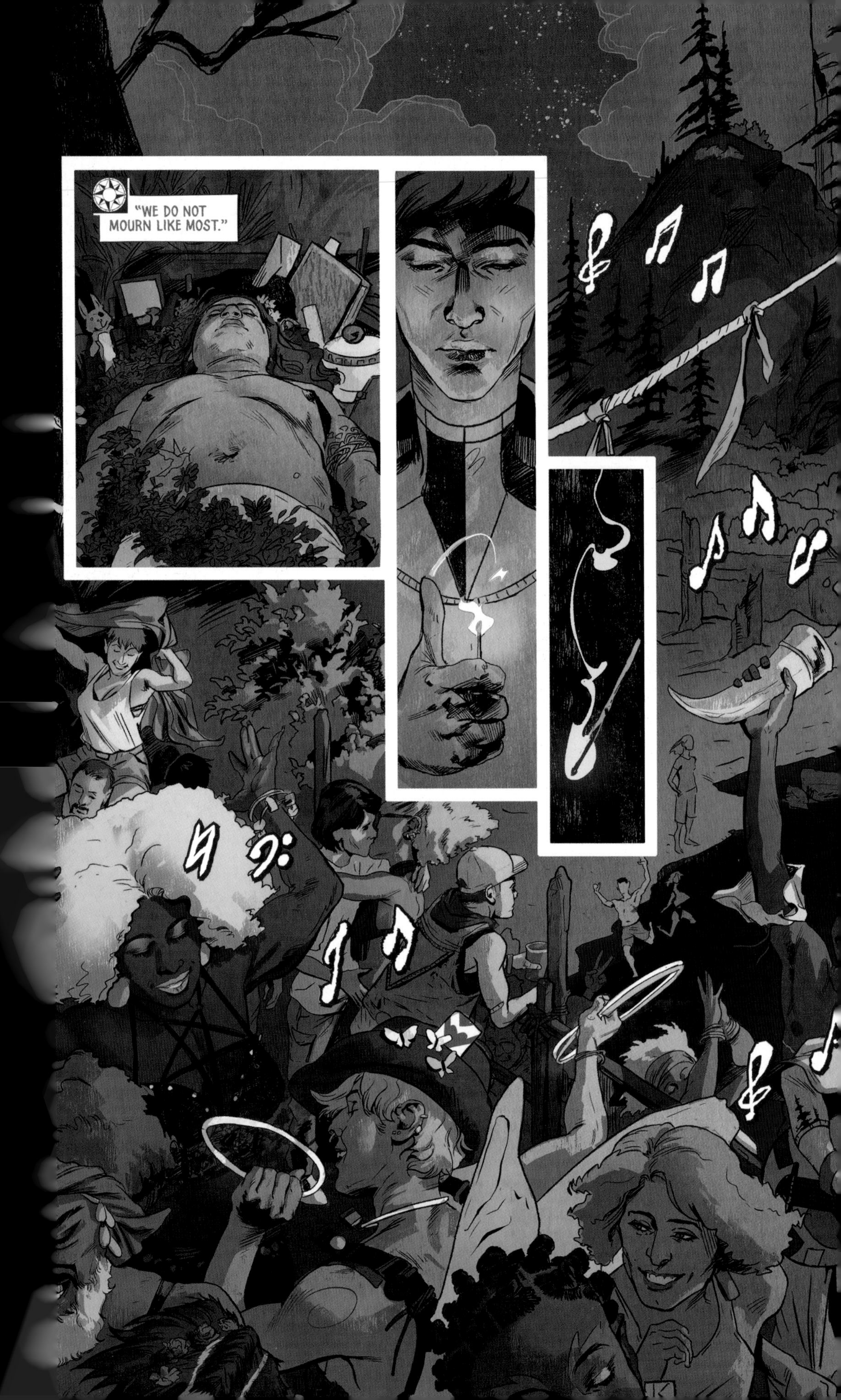
"WE DO NOT
MOURN LIKE MOST."

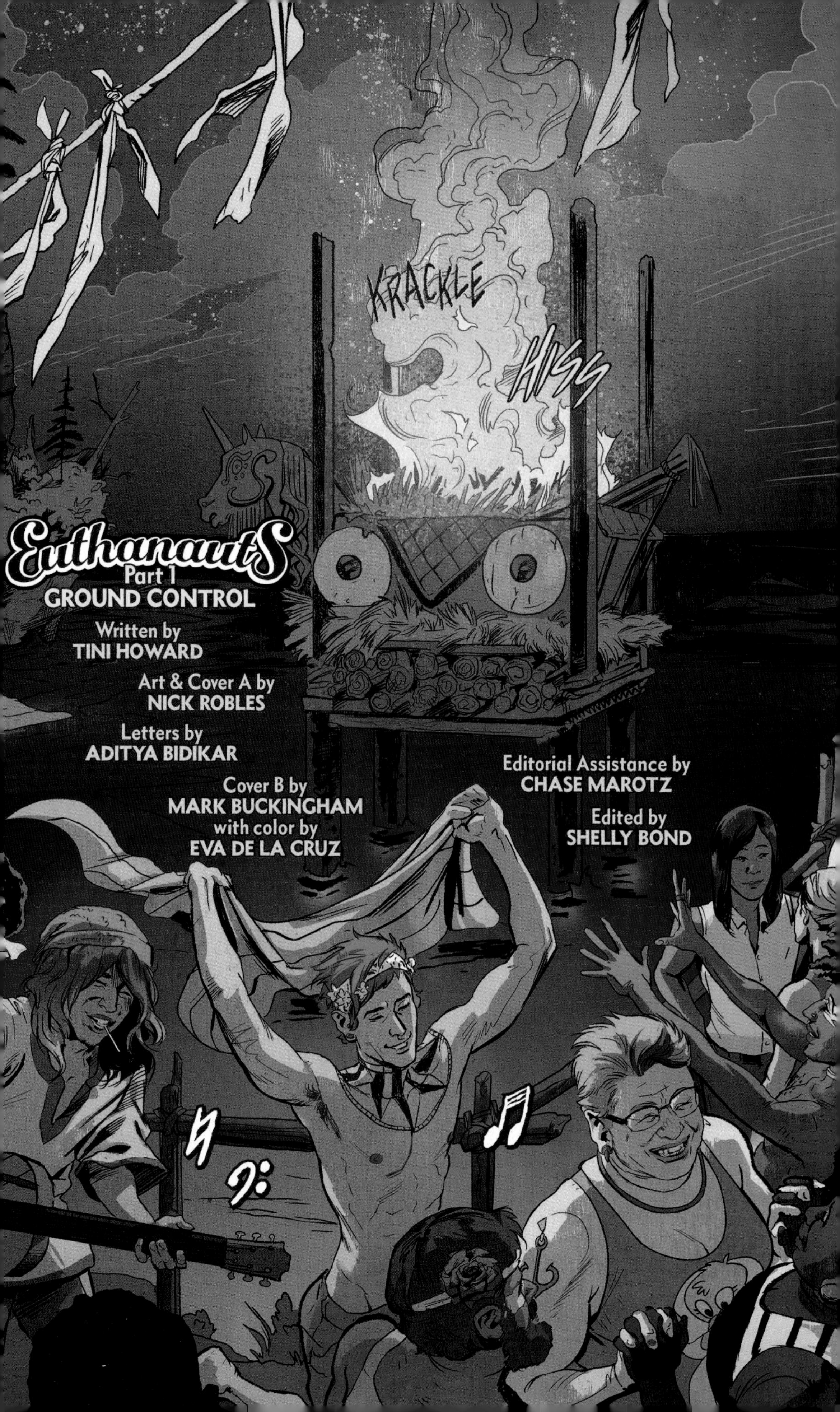
KRACKLE
HISS
Euthanauts
Part 1
GROUND CONTROL
Written by
TINI HOWARD
Art & Cover A by
NICK ROBLES
Letters by
ADITYA BIDIKAR
Cover B by
MARK BUCKINGHAM
with color by
EVA DE LA CRUZ
Editorial Assistance by
CHASE MAROTZ
Edited by
SHELLY BOND

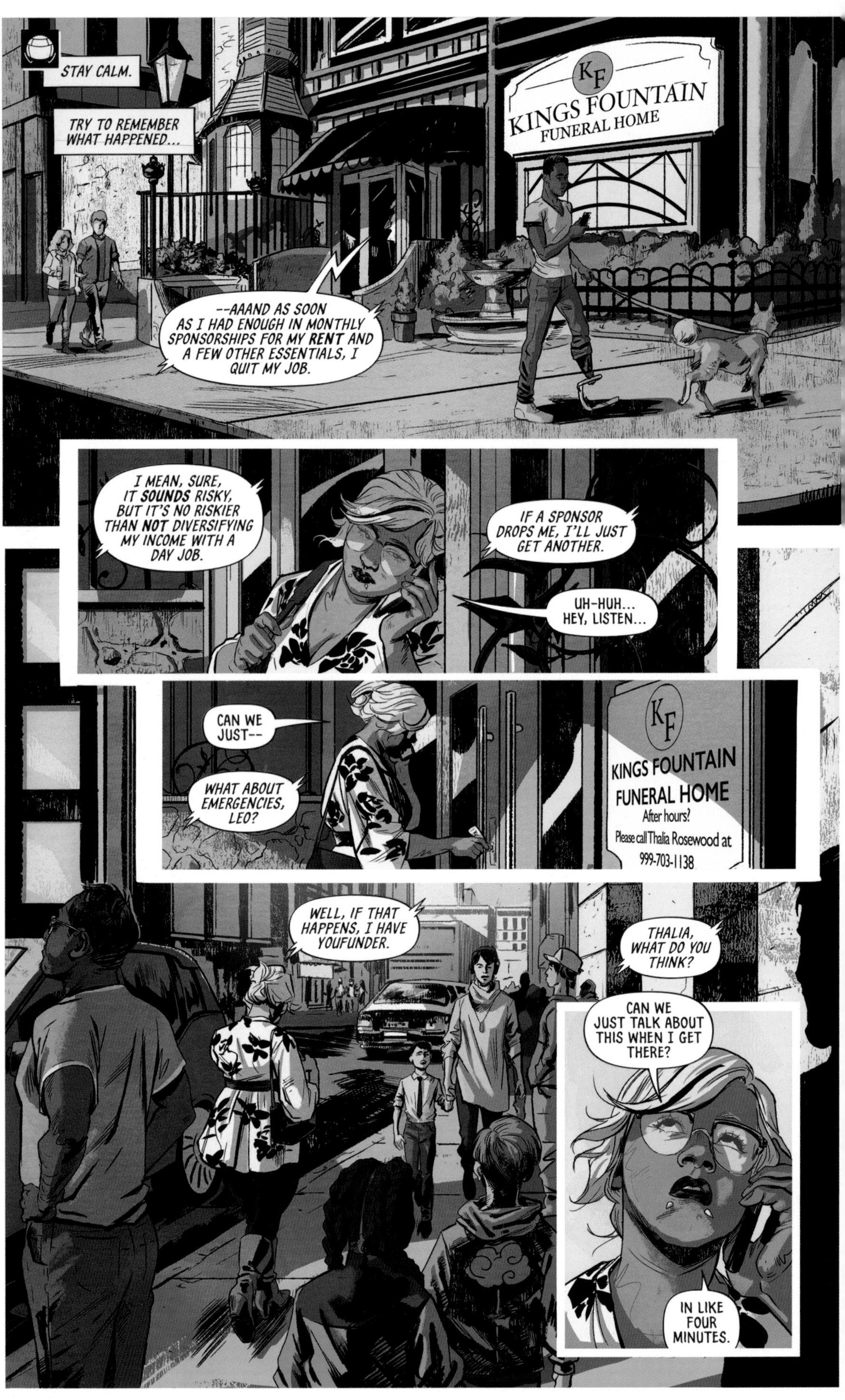
STAY CALM.
TRY TO REMEMBER WHAT HAPPENED...
KF KINGS FOUNTAIN FUNERAL HOME
--AAAND AS SOON AS I HAD ENOUGH IN MONTHLY SPONSORSHIPS FOR MY RENT AND A FEW OTHER ESSENTIALS, I QUIT MY JOB.
I MEAN, SURE, IT SOUNDS RISKY, BUT IT'S NO RISKIER THAN NOT DIVERSIFYING MY INCOME WITH A DAY JOB.
IF A SPONSOR DROPS ME, I'LL JUST GET ANOTHER.
UH-HUH... HEY, LISTEN...
CAN WE JUST--
WHAT ABOUT EMERGENCIES, LEO?
KF KINGS FOUNTAIN FUNERAL HOME After hours? Please call Thalia Rosewood at 999-703-1138
WELL, IF THAT HAPPENS, I HAVE YOUFUNDER.
THALIA, WHAT DO YOU THINK?
CAN WE JUST TALK ABOUT THIS WHEN I GET THERE?
IN LIKE FOUR MINUTES.

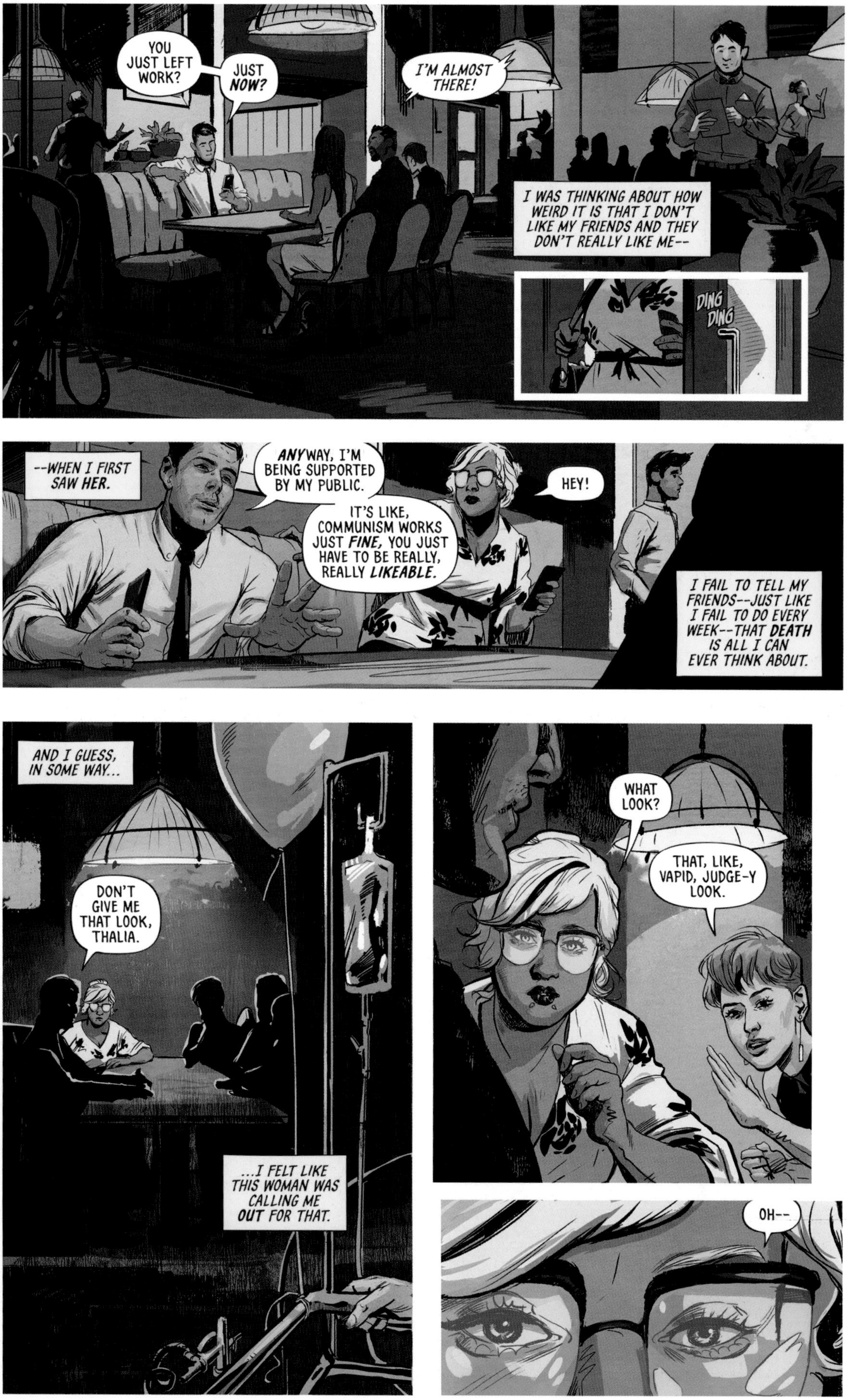

YOU JUST LEFT WORK?
JUST NOW?
I'M ALMOST THERE!
I WAS THINKING ABOUT HOW WEIRD IT IS THAT I DON'T LIKE MY FRIENDS AND THEY DON'T REALLY LIKE ME--
DING DING
--WHEN I FIRST SAW HER.
ANYWAY, I'M BEING SUPPORTED BY MY PUBLIC.
IT'S LIKE, COMMUNISM WORKS JUST FINE, YOU JUST HAVE TO BE REALLY, REALLY LIKEABLE.
HEY!
I FAIL TO TELL MY FRIENDS--JUST LIKE I FAIL TO DO EVERY WEEK--THAT DEATH IS ALL I CAN EVER THINK ABOUT.
AND I GUESS, IN SOME WAY...
DON'T GIVE ME THAT LOOK, THALIA.
...I FELT LIKE THIS WOMAN WAS CALLING ME OUT FOR THAT.
WHAT LOOK?
THAT, LIKE, VAPID, JUDGE-Y LOOK.
OH--

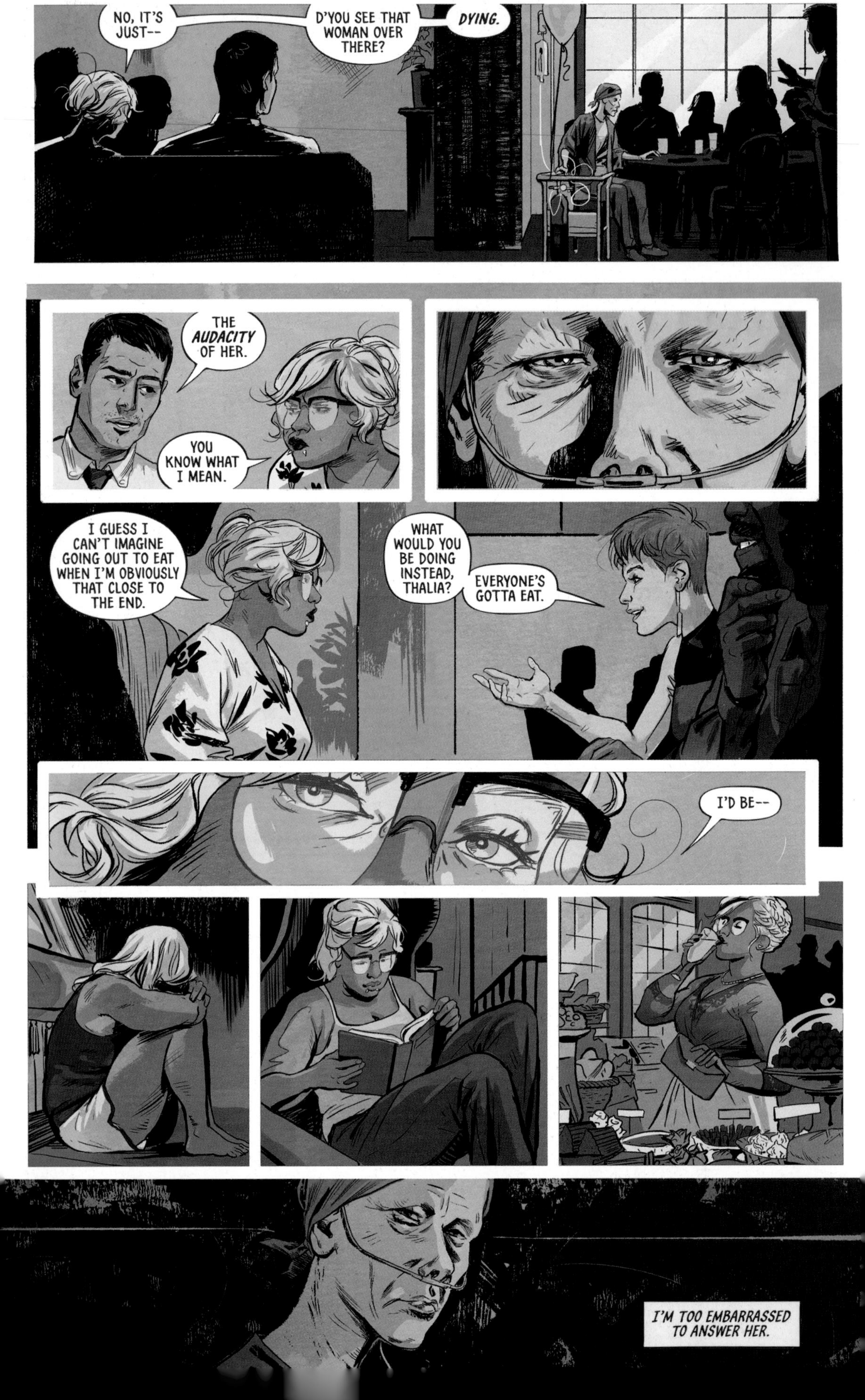

NO, IT'S JUST--
D'YOU SEE THAT WOMAN OVER THERE?
DYING.
THE AUDACITY OF HER.
YOU KNOW WHAT I MEAN.
I GUESS I CAN'T IMAGINE GOING OUT TO EAT WHEN I'M OBVIOUSLY THAT CLOSE TO THE END.
WHAT WOULD YOU BE DOING INSTEAD, THALIA?
EVERYONE'S GOTTA EAT.
I'D BE--
I'M TOO EMBARRASSED TO ANSWER HER.

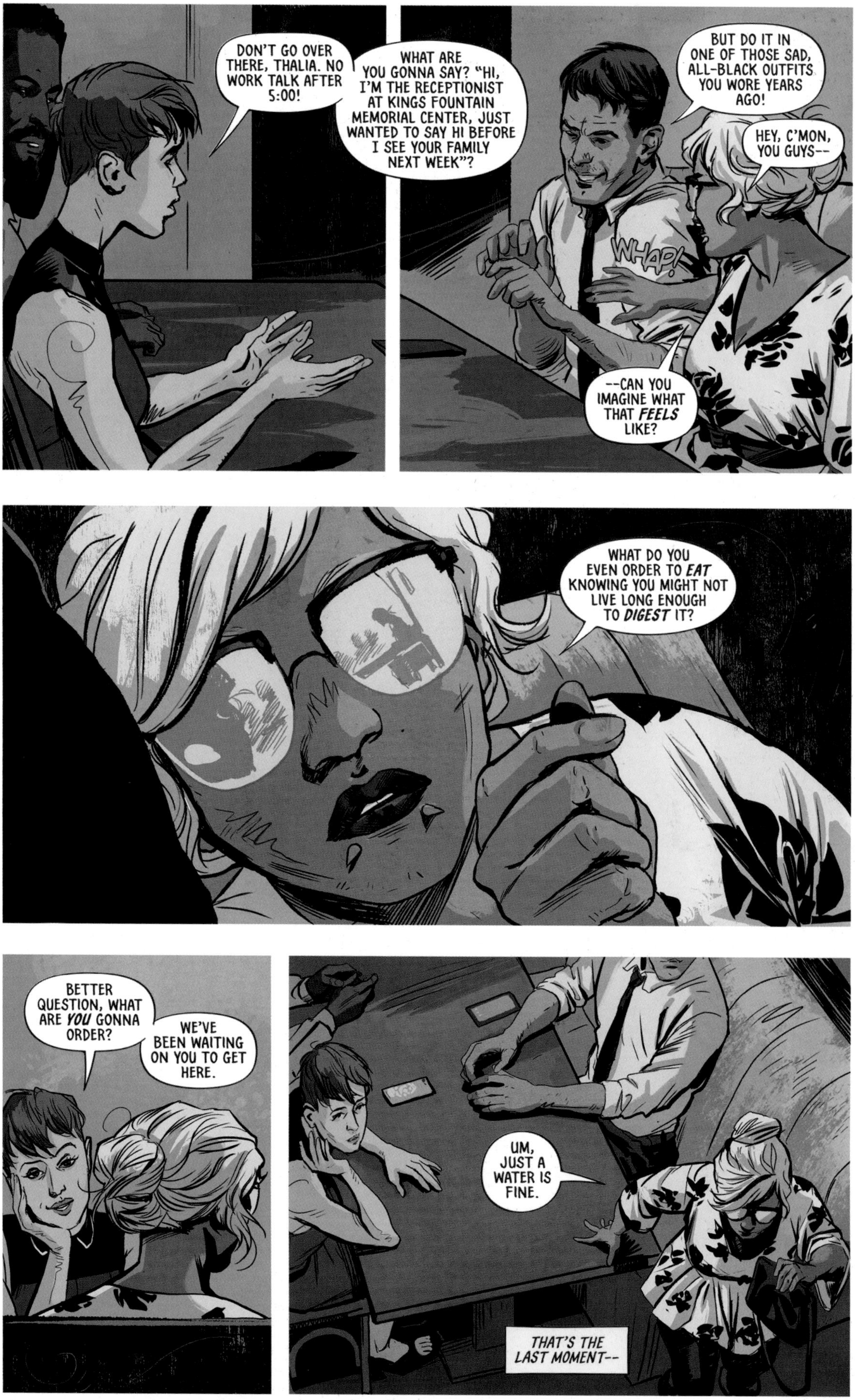
DON'T GO OVER THERE, THALIA. NO WORK TALK AFTER 5:00!
WHAT ARE YOU GONNA SAY? "HI, I'M THE RECEPTIONIST AT KINGS FOUNTAIN MEMORIAL CENTER, JUST WANTED TO SAY HI BEFORE I SEE YOUR FAMILY NEXT WEEK"?
BUT DO IT IN ONE OF THOSE SAD, ALL-BLACK OUTFITS YOU WORE YEARS AGO!
HEY, C'MON, YOU GUYS--
WHAP!
--CAN YOU IMAGINE WHAT THAT *FEELS* LIKE?
WHAT DO YOU EVEN ORDER TO *EAT* KNOWING YOU MIGHT NOT LIVE LONG ENOUGH TO *DIGEST* IT?
BETTER QUESTION, WHAT ARE *YOU* GONNA ORDER?
WE'VE BEEN WAITING ON YOU TO GET HERE.
UM, JUST A WATER IS FINE.
THAT'S THE LAST MOMENT--

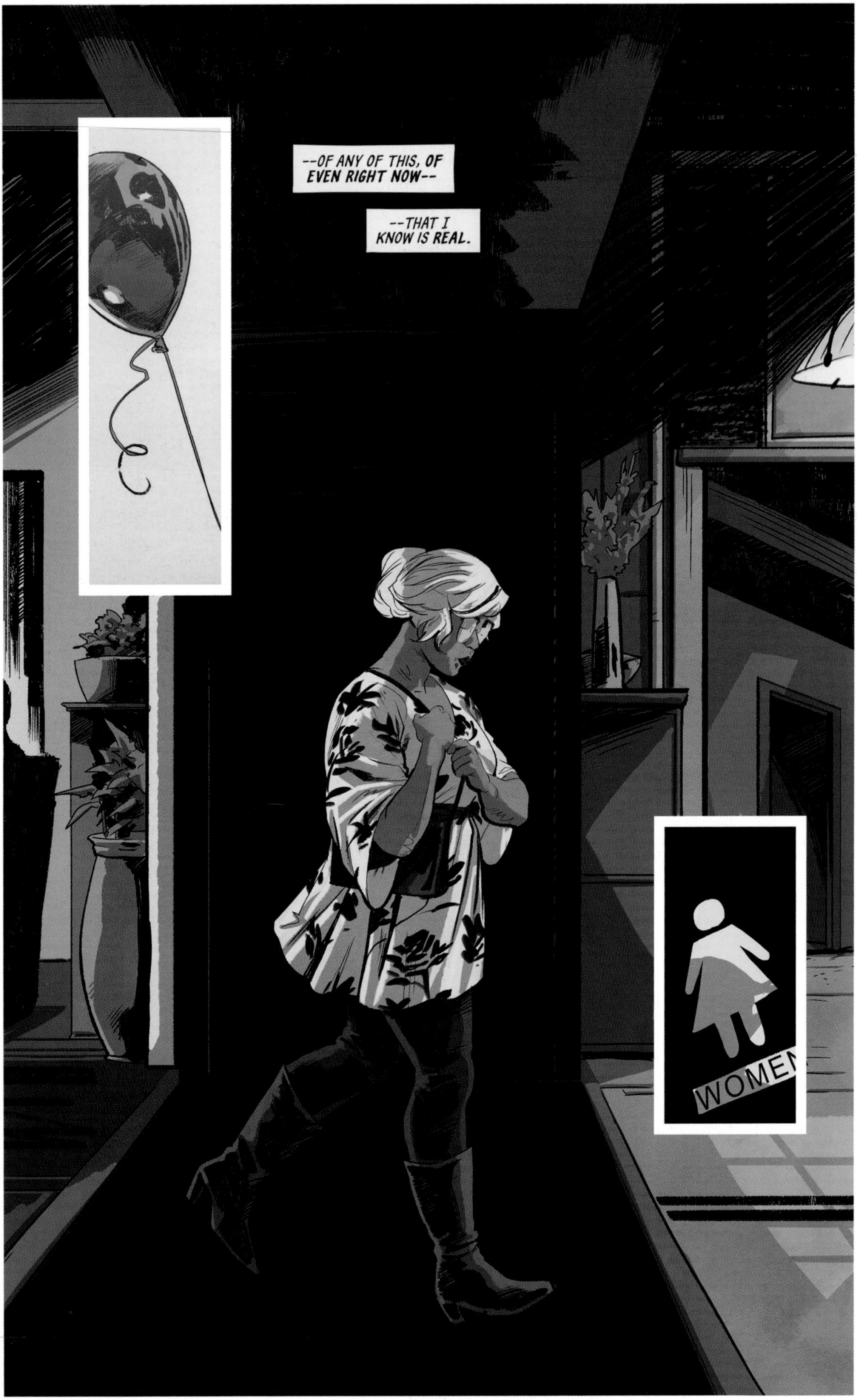
--OF ANY OF THIS, OF EVEN RIGHT NOW--
--THAT I KNOW IS REAL.
WOMEN

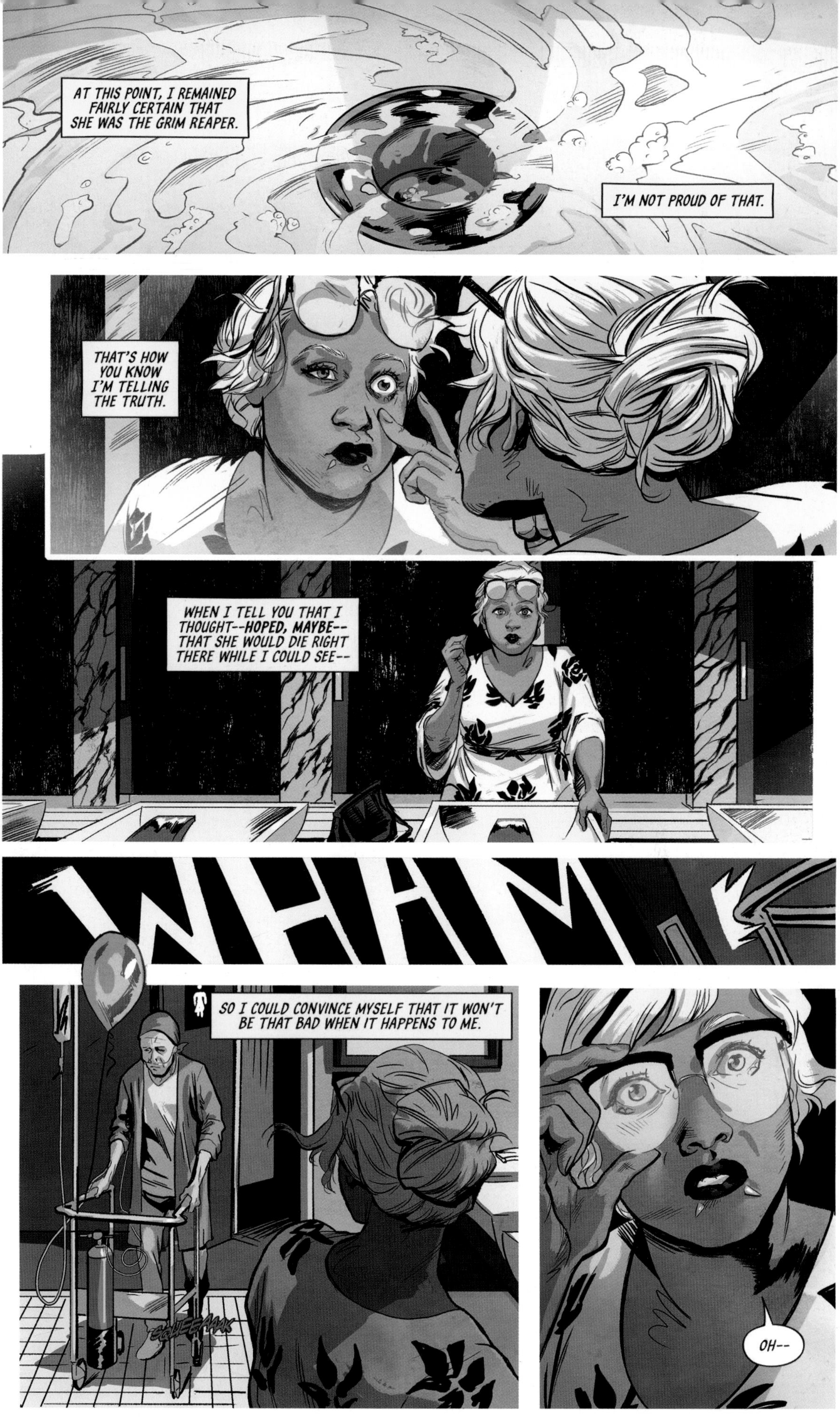
AT THIS POINT, I REMAINED FAIRLY CERTAIN THAT SHE WAS THE GRIM REAPER.
I'M NOT PROUD OF THAT.
THAT'S HOW YOU KNOW I'M TELLING THE TRUTH.
WHEN I TELL YOU THAT I THOUGHT--HOPED, MAYBE--THAT SHE WOULD DIE RIGHT THERE WHILE I COULD SEE--
WHAM
SO I COULD CONVINCE MYSELF THAT IT WON'T BE THAT BAD WHEN IT HAPPENS TO ME.
SQUEEAAAK
OH--

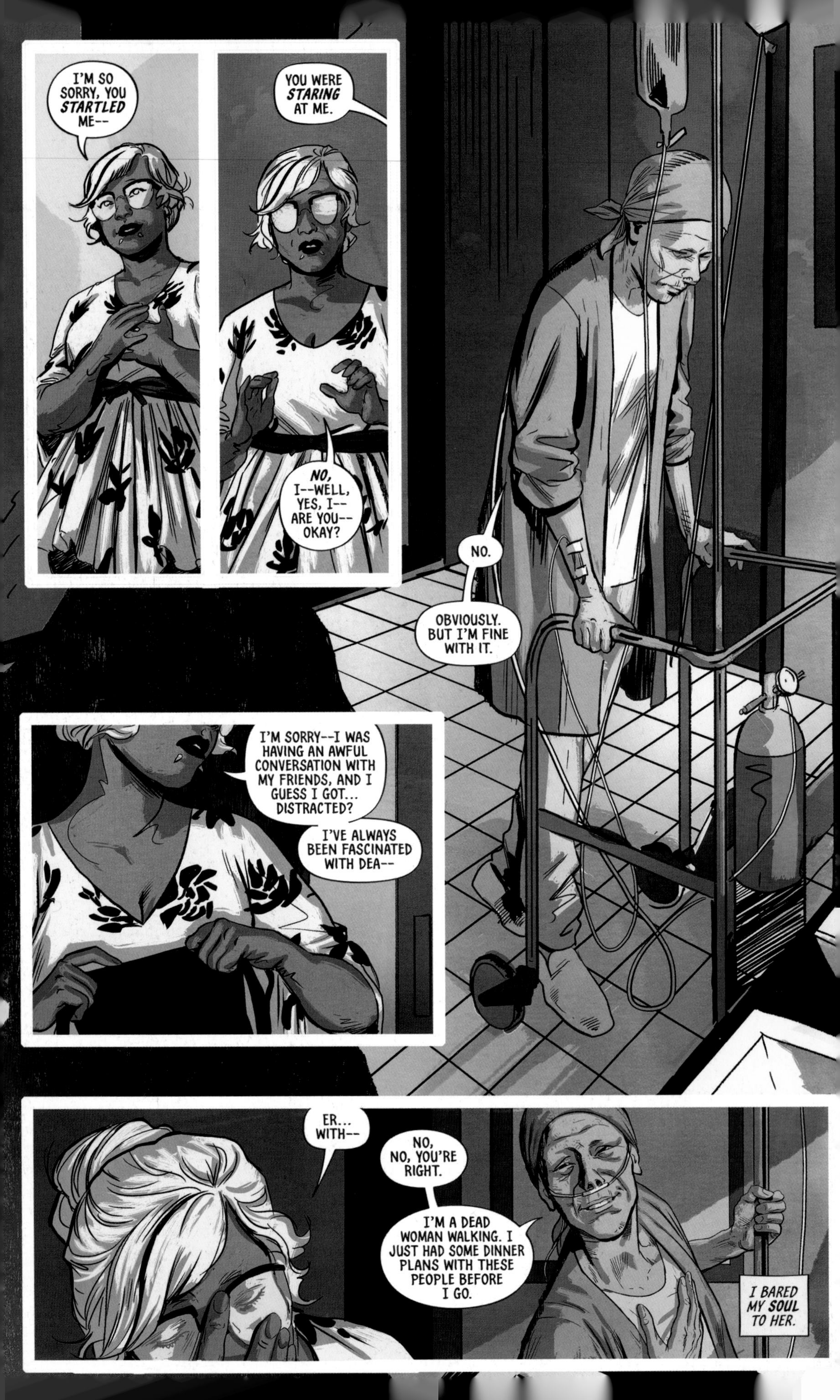
I'M SO SORRY, YOU STARTLED ME--
YOU WERE STARING AT ME.
NO, I--WELL, YES, I-- ARE YOU-- OKAY?
NO.
OBVIOUSLY. BUT I'M FINE WITH IT.
I'M SORRY--I WAS HAVING AN AWFUL CONVERSATION WITH MY FRIENDS, AND I GUESS I GOT... DISTRACTED?
I'VE ALWAYS BEEN FASCINATED WITH DEA--
ER... WITH--
NO, NO, YOU'RE RIGHT.
I'M A DEAD WOMAN WALKING. I JUST HAD SOME DINNER PLANS WITH THESE PEOPLE BEFORE I GO.
I BARED MY SOUL TO HER.

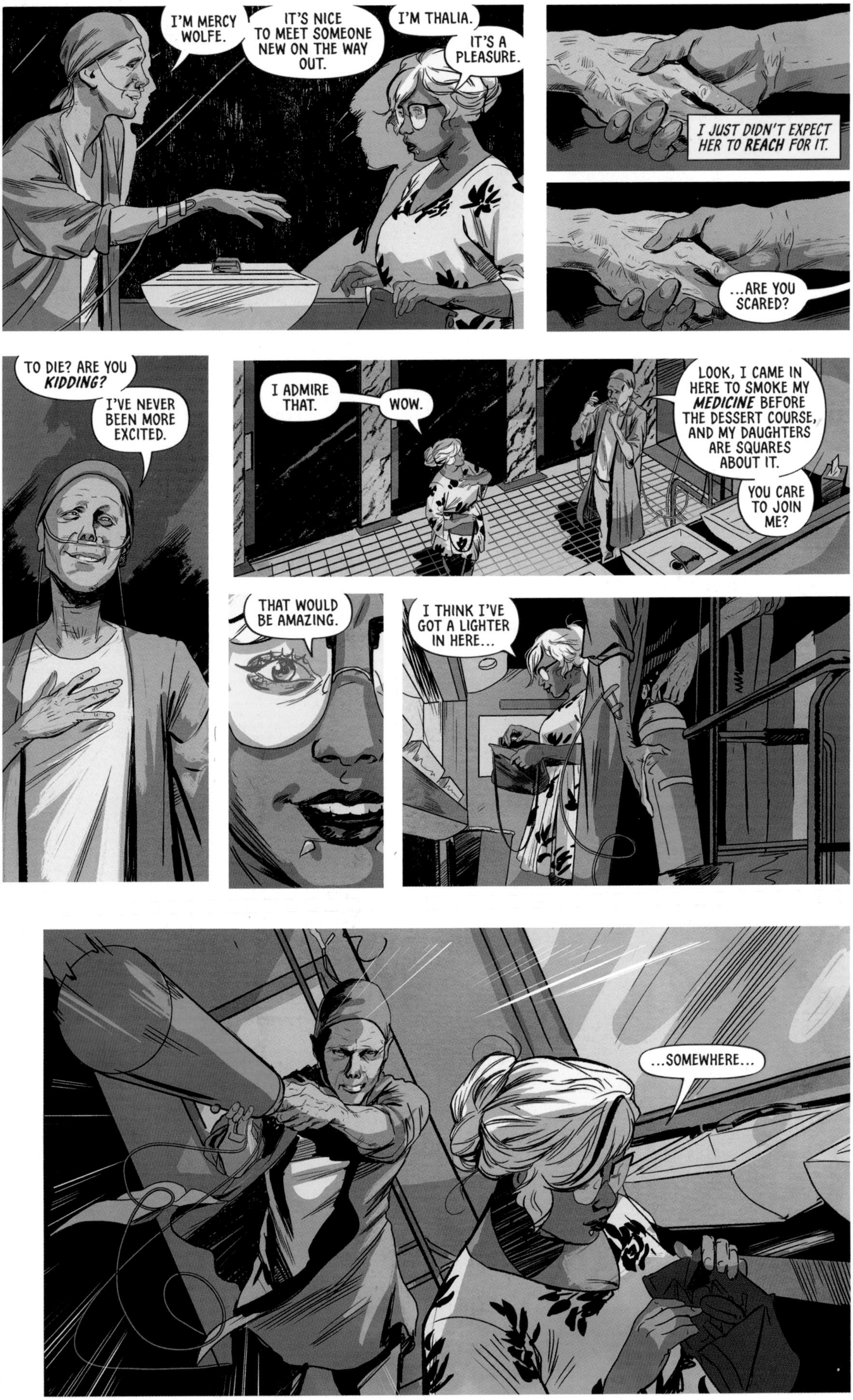
I'M MERCY WOLFE.
IT'S NICE TO MEET SOMEONE NEW ON THE WAY OUT.
I'M THALIA.
IT'S A PLEASURE.
I JUST DIDN'T EXPECT HER TO REACH FOR IT.
...ARE YOU SCARED?
TO DIE? ARE YOU KIDDING?
I'VE NEVER BEEN MORE EXCITED.
I ADMIRE THAT.
WOW.
LOOK, I CAME IN HERE TO SMOKE MY MEDICINE BEFORE THE DESSERT COURSE, AND MY DAUGHTERS ARE SQUARES ABOUT IT.
YOU CARE TO JOIN ME?
THAT WOULD BE AMAZING.
I THINK I'VE GOT A LIGHTER IN HERE...
...SOMEWHERE...

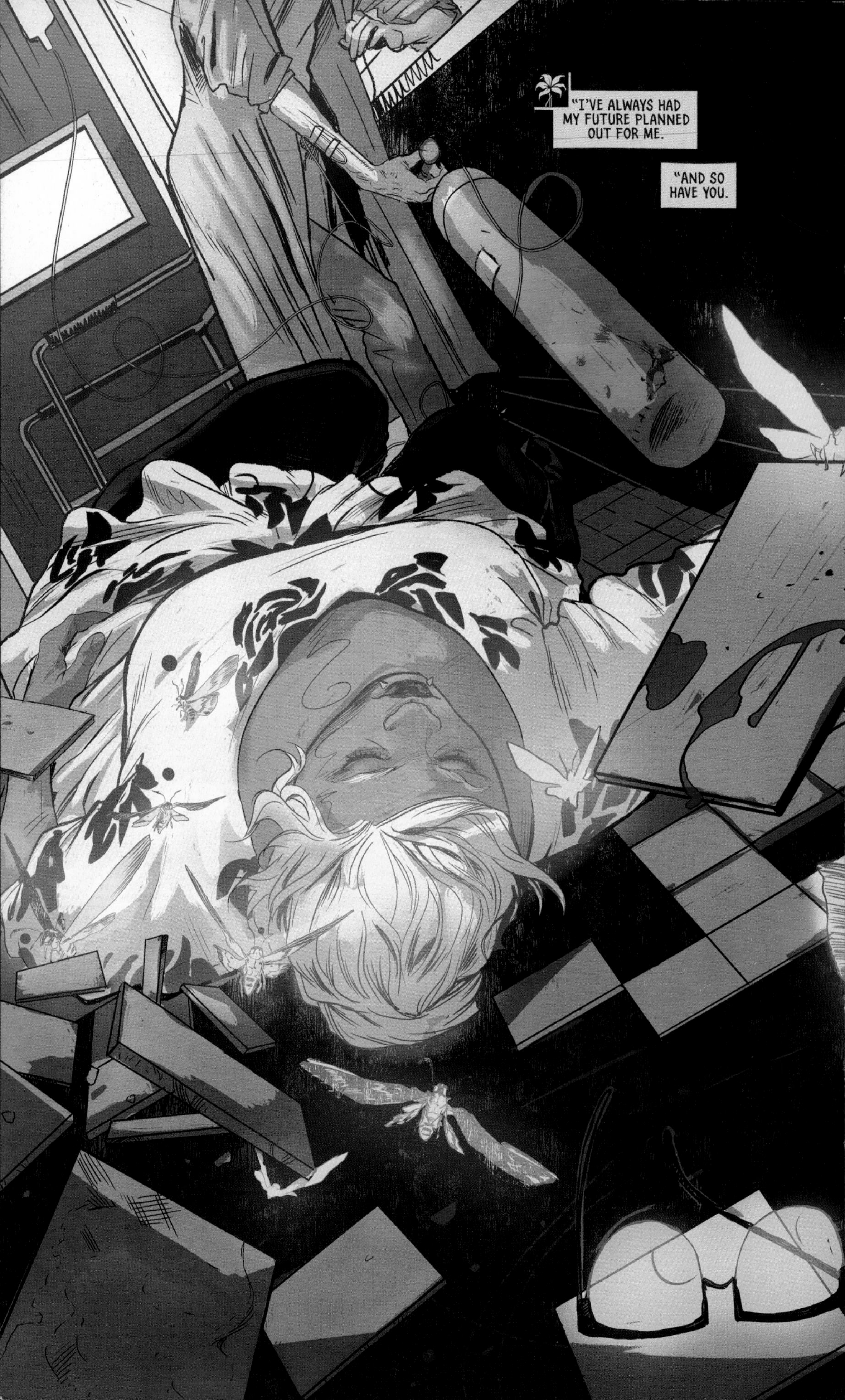
"I'VE ALWAYS HAD MY FUTURE PLANNED OUT FOR ME.
"AND SO HAVE YOU.

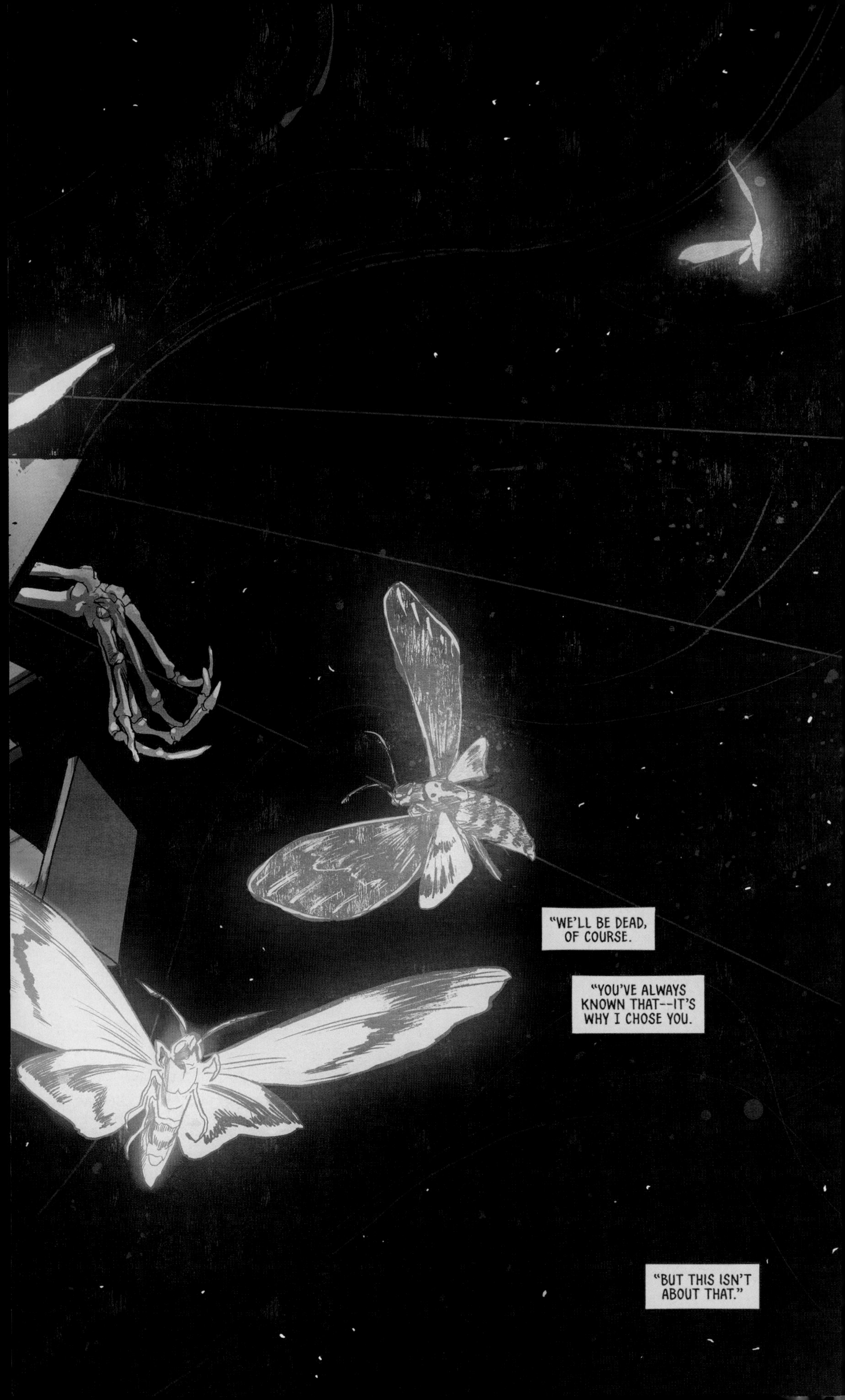
"WE'LL BE DEAD, OF COURSE.
"YOU'VE ALWAYS KNOWN THAT--IT'S WHY I CHOSE YOU.
"BUT THIS ISN'T ABOUT THAT."

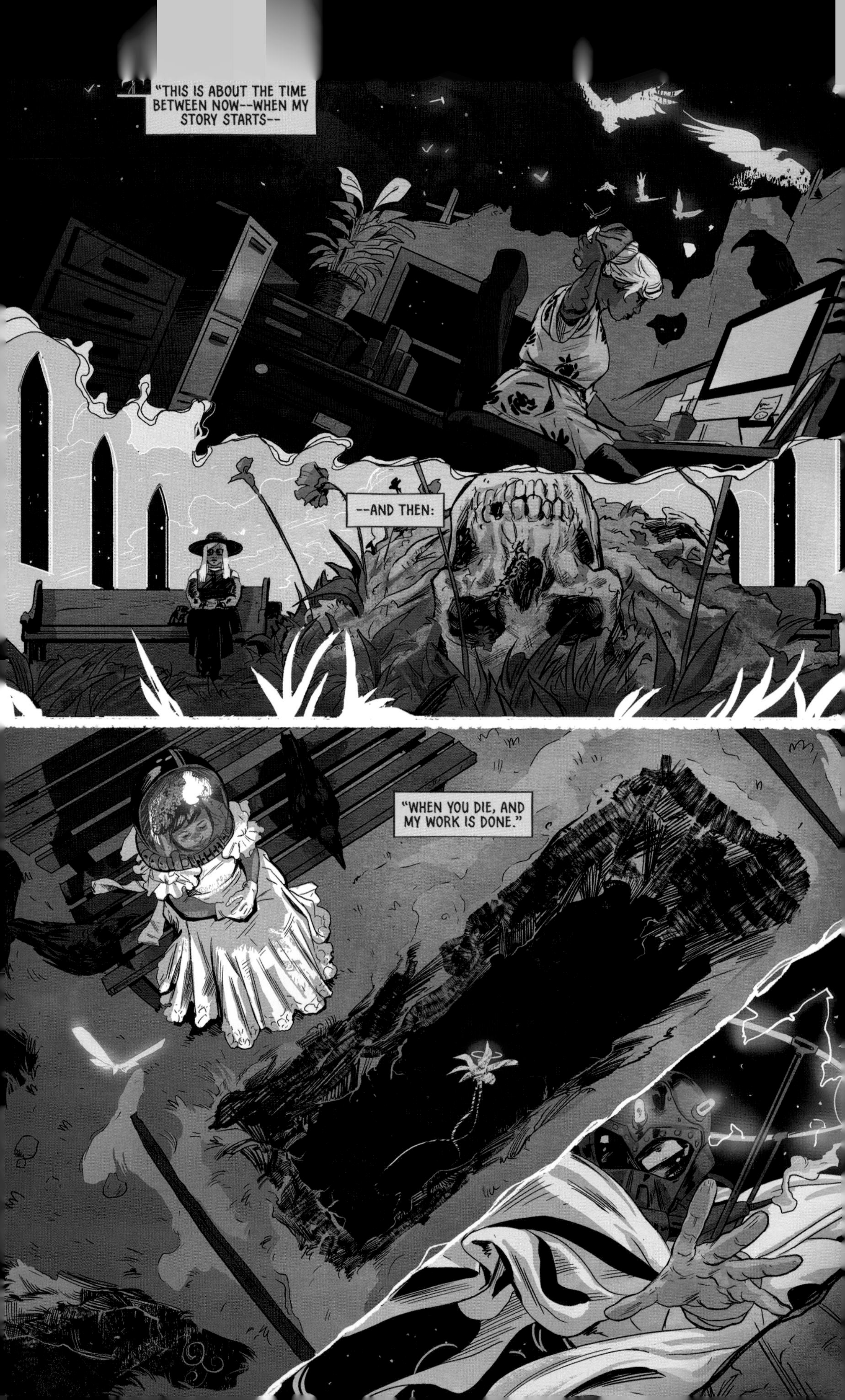
"THIS IS ABOUT THE TIME BETWEEN NOW--WHEN MY STORY STARTS--
--AND THEN:
"WHEN YOU DIE, AND MY WORK IS DONE."

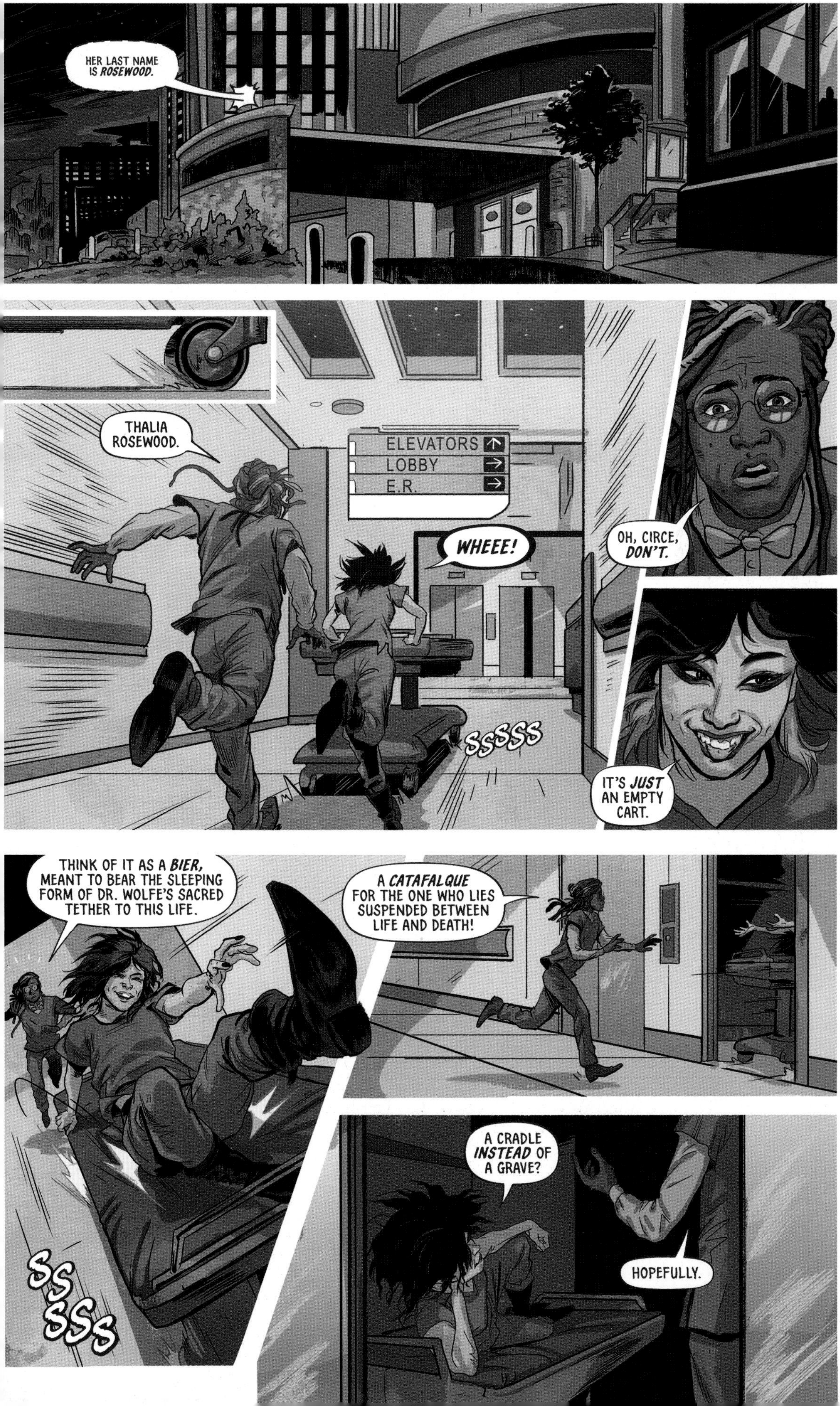
HER LAST NAME IS ROSEWOOD.
THALIA ROSEWOOD.
ELEVATORS
LOBBY
E.R.
WHEEE!
SSSSS
OH, CIRCE, DON'T.
IT'S JUST AN EMPTY CART.
THINK OF IT AS A BIER, MEANT TO BEAR THE SLEEPING FORM OF DR. WOLFE'S SACRED TETHER TO THIS LIFE.
SS SSS
A CATAFALQUE FOR THE ONE WHO LIES SUSPENDED BETWEEN LIFE AND DEATH!
A CRADLE INSTEAD OF A GRAVE?
HOPEFULLY.

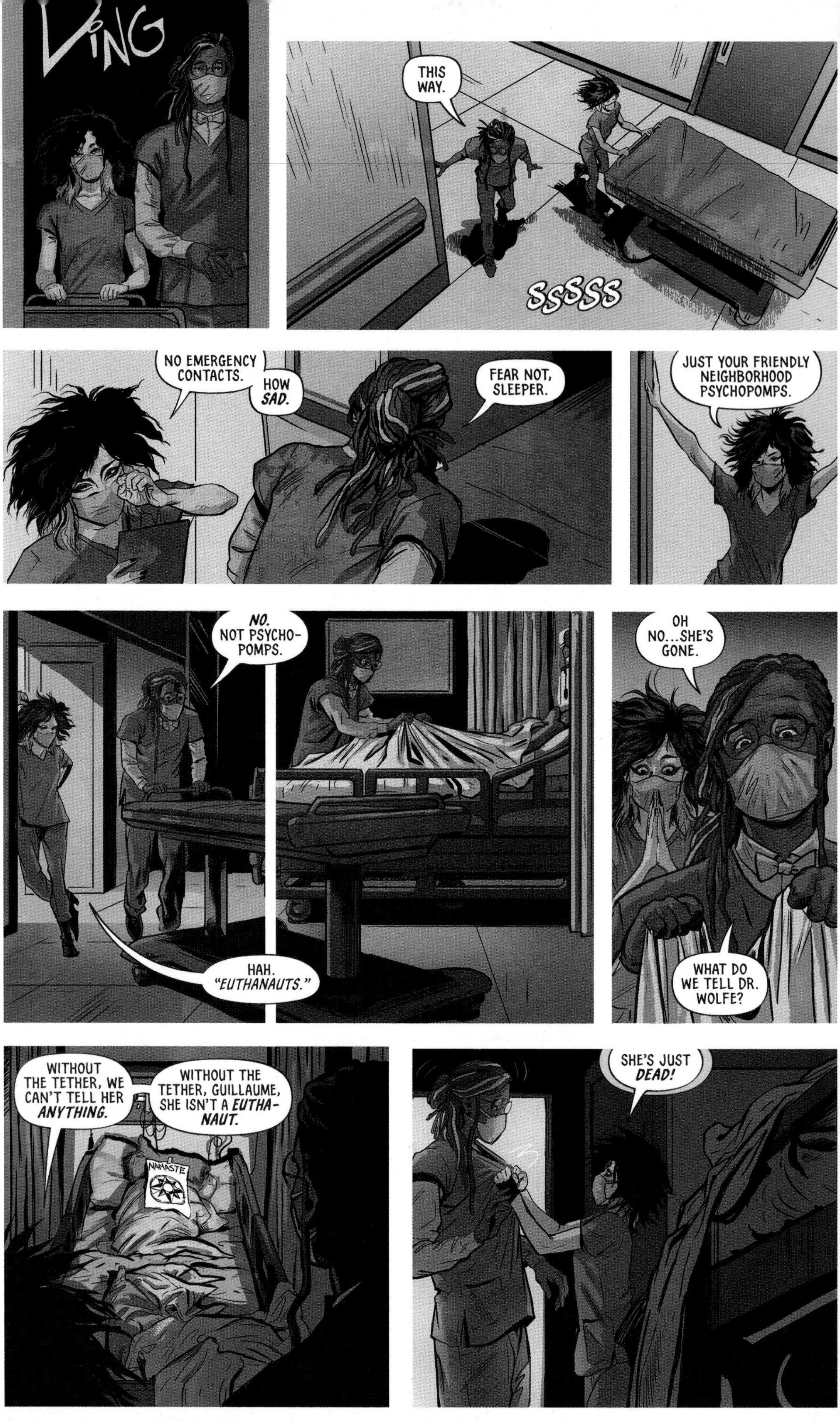
VING
THIS WAY.
SSSSS
NO EMERGENCY CONTACTS.
HOW *SAD.*
FEAR NOT, SLEEPER.
JUST YOUR FRIENDLY NEIGHBORHOOD PSYCHOPOMPS.
NO. NOT PSYCHO-POMPS.
HAH. "*EUTHANAUTS.*"
OH NO...SHE'S GONE.
WHAT DO WE TELL DR. WOLFE?
WITHOUT THE TETHER, WE CAN'T TELL HER *ANYTHING.*
WITHOUT THE TETHER, GUILLAUME, SHE ISN'T A *EUTHA-NAUT.*
NAMASTE
SHE'S JUST *DEAD!*

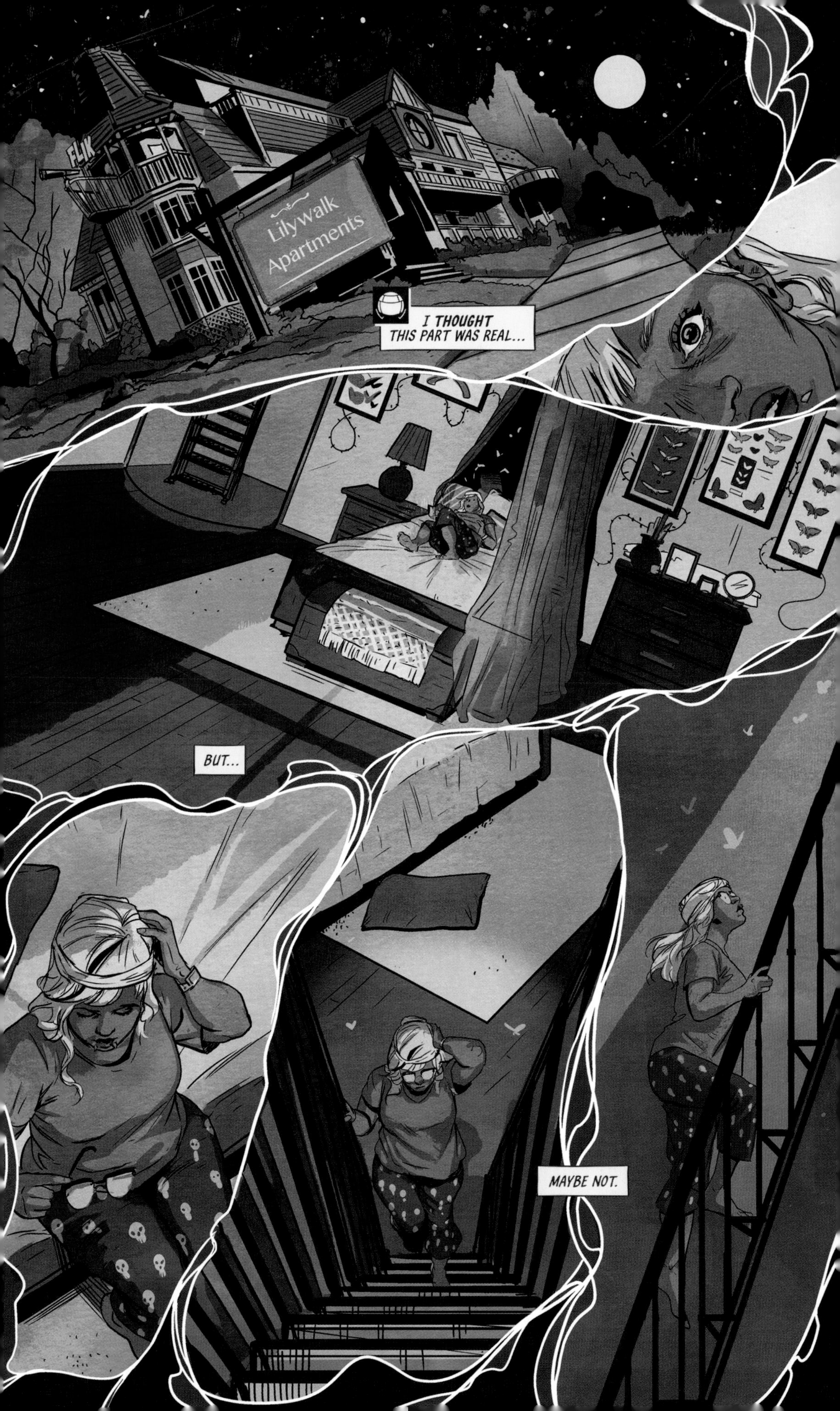
Lilywalk Apartments
FLiK
I THOUGHT THIS PART WAS REAL...
BUT...
MAYBE NOT.

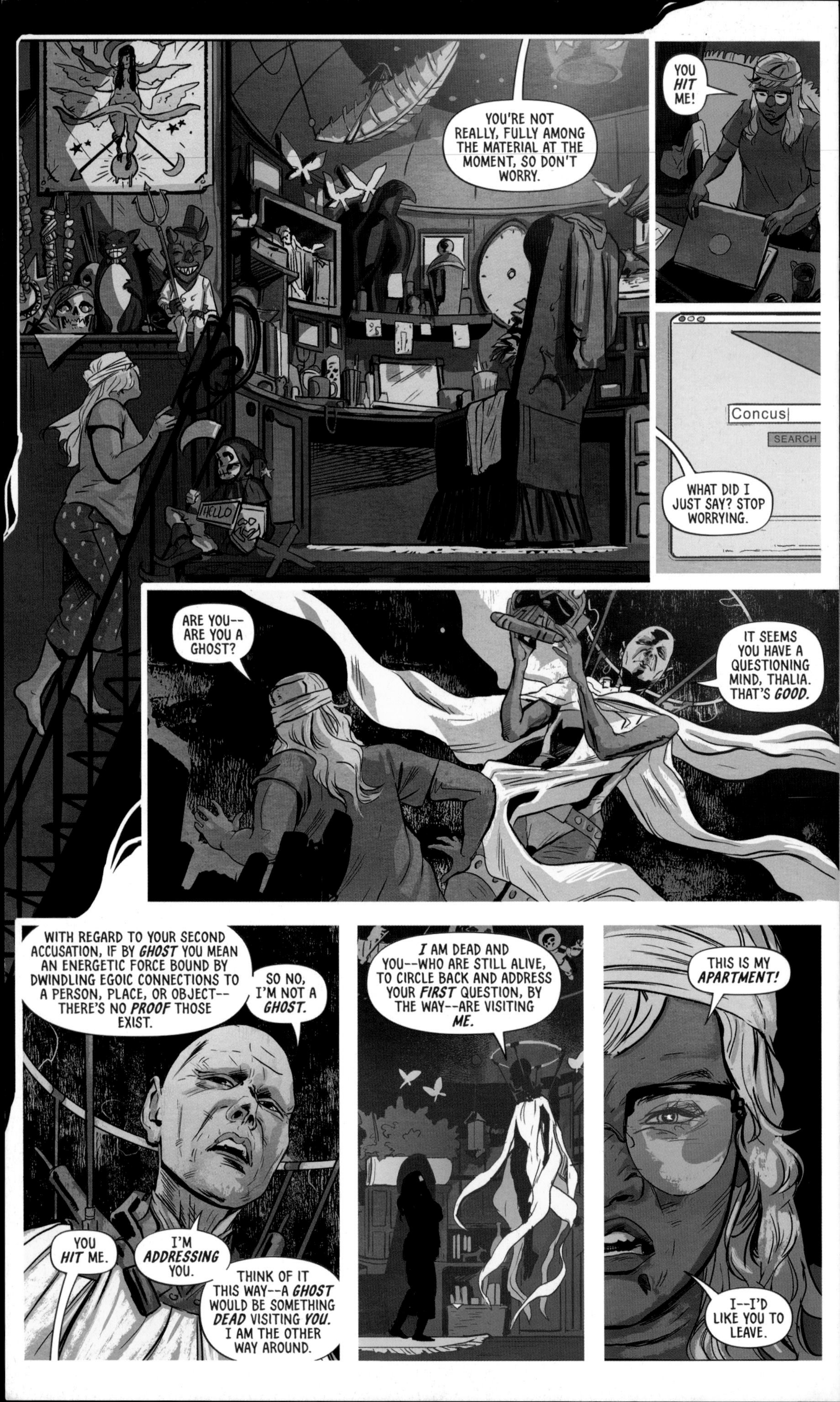
YOU'RE NOT REALLY, FULLY AMONG THE MATERIAL AT THE MOMENT, SO DON'T WORRY.
HELLO
YOU HIT ME!
Concus
SEARCH
WHAT DID I JUST SAY? STOP WORRYING.
ARE YOU-- ARE YOU A GHOST?
IT SEEMS YOU HAVE A QUESTIONING MIND, THALIA. THAT'S GOOD.
WITH REGARD TO YOUR SECOND ACCUSATION, IF BY GHOST YOU MEAN AN ENERGETIC FORCE BOUND BY DWINDLING EGOIC CONNECTIONS TO A PERSON, PLACE, OR OBJECT-- THERE'S NO PROOF THOSE EXIST.
SO NO, I'M NOT A GHOST.
YOU HIT ME.
I'M ADDRESSING YOU.
THINK OF IT THIS WAY--A GHOST WOULD BE SOMETHING DEAD VISITING YOU. I AM THE OTHER WAY AROUND.
I AM DEAD AND YOU--WHO ARE STILL ALIVE, TO CIRCLE BACK AND ADDRESS YOUR FIRST QUESTION, BY THE WAY--ARE VISITING ME.
THIS IS MY APARTMENT!
I--I'D LIKE YOU TO LEAVE.

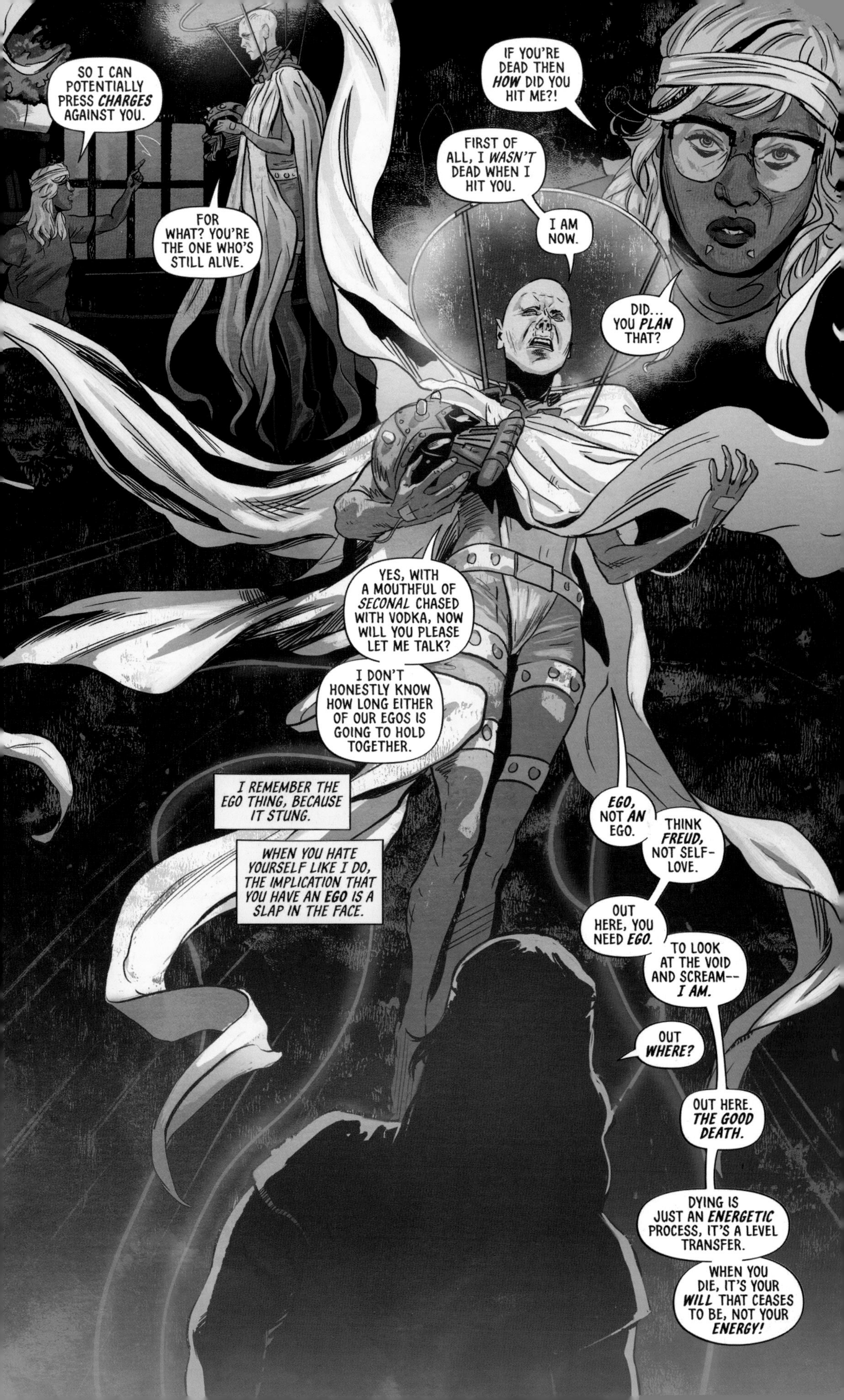
SO I CAN POTENTIALLY PRESS *CHARGES* AGAINST YOU.
FOR WHAT? YOU'RE THE ONE WHO'S STILL ALIVE.
IF YOU'RE DEAD THEN *HOW* DID YOU HIT ME?!
FIRST OF ALL, I *WASN'T* DEAD WHEN I HIT YOU.
I AM NOW.
DID... YOU *PLAN* THAT?
YES, WITH A MOUTHFUL OF *SECONAL* CHASED WITH VODKA, NOW WILL YOU PLEASE LET ME TALK?
I DON'T HONESTLY KNOW HOW LONG EITHER OF OUR EGOS IS GOING TO HOLD TOGETHER.
I REMEMBER THE EGO THING, BECAUSE IT STUNG.
WHEN YOU HATE YOURSELF LIKE I DO, THE IMPLICATION THAT YOU HAVE AN *EGO* IS A SLAP IN THE FACE.
EGO, NOT *AN* EGO.
THINK *FREUD*, NOT SELF-LOVE.
OUT HERE, YOU NEED *EGO*.
TO LOOK AT THE VOID AND SCREAM-- *I AM*.
OUT *WHERE?*
OUT HERE. ***THE GOOD DEATH.***
DYING IS JUST AN *ENERGETIC* PROCESS, IT'S A LEVEL TRANSFER.
WHEN YOU DIE, IT'S YOUR *WILL* THAT CEASES TO BE, NOT YOUR *ENERGY!*

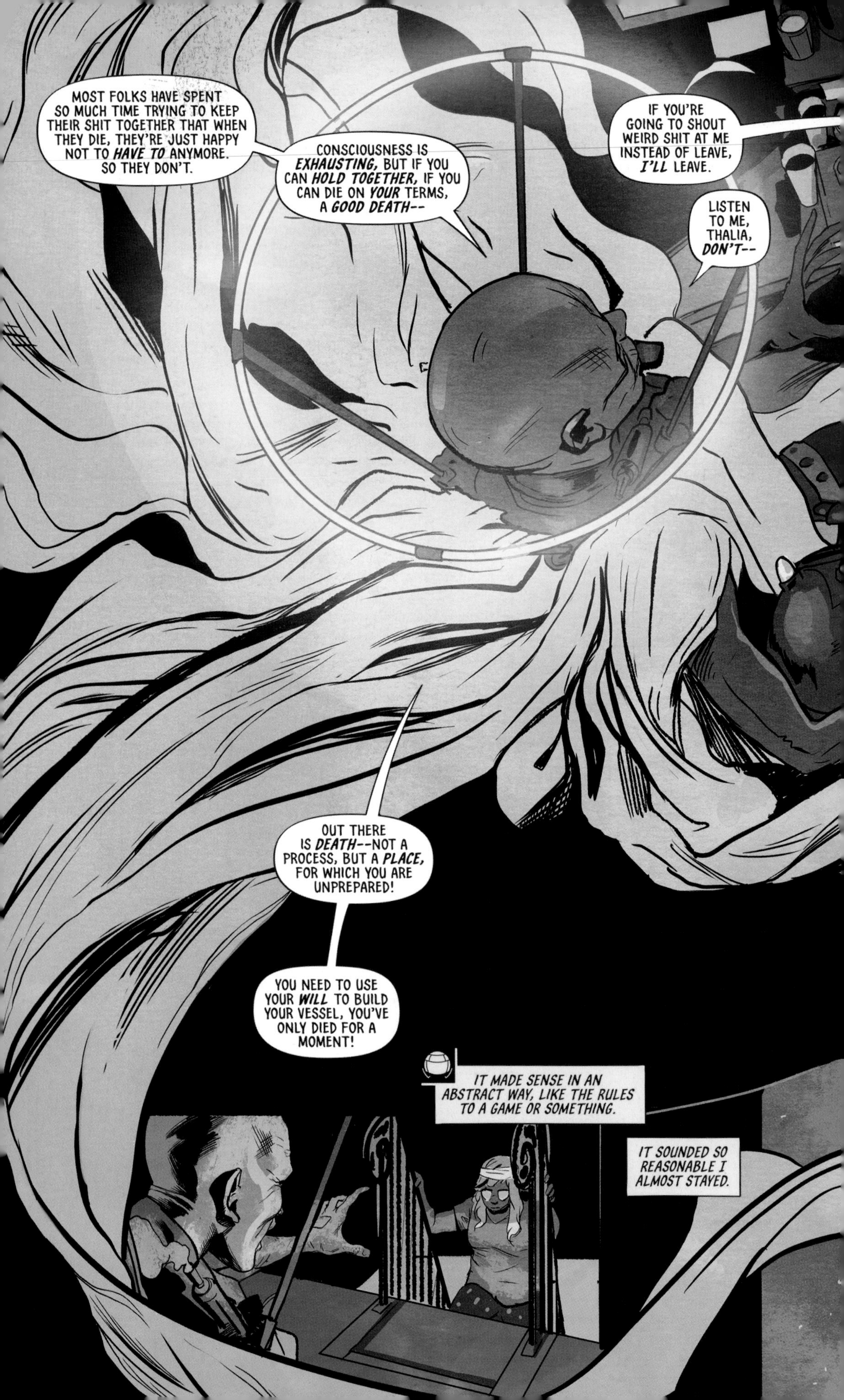
MOST FOLKS HAVE SPENT SO MUCH TIME TRYING TO KEEP THEIR SHIT TOGETHER THAT WHEN THEY DIE, THEY'RE JUST HAPPY NOT TO *HAVE TO* ANYMORE. SO THEY DON'T.
CONSCIOUSNESS IS *EXHAUSTING,* BUT IF YOU CAN *HOLD TOGETHER,* IF YOU CAN DIE ON *YOUR* TERMS, A *GOOD DEATH*--
IF YOU'RE GOING TO SHOUT WEIRD SHIT AT ME INSTEAD OF LEAVE, *I'LL* LEAVE.
LISTEN TO ME, THALIA, *DON'T*--
OUT THERE IS *DEATH*--NOT A PROCESS, BUT A *PLACE,* FOR WHICH YOU ARE UNPREPARED!
YOU NEED TO USE YOUR *WILL* TO BUILD YOUR VESSEL, YOU'VE ONLY DIED FOR A MOMENT!
IT MADE SENSE IN AN ABSTRACT WAY, LIKE THE RULES TO A GAME OR SOMETHING.
IT SOUNDED SO REASONABLE I ALMOST STAYED.

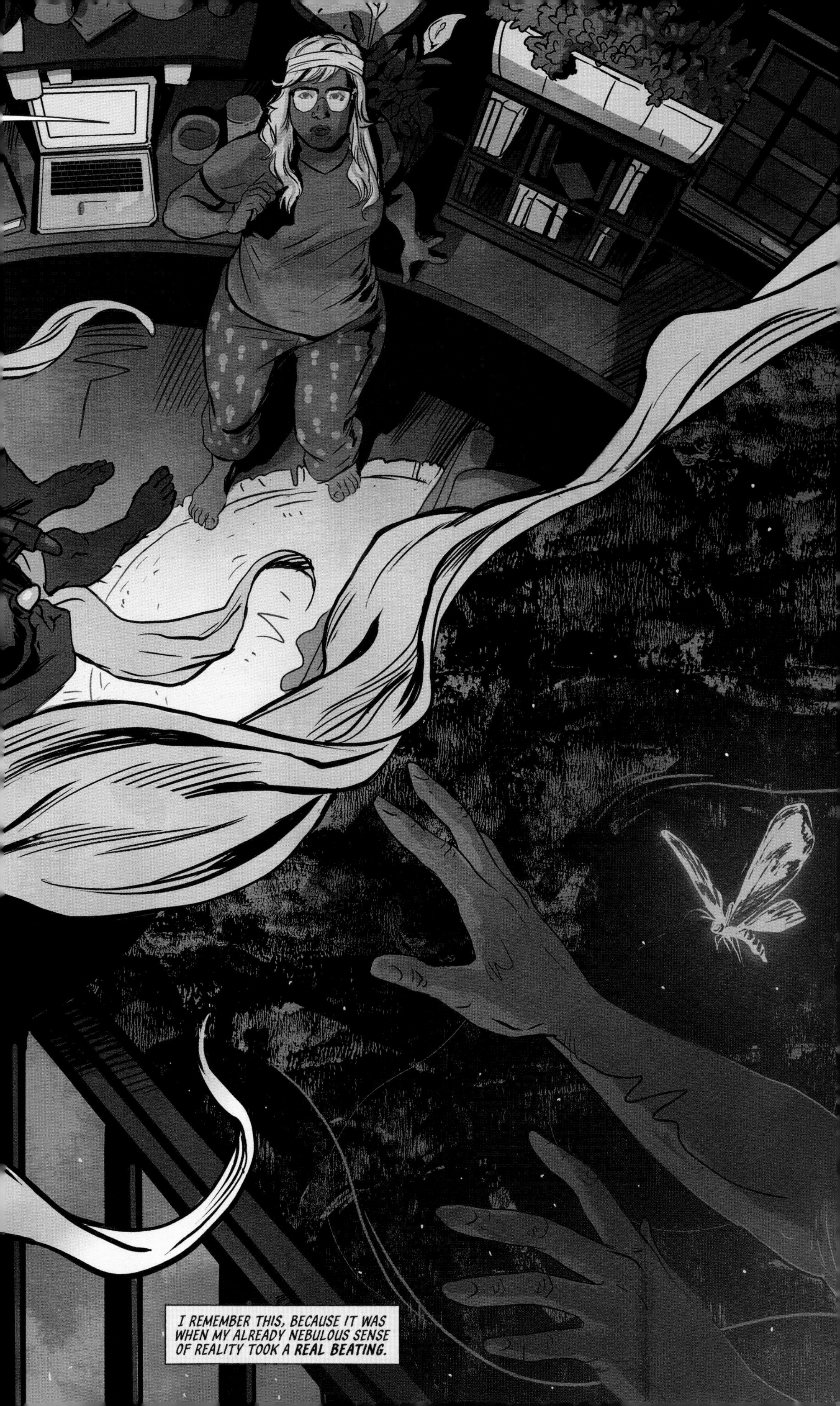
I REMEMBER THIS, BECAUSE IT WAS WHEN MY ALREADY NEBULOUS SENSE OF REALITY TOOK A **REAL BEATING.**

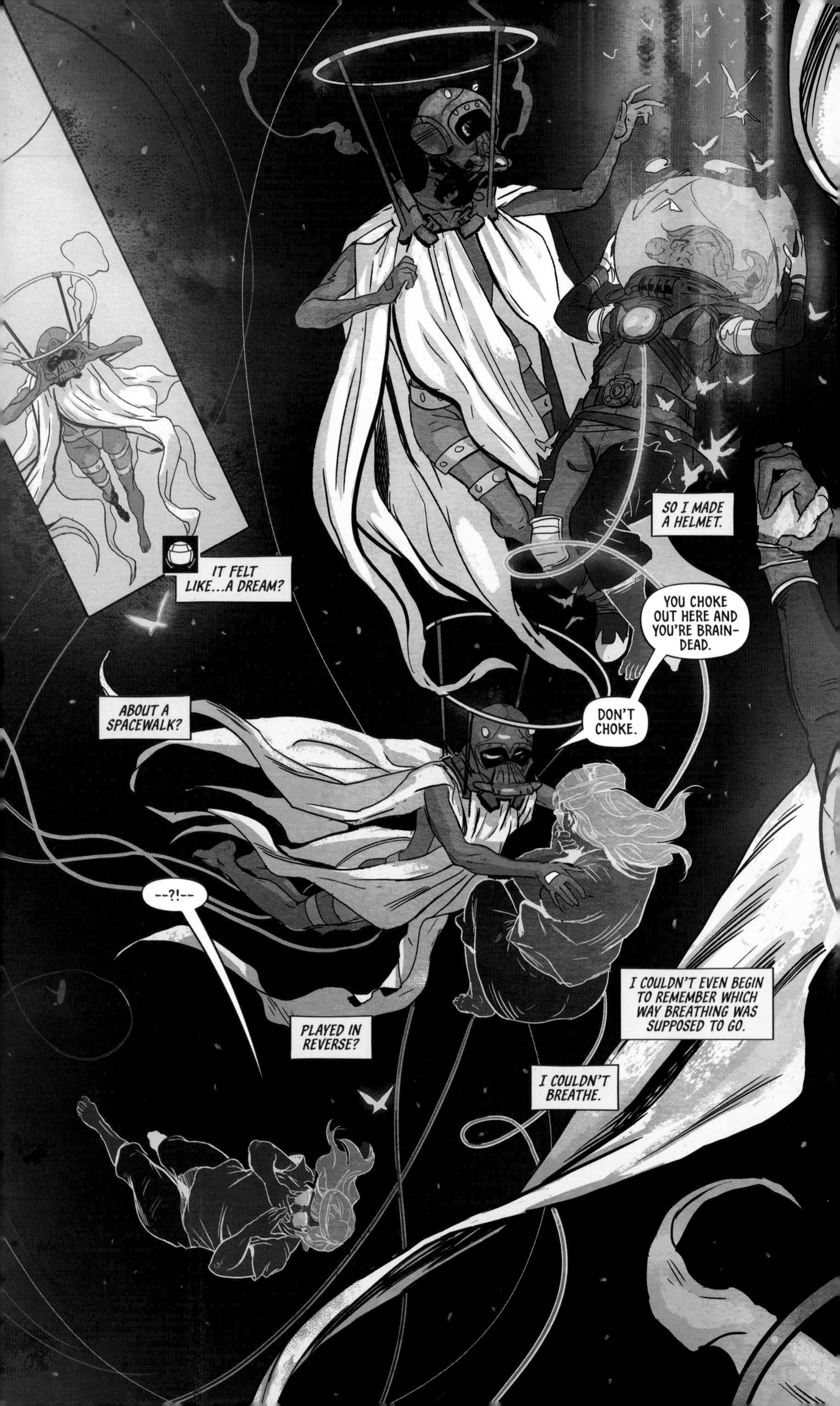
IT FELT LIKE...A DREAM?
ABOUT A SPACEWALK?
PLAYED IN REVERSE?
SO I MADE A HELMET.
YOU CHOKE OUT HERE AND YOU'RE BRAIN-DEAD.
DON'T CHOKE.
--?!--
I COULDN'T EVEN BEGIN TO REMEMBER WHICH WAY BREATHING WAS SUPPOSED TO GO.
I COULDN'T BREATHE.

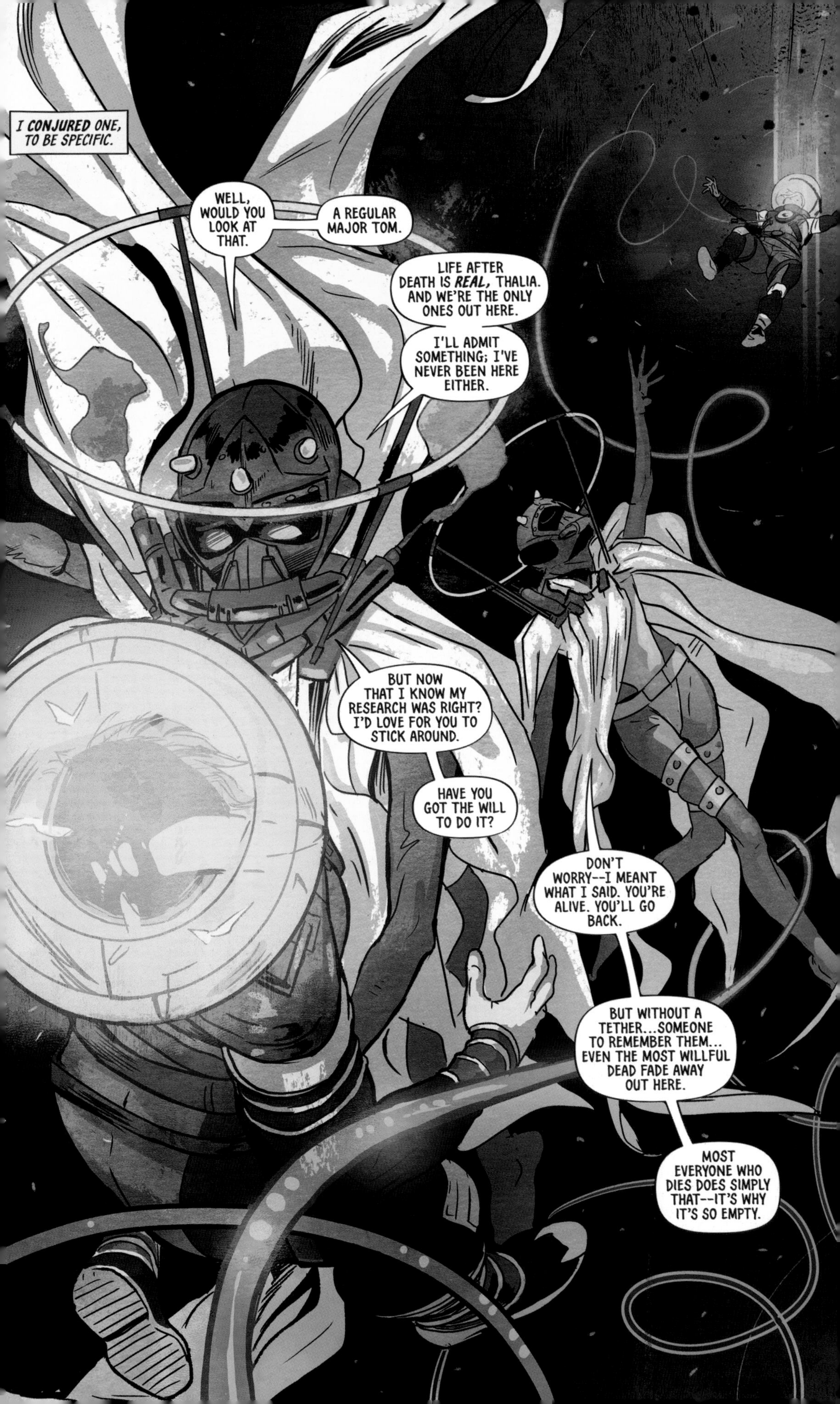
I CONJURED ONE, TO BE SPECIFIC.
WELL, WOULD YOU LOOK AT THAT.
A REGULAR MAJOR TOM.
LIFE AFTER DEATH IS REAL, THALIA. AND WE'RE THE ONLY ONES OUT HERE.
I'LL ADMIT SOMETHING; I'VE NEVER BEEN HERE EITHER.
BUT NOW THAT I KNOW MY RESEARCH WAS RIGHT? I'D LOVE FOR YOU TO STICK AROUND.
HAVE YOU GOT THE WILL TO DO IT?
DON'T WORRY--I MEANT WHAT I SAID. YOU'RE ALIVE. YOU'LL GO BACK.
BUT WITHOUT A TETHER...SOMEONE TO REMEMBER THEM... EVEN THE MOST WILLFUL DEAD FADE AWAY OUT HERE.
MOST EVERYONE WHO DIES DOES SIMPLY THAT--IT'S WHY IT'S SO EMPTY.

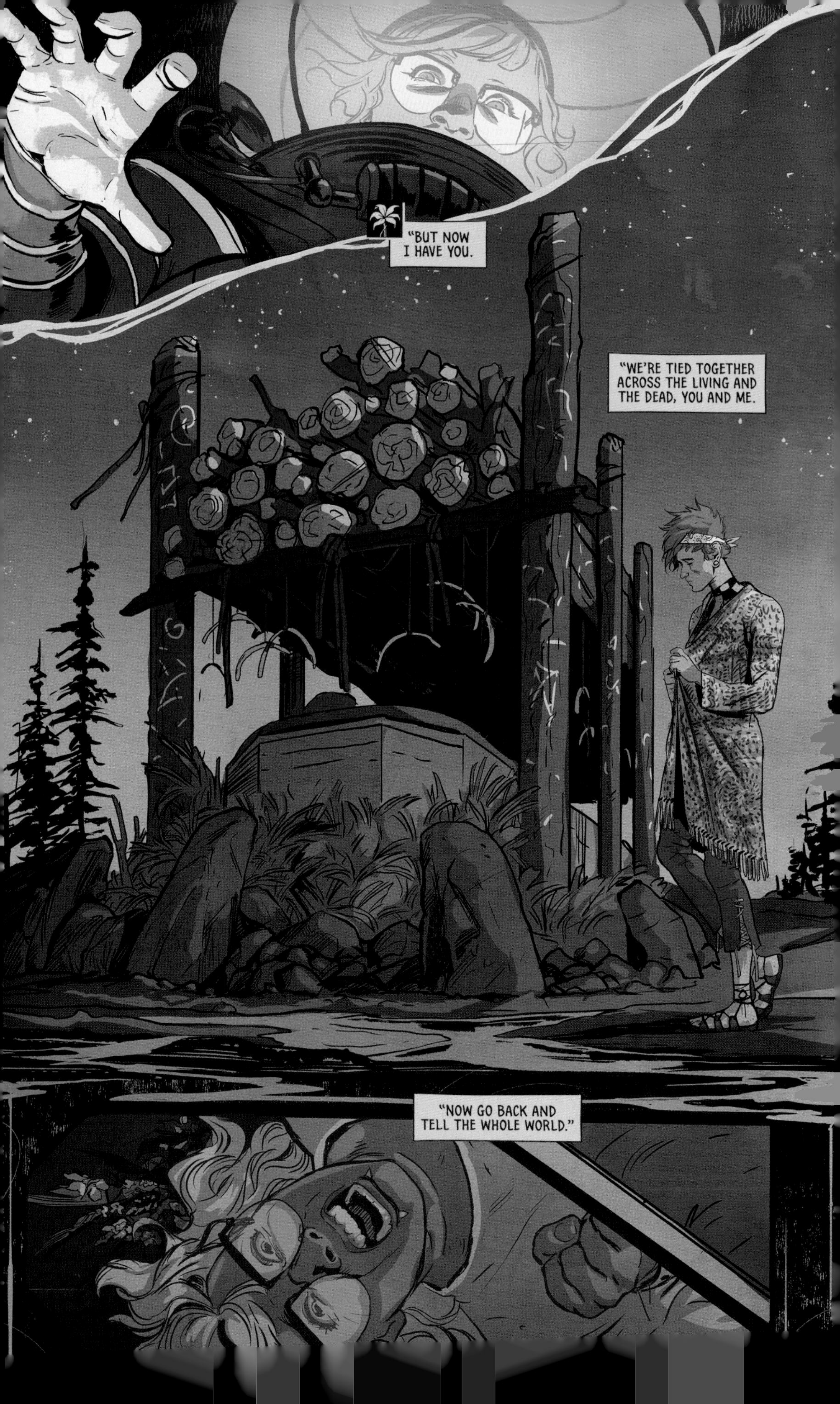
"BUT NOW
I HAVE YOU.
"WE'RE TIED TOGETHER
ACROSS THE LIVING AND
THE DEAD, YOU AND ME.
"NOW GO BACK AND
TELL THE WHOLE WORLD."

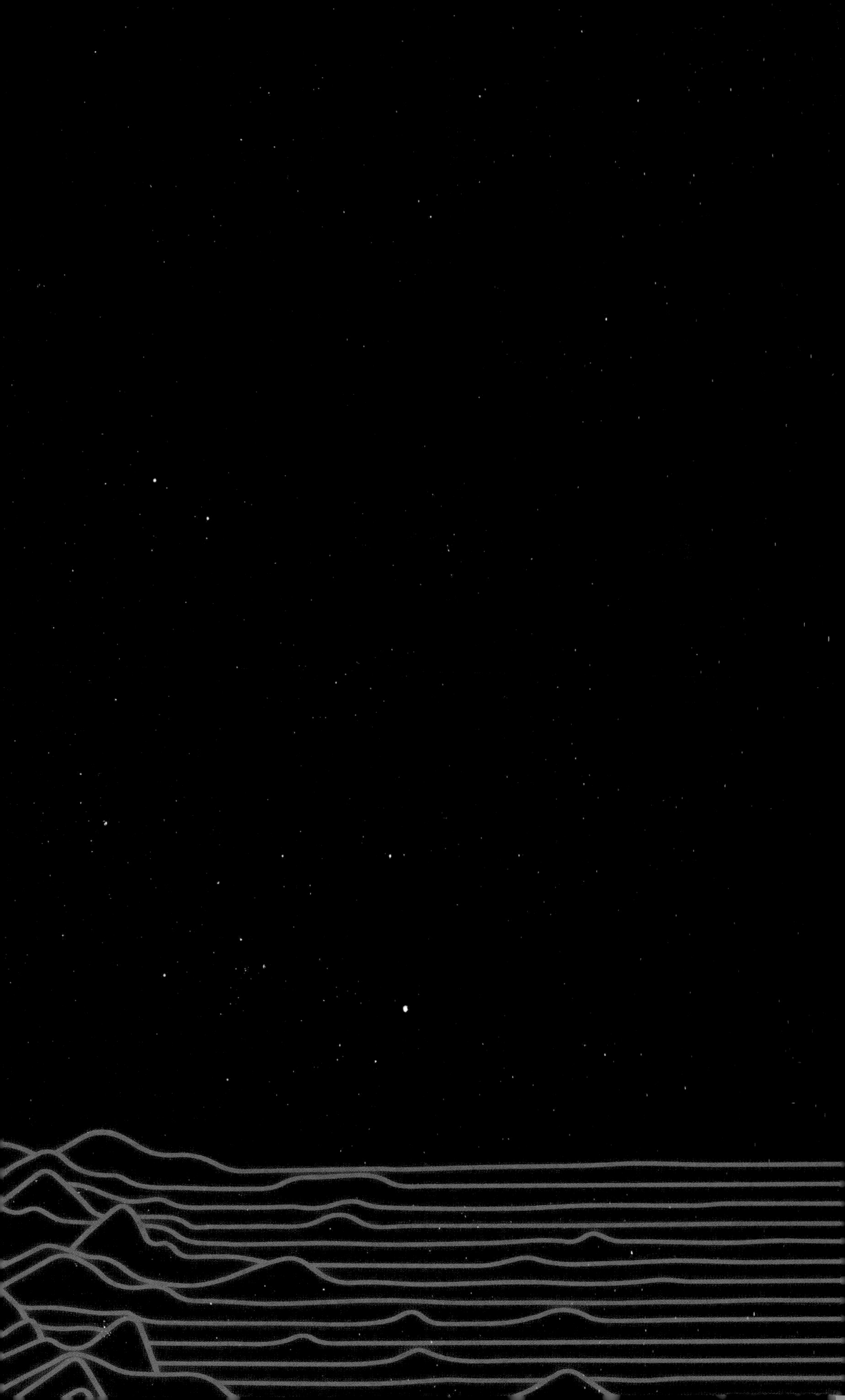

"ALL RIGHT, THALIA ROSEWOOD. LET'S HOPE YOU'RE THE KIND OF GIRL WHO COMES TO WORK WITH A CONCUSSION."

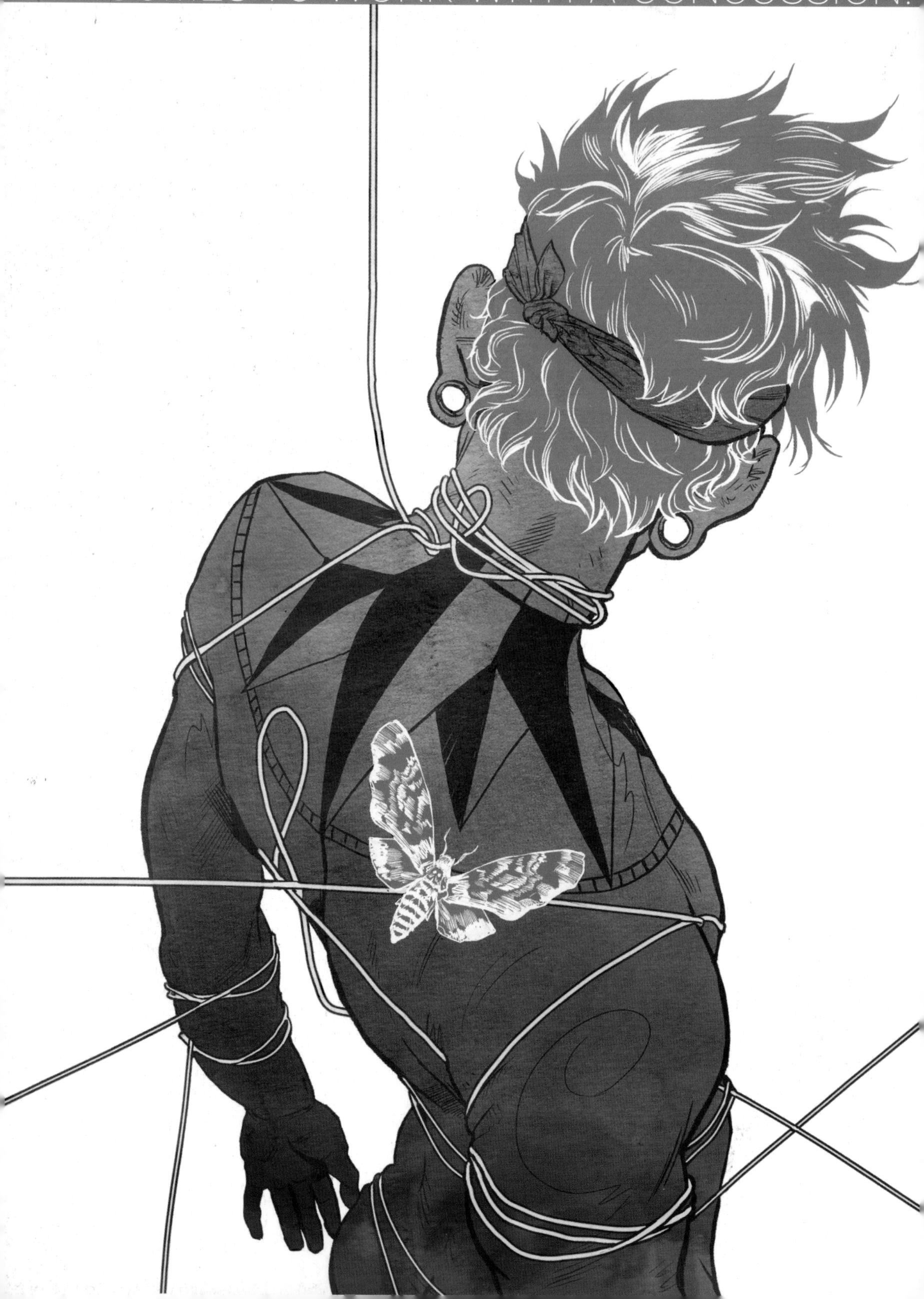

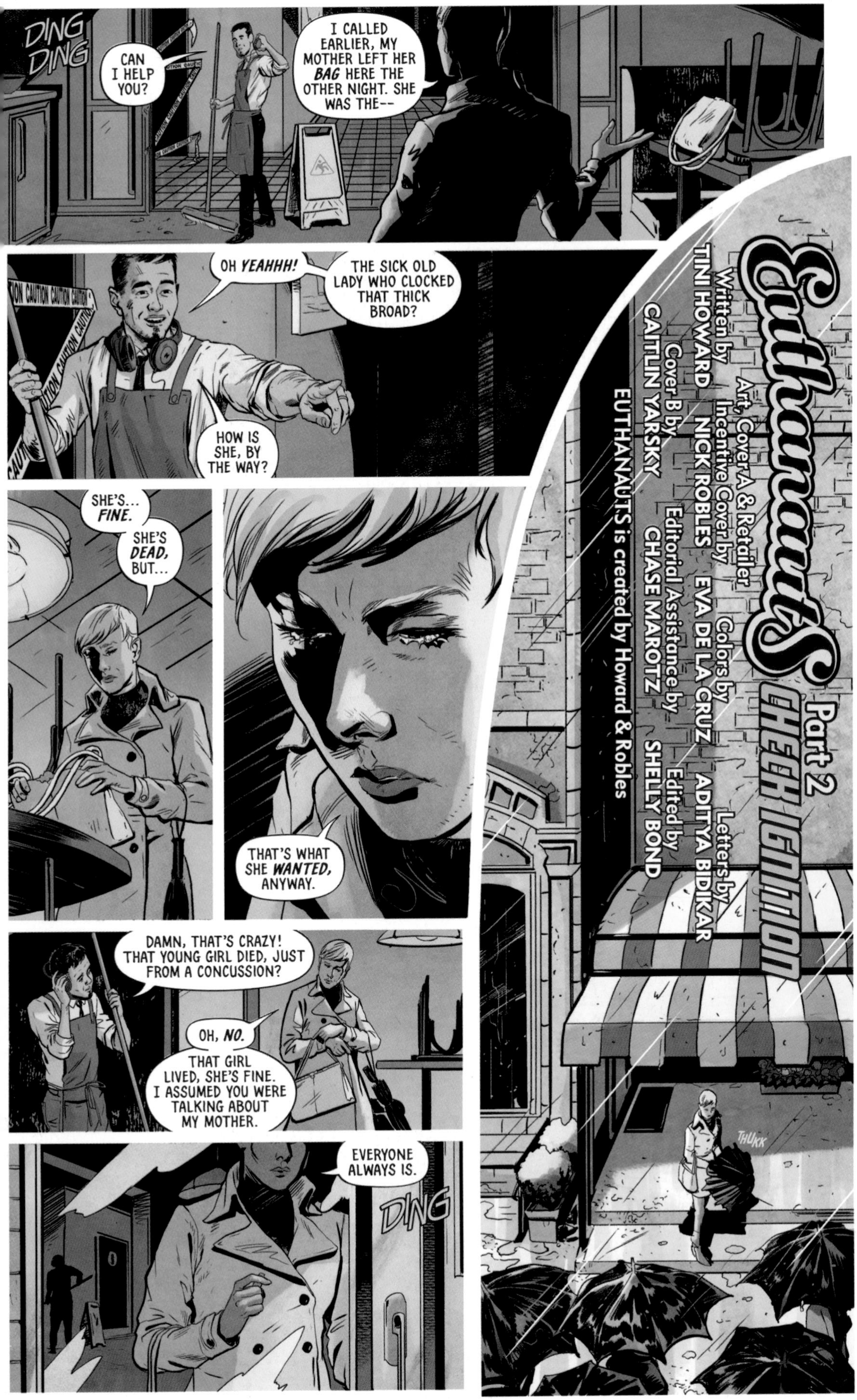
DING DING
CAN I HELP YOU?
I CALLED EARLIER, MY MOTHER LEFT HER BAG HERE THE OTHER NIGHT. SHE WAS THE--
OH YEAHHH!
THE SICK OLD LADY WHO CLOCKED THAT THICK BROAD?
HOW IS SHE, BY THE WAY?
SHE'S... FINE.
SHE'S DEAD, BUT...
THAT'S WHAT SHE WANTED, ANYWAY.
DAMN, THAT'S CRAZY! THAT YOUNG GIRL DIED, JUST FROM A CONCUSSION?
OH, NO.
THAT GIRL LIVED, SHE'S FINE. I ASSUMED YOU WERE TALKING ABOUT MY MOTHER.
EVERYONE ALWAYS IS.
DING
THUKK
Euthanauts
Part 2
CHECK IGNITION
Written by TINI HOWARD
Art, Cover A & Retailer Incentive Cover by NICK ROBLES
Colors by EVA DE LA CRUZ
Letters by ADITYA BIDIKAR
Cover B by CAITLIN YARSKY
Editorial Assistance by CHASE MAROTZ
Edited by SHELLY BOND
EUTHANAUTS is created by Howard & Robles

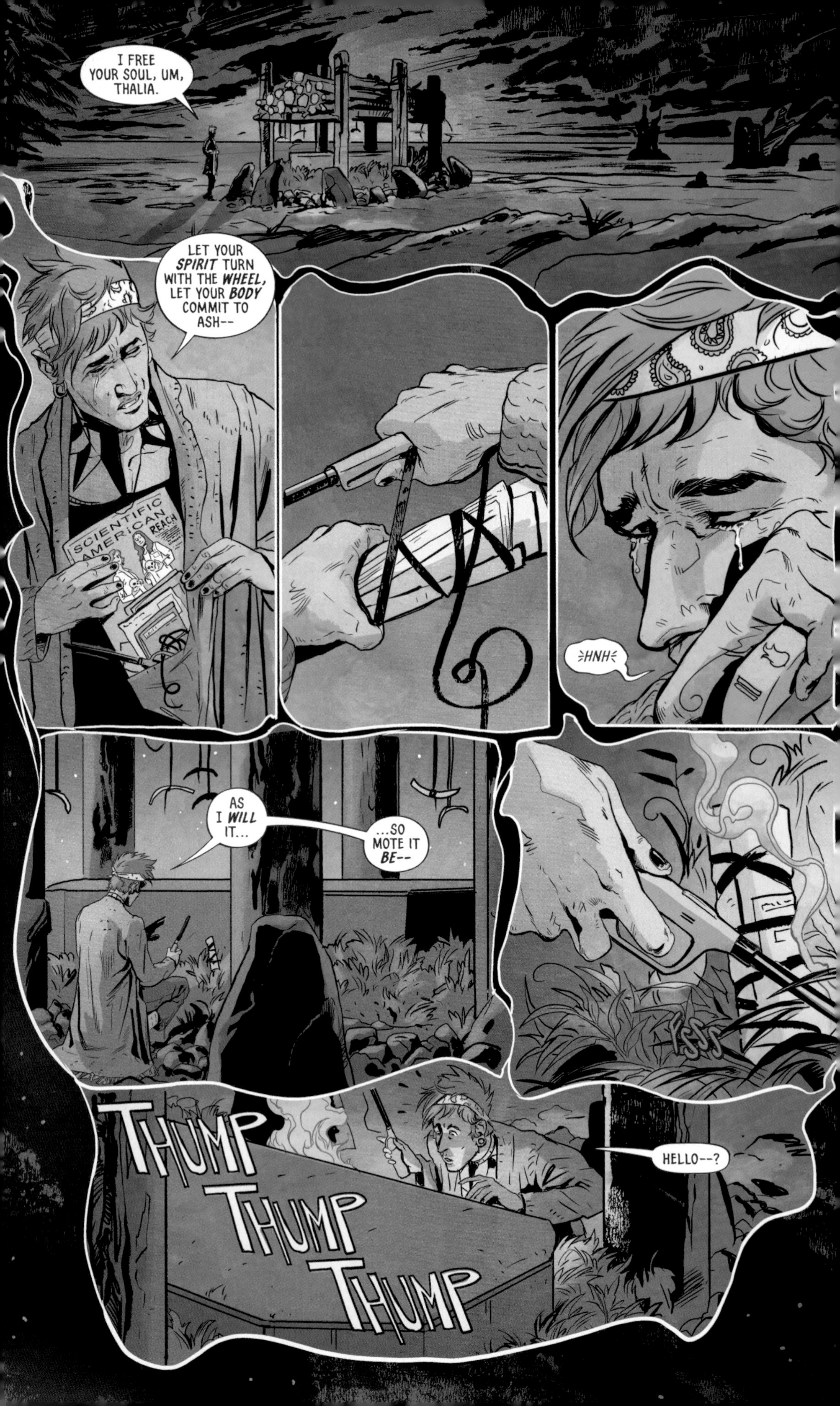
I FREE YOUR SOUL, UM, THALIA.
LET YOUR SPIRIT TURN WITH THE WHEEL, LET YOUR BODY COMMIT TO ASH--
SCIENTIFIC AMERICAN
REACH
HNH
AS I WILL IT...
...SO MOTE IT BE--
TSSS
THUMP THUMP THUMP
HELLO--?

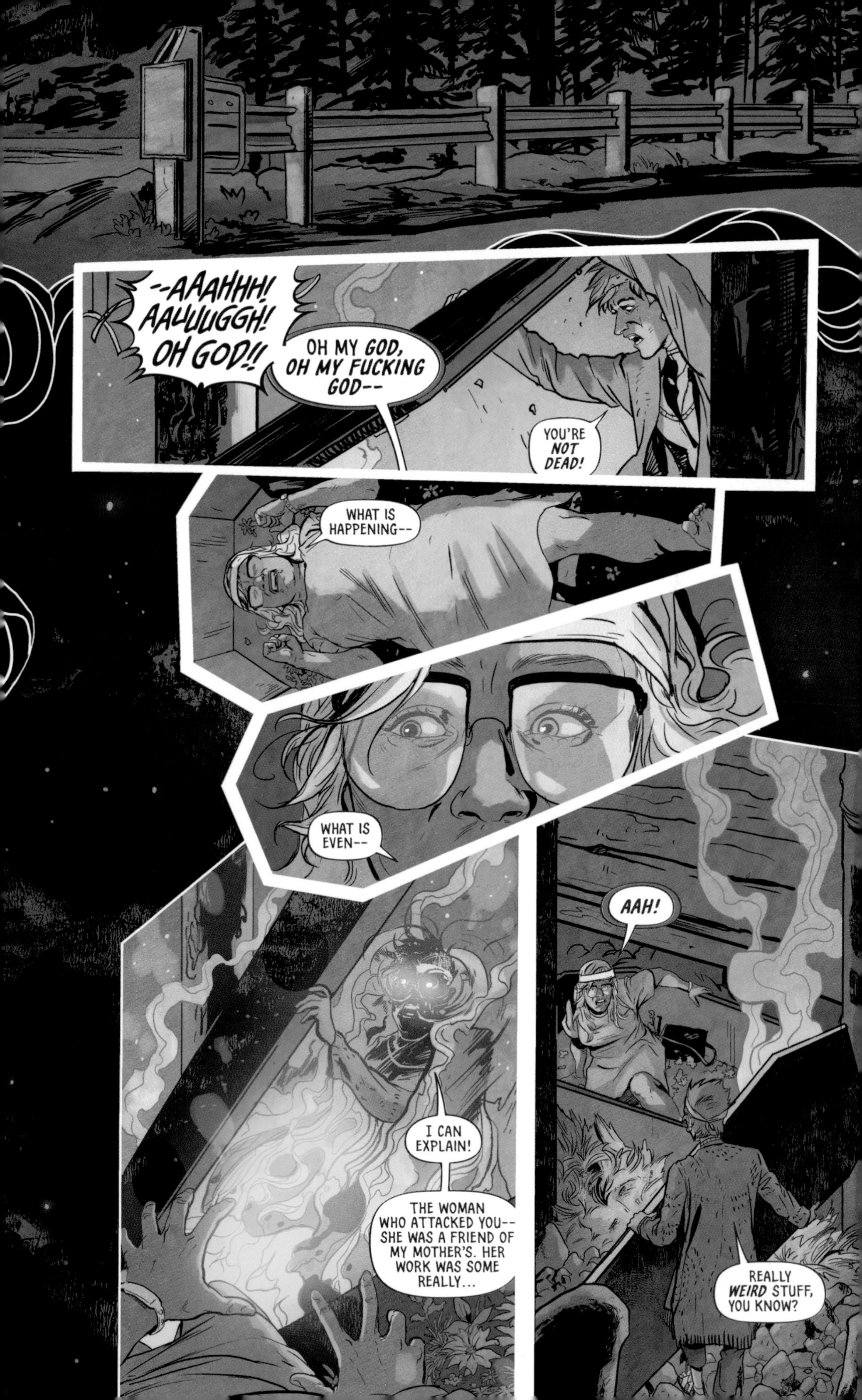

--AAAHHH! AAUUUGGH! OH GOD!!
OH MY GOD, OH MY FUCKING GOD--
YOU'RE NOT DEAD!
WHAT IS HAPPENING--
WHAT IS EVEN--
AAH!
I CAN EXPLAIN!
THE WOMAN WHO ATTACKED YOU-- SHE WAS A FRIEND OF MY MOTHER'S. HER WORK WAS SOME REALLY...
REALLY WEIRD STUFF, YOU KNOW?

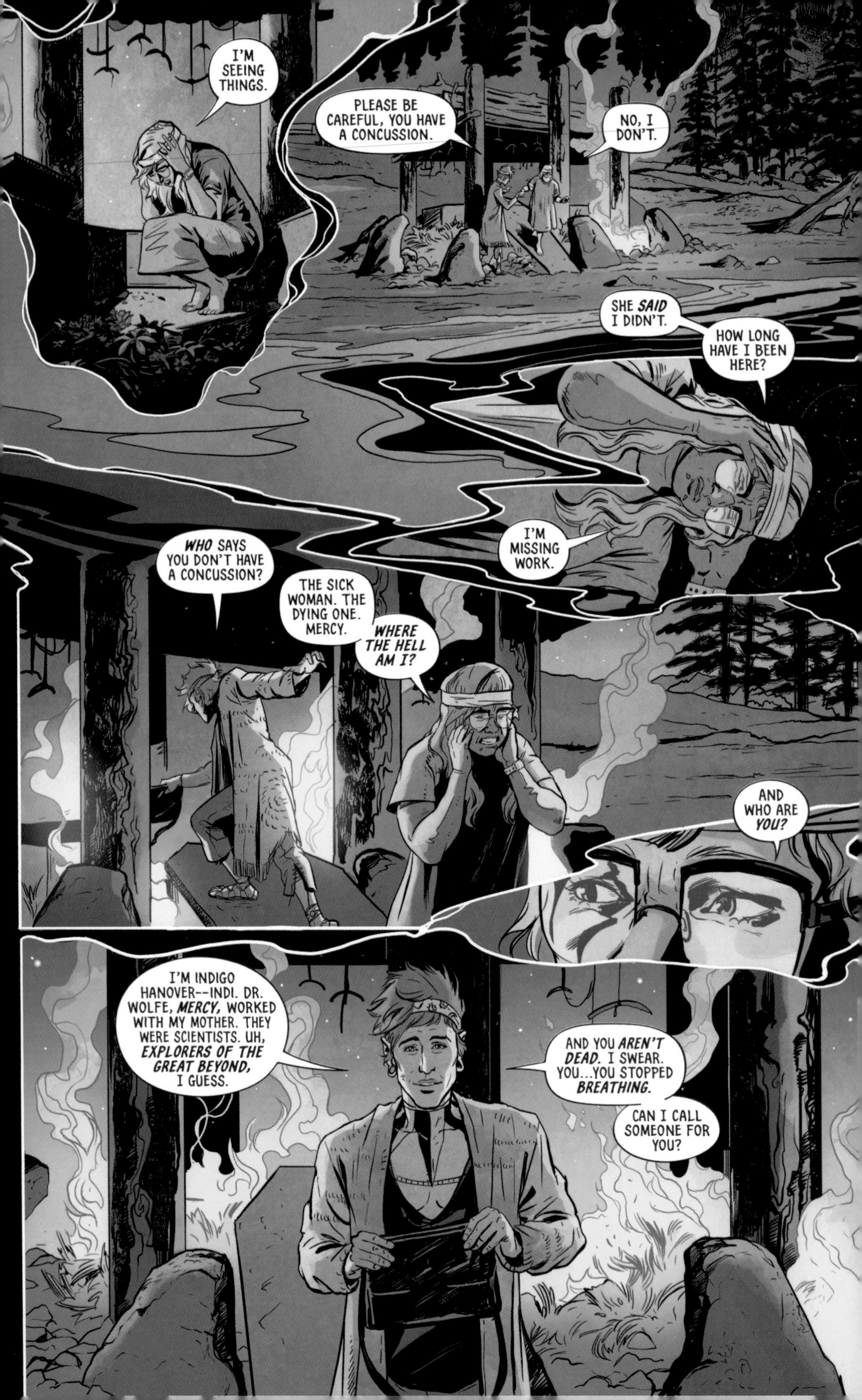
I'M SEEING THINGS.
PLEASE BE CAREFUL, YOU HAVE A CONCUSSION.
NO, I DON'T.
SHE *SAID* I DIDN'T.
HOW LONG HAVE I BEEN HERE?
I'M MISSING WORK.
WHO SAYS YOU DON'T HAVE A CONCUSSION?
THE SICK WOMAN. THE DYING ONE. MERCY.
WHERE THE HELL AM I?
AND WHO ARE *YOU?*
I'M INDIGO HANOVER--INDI. DR. WOLFE, *MERCY,* WORKED WITH MY MOTHER. THEY WERE SCIENTISTS. UH, *EXPLORERS OF THE GREAT BEYOND,* I GUESS.
AND YOU *AREN'T DEAD.* I SWEAR. YOU...YOU STOPPED *BREATHING.*
CAN I CALL SOMEONE FOR YOU?

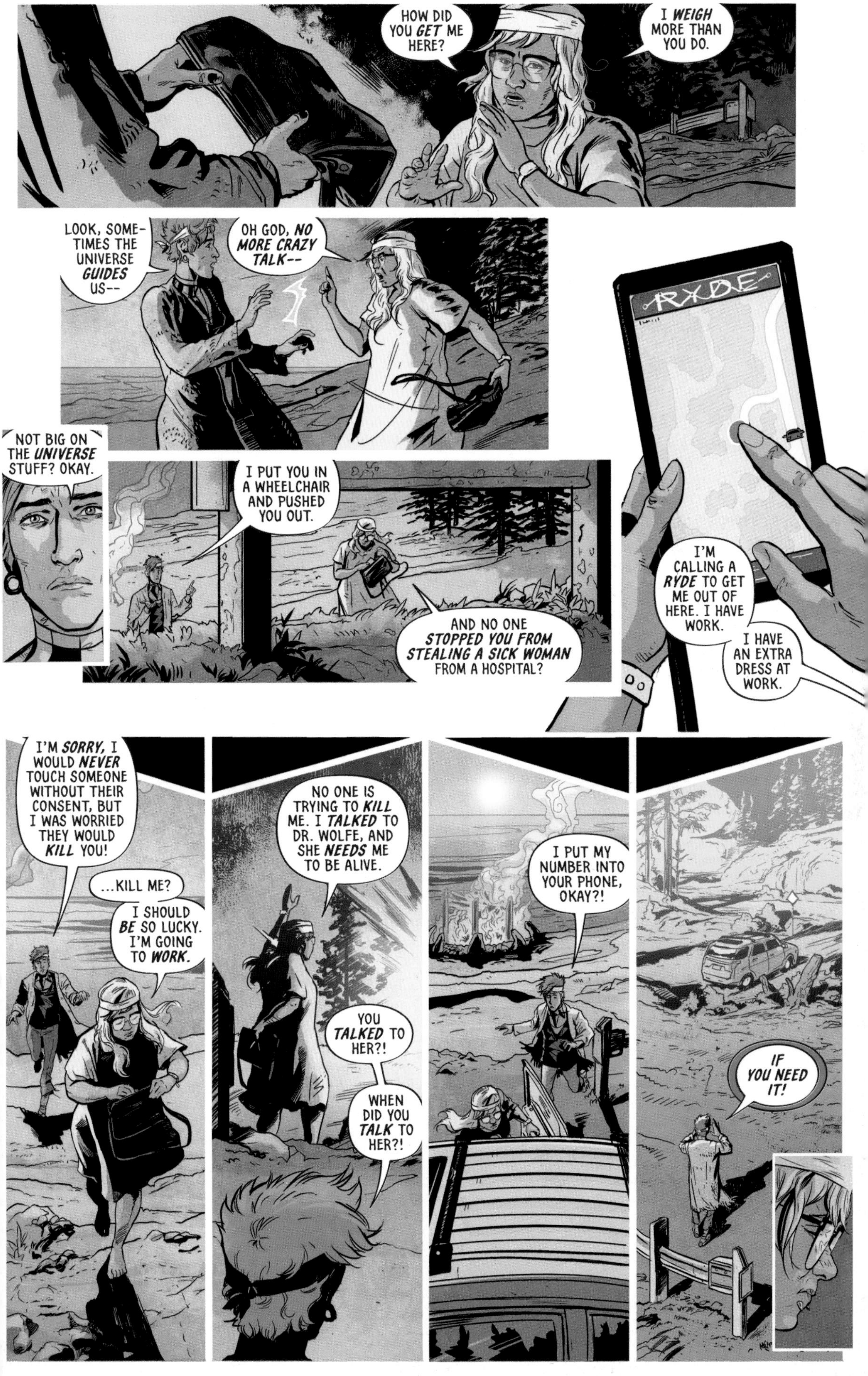
HOW DID YOU GET ME HERE?
I WEIGH MORE THAN YOU DO.
LOOK, SOMETIMES THE UNIVERSE GUIDES US--
OH GOD, NO MORE CRAZY TALK--
NOT BIG ON THE UNIVERSE STUFF? OKAY.
I PUT YOU IN A WHEELCHAIR AND PUSHED YOU OUT.
AND NO ONE STOPPED YOU FROM STEALING A SICK WOMAN FROM A HOSPITAL?
RYDE
I'M CALLING A RYDE TO GET ME OUT OF HERE. I HAVE WORK.
I HAVE AN EXTRA DRESS AT WORK.
I'M SORRY, I WOULD NEVER TOUCH SOMEONE WITHOUT THEIR CONSENT, BUT I WAS WORRIED THEY WOULD KILL YOU!
...KILL ME?
I SHOULD BE SO LUCKY. I'M GOING TO WORK.
NO ONE IS TRYING TO KILL ME. I TALKED TO DR. WOLFE, AND SHE NEEDS ME TO BE ALIVE.
YOU TALKED TO HER?!
WHEN DID YOU TALK TO HER?!
I PUT MY NUMBER INTO YOUR PHONE, OKAY?!
IF YOU NEED IT!

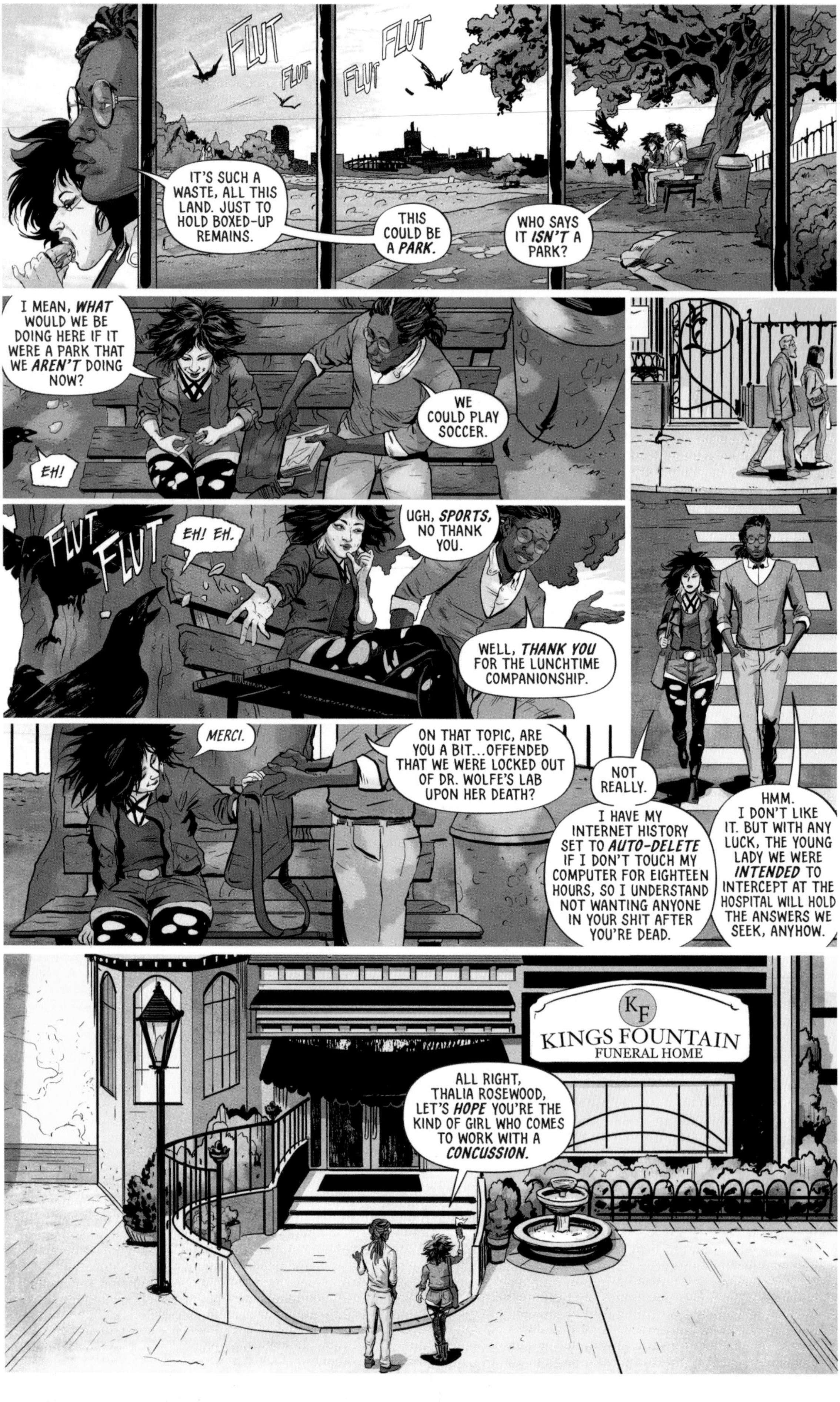
FLUT
FLUT
FLUT FLUT
IT'S SUCH A WASTE, ALL THIS LAND. JUST TO HOLD BOXED-UP REMAINS.
THIS COULD BE A PARK.
WHO SAYS IT ISN'T A PARK?
I MEAN, WHAT WOULD WE BE DOING HERE IF IT WERE A PARK THAT WE AREN'T DOING NOW?
WE COULD PLAY SOCCER.
EH!
FLUT FLUT
EH! EH.
UGH, SPORTS, NO THANK YOU.
WELL, THANK YOU FOR THE LUNCHTIME COMPANIONSHIP.
MERCI.
ON THAT TOPIC, ARE YOU A BIT...OFFENDED THAT WE WERE LOCKED OUT OF DR. WOLFE'S LAB UPON HER DEATH?
NOT REALLY.
I HAVE MY INTERNET HISTORY SET TO AUTO-DELETE IF I DON'T TOUCH MY COMPUTER FOR EIGHTEEN HOURS, SO I UNDERSTAND NOT WANTING ANYONE IN YOUR SHIT AFTER YOU'RE DEAD.
HMM. I DON'T LIKE IT. BUT WITH ANY LUCK, THE YOUNG LADY WE WERE INTENDED TO INTERCEPT AT THE HOSPITAL WILL HOLD THE ANSWERS WE SEEK, ANYHOW.
KF
KINGS FOUNTAIN
FUNERAL HOME
ALL RIGHT, THALIA ROSEWOOD, LET'S HOPE YOU'RE THE KIND OF GIRL WHO COMES TO WORK WITH A CONCUSSION.

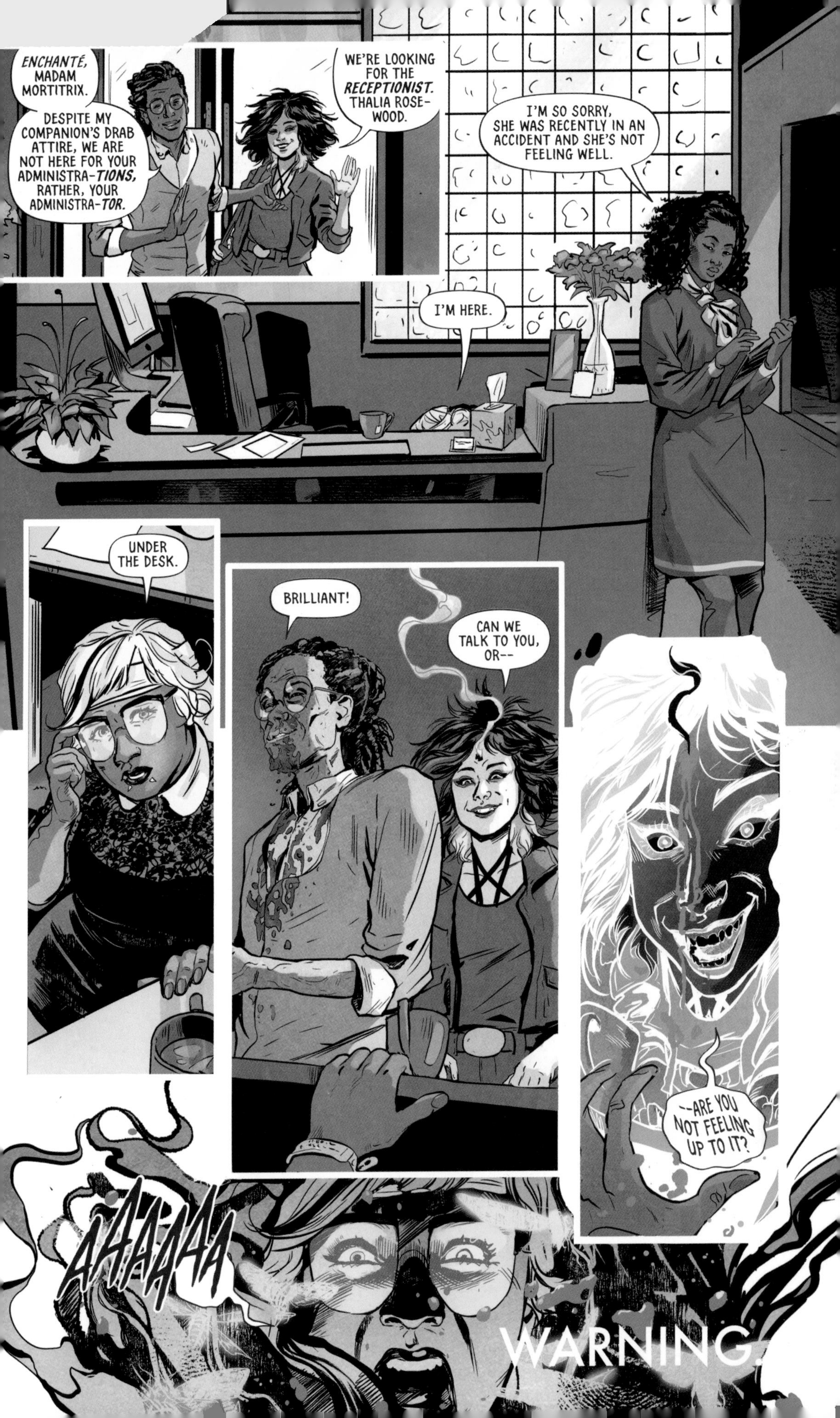
ENCHANTÉ, MADAM MORTITRIX.
DESPITE MY COMPANION'S DRAB ATTIRE, WE ARE NOT HERE FOR YOUR ADMINISTRA-TIONS, RATHER, YOUR ADMINISTRA-TOR.
WE'RE LOOKING FOR THE RECEPTIONIST. THALIA ROSE-WOOD.
I'M SO SORRY, SHE WAS RECENTLY IN AN ACCIDENT AND SHE'S NOT FEELING WELL.
I'M HERE.
UNDER THE DESK.
BRILLIANT!
CAN WE TALK TO YOU, OR--
--ARE YOU NOT FEELING UP TO IT?
AHAAAAA
WARNING.

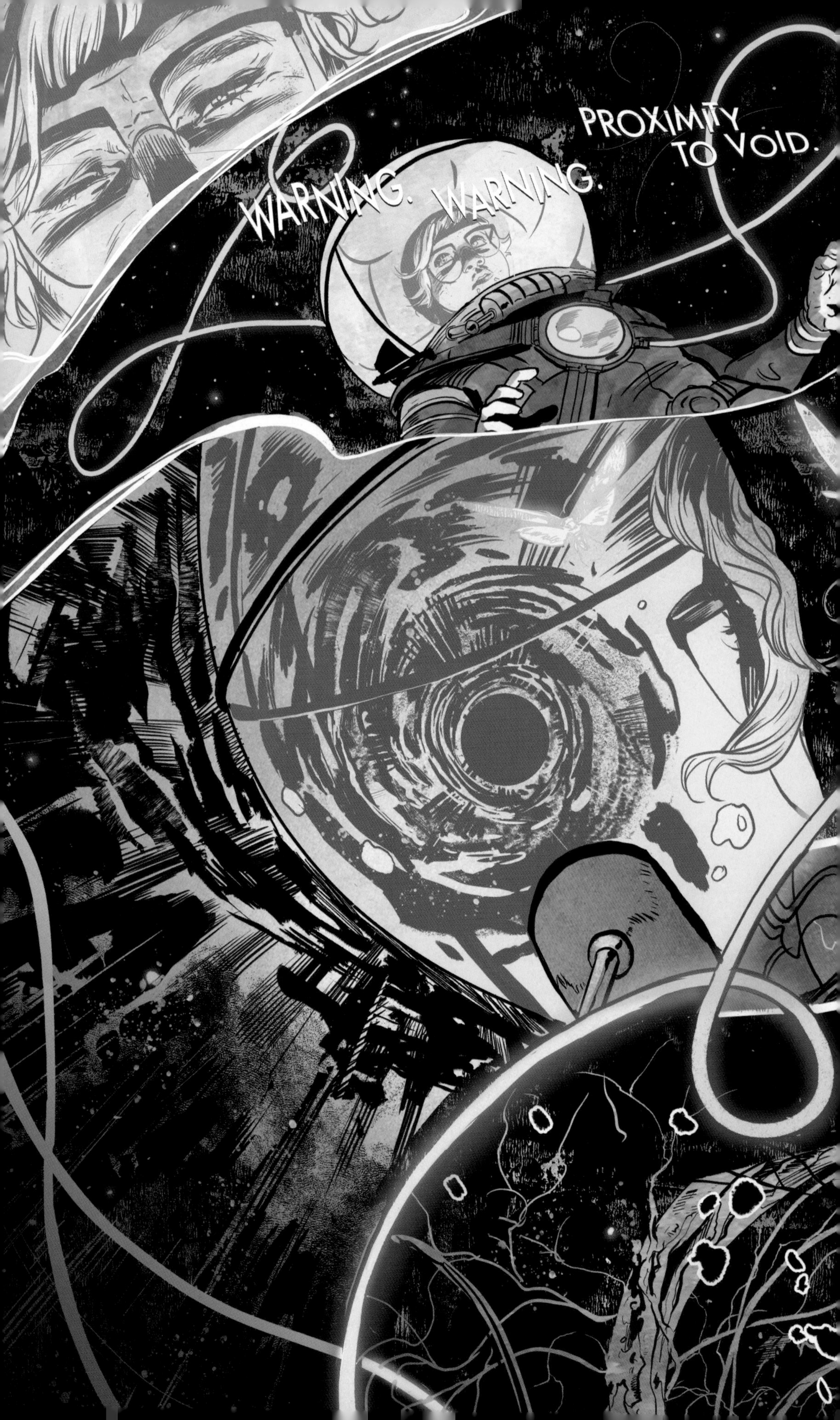
WARNING. WARNING.
PROXIMITY TO VOID.

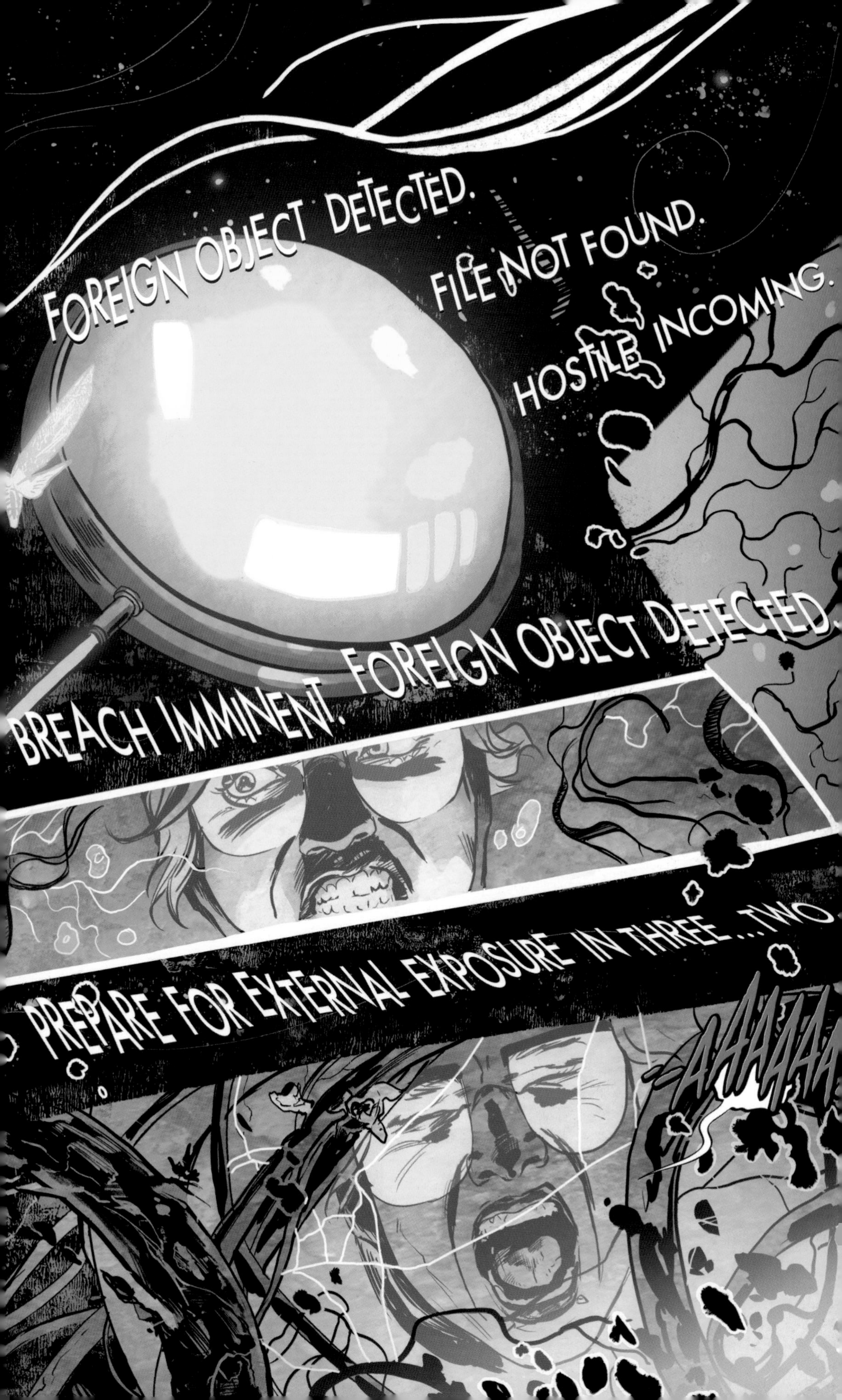
FOREIGN OBJECT DETECTED.
FILE NOT FOUND.
HOSTILE INCOMING.
BREACH IMMINENT. FOREIGN OBJECT DETECTED.
PREPARE FOR EXTERNAL EXPOSURE IN THREE...TWO
AAAAAA

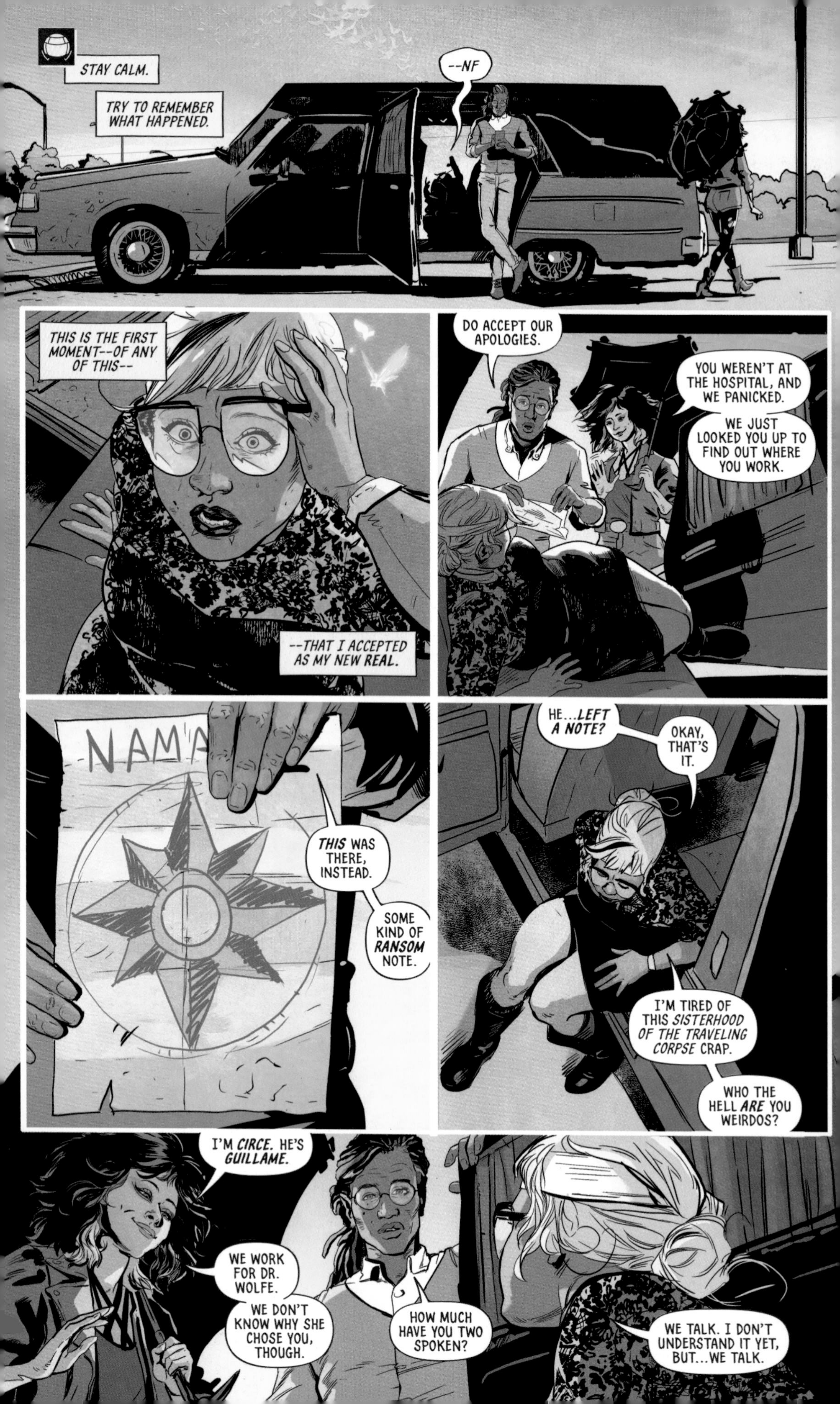
STAY CALM.
TRY TO REMEMBER WHAT HAPPENED.
--NF
THIS IS THE FIRST MOMENT--OF ANY OF THIS--
--THAT I ACCEPTED AS MY NEW REAL.
DO ACCEPT OUR APOLOGIES.
YOU WEREN'T AT THE HOSPITAL, AND WE PANICKED.
WE JUST LOOKED YOU UP TO FIND OUT WHERE YOU WORK.
NAMA
THIS WAS THERE, INSTEAD.
SOME KIND OF RANSOM NOTE.
HE...LEFT A NOTE?
OKAY, THAT'S IT.
I'M TIRED OF THIS SISTERHOOD OF THE TRAVELING CORPSE CRAP.
WHO THE HELL ARE YOU WEIRDOS?
I'M CIRCE. HE'S GUILLAME.
WE WORK FOR DR. WOLFE.
WE DON'T KNOW WHY SHE CHOSE YOU, THOUGH.
HOW MUCH HAVE YOU TWO SPOKEN?
WE TALK. I DON'T UNDERSTAND IT YET, BUT...WE TALK.

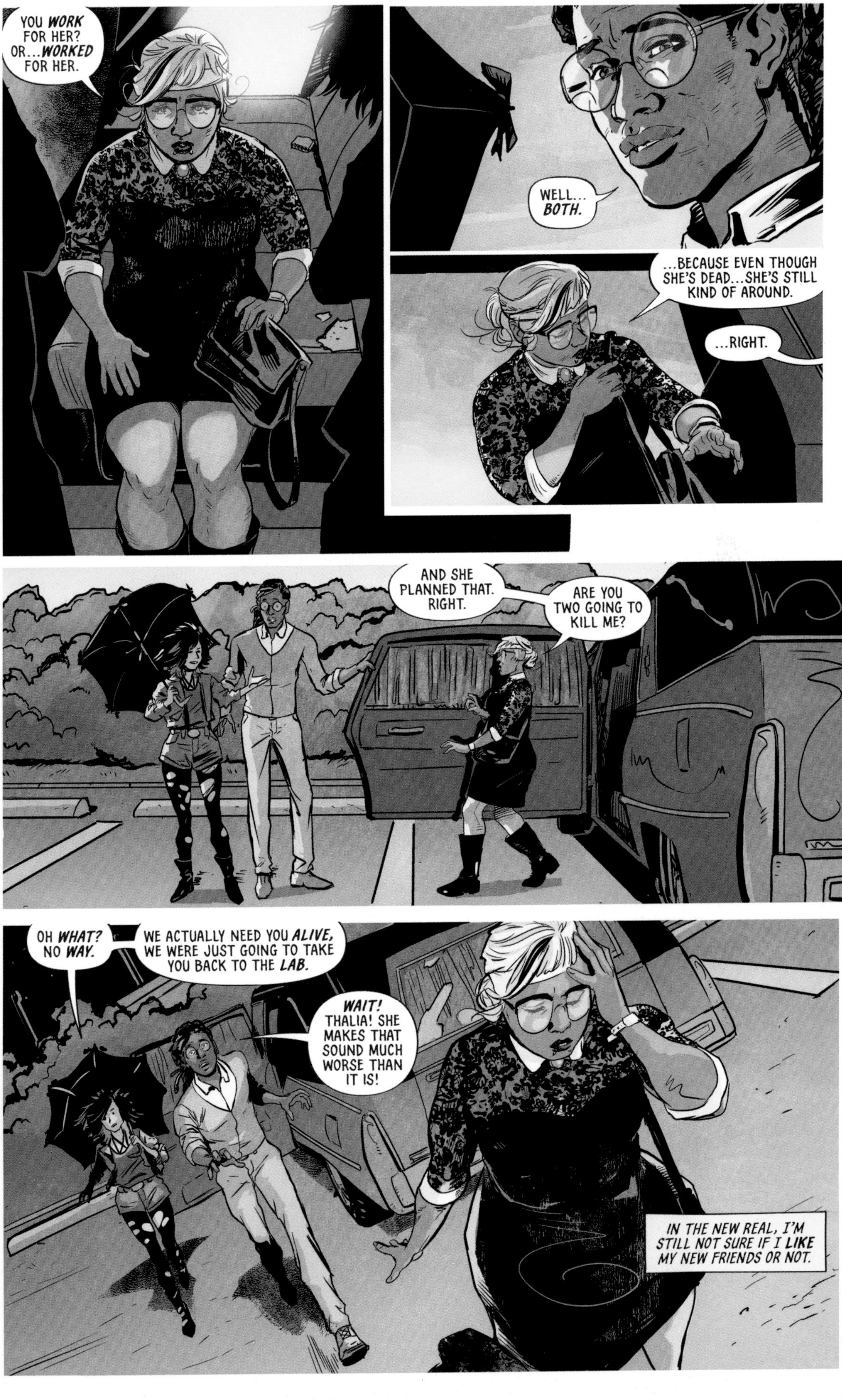
YOU WORK FOR HER? OR...WORKED FOR HER.
WELL... BOTH.
...BECAUSE EVEN THOUGH SHE'S DEAD...SHE'S STILL KIND OF AROUND.
...RIGHT.
AND SHE PLANNED THAT. RIGHT.
ARE YOU TWO GOING TO KILL ME?
OH WHAT? NO WAY.
WE ACTUALLY NEED YOU ALIVE, WE WERE JUST GOING TO TAKE YOU BACK TO THE LAB.
WAIT! THALIA! SHE MAKES THAT SOUND MUCH WORSE THAN IT IS!
IN THE NEW REAL, I'M STILL NOT SURE IF I LIKE MY NEW FRIENDS OR NOT.

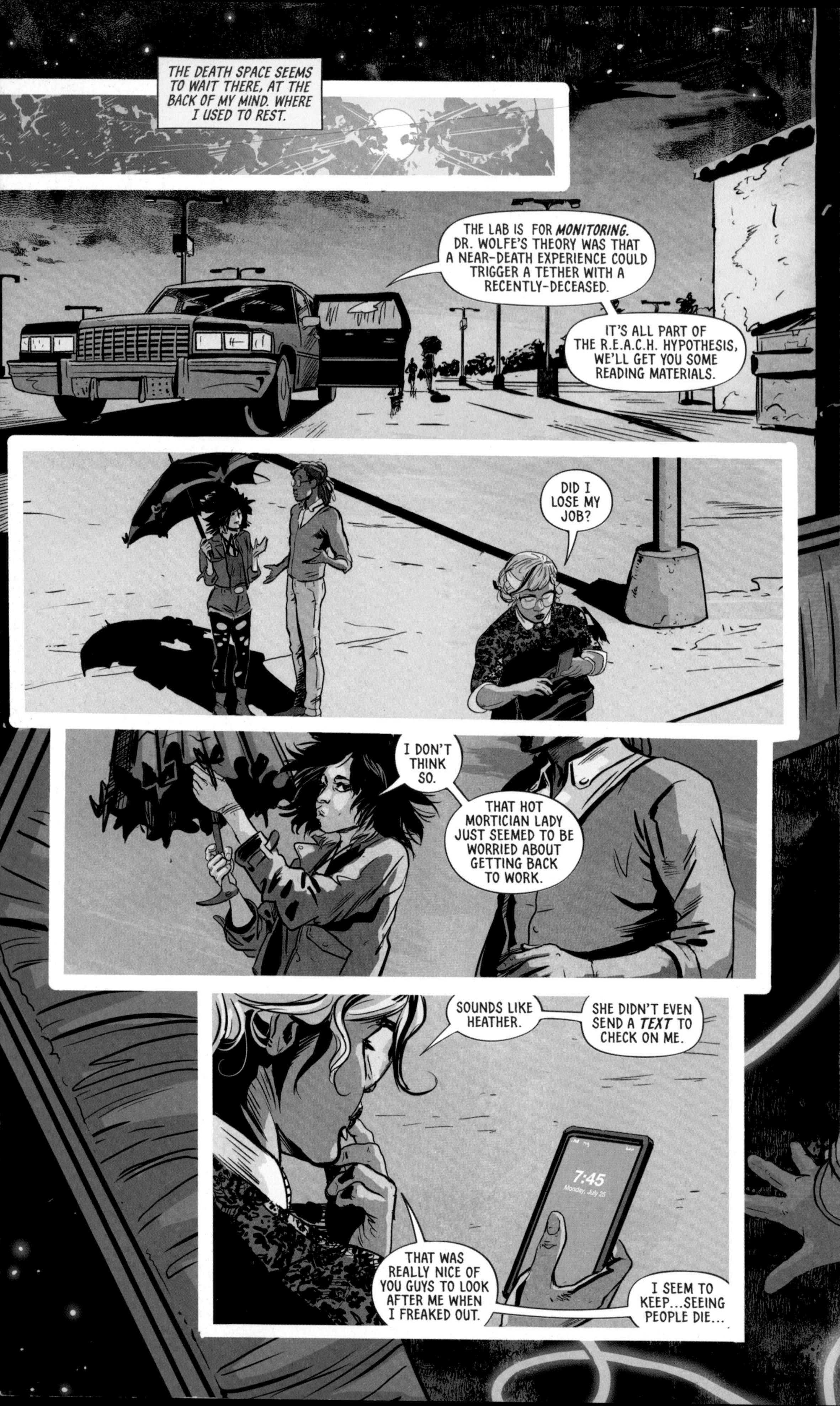
THE DEATH SPACE SEEMS TO WAIT THERE, AT THE BACK OF MY MIND. WHERE I USED TO REST.
THE LAB IS FOR *MONITORING.* DR. WOLFE'S THEORY WAS THAT A NEAR-DEATH EXPERIENCE COULD TRIGGER A TETHER WITH A RECENTLY-DECEASED.
IT'S ALL PART OF THE R.E.A.C.H. HYPOTHESIS, WE'LL GET YOU SOME READING MATERIALS.
DID I LOSE MY JOB?
I DON'T THINK SO.
THAT HOT MORTICIAN LADY JUST SEEMED TO BE WORRIED ABOUT GETTING BACK TO WORK.
SOUNDS LIKE HEATHER.
SHE DIDN'T EVEN SEND A *TEXT* TO CHECK ON ME.
7:45
Monday, July 25
THAT WAS REALLY NICE OF YOU GUYS TO LOOK AFTER ME WHEN I FREAKED OUT.
I SEEM TO KEEP...SEEING PEOPLE DIE...

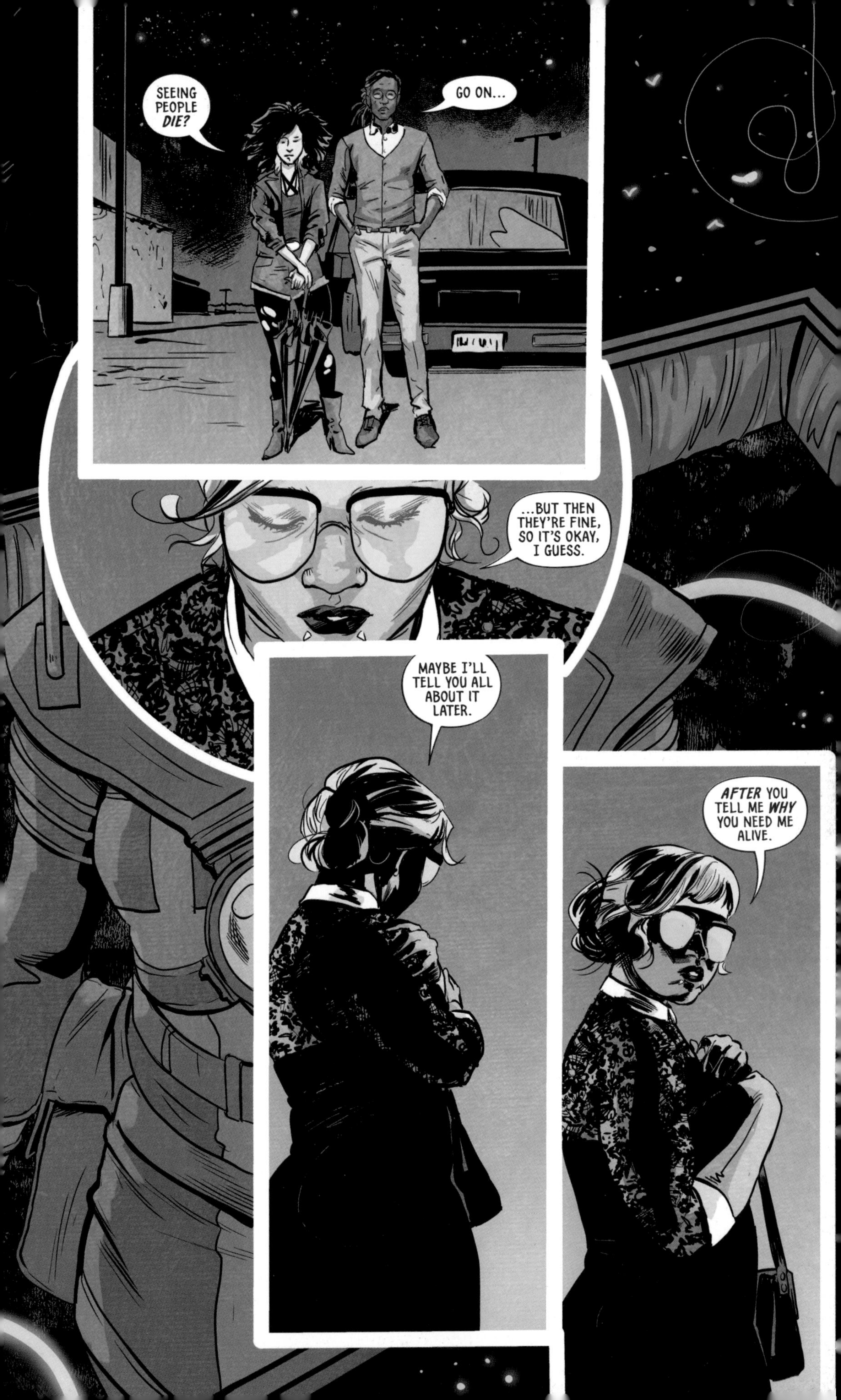
SEEING PEOPLE DIE?
GO ON...
...BUT THEN THEY'RE FINE, SO IT'S OKAY, I GUESS.
MAYBE I'LL TELL YOU ALL ABOUT IT LATER.
AFTER YOU TELL ME WHY YOU NEED ME ALIVE.

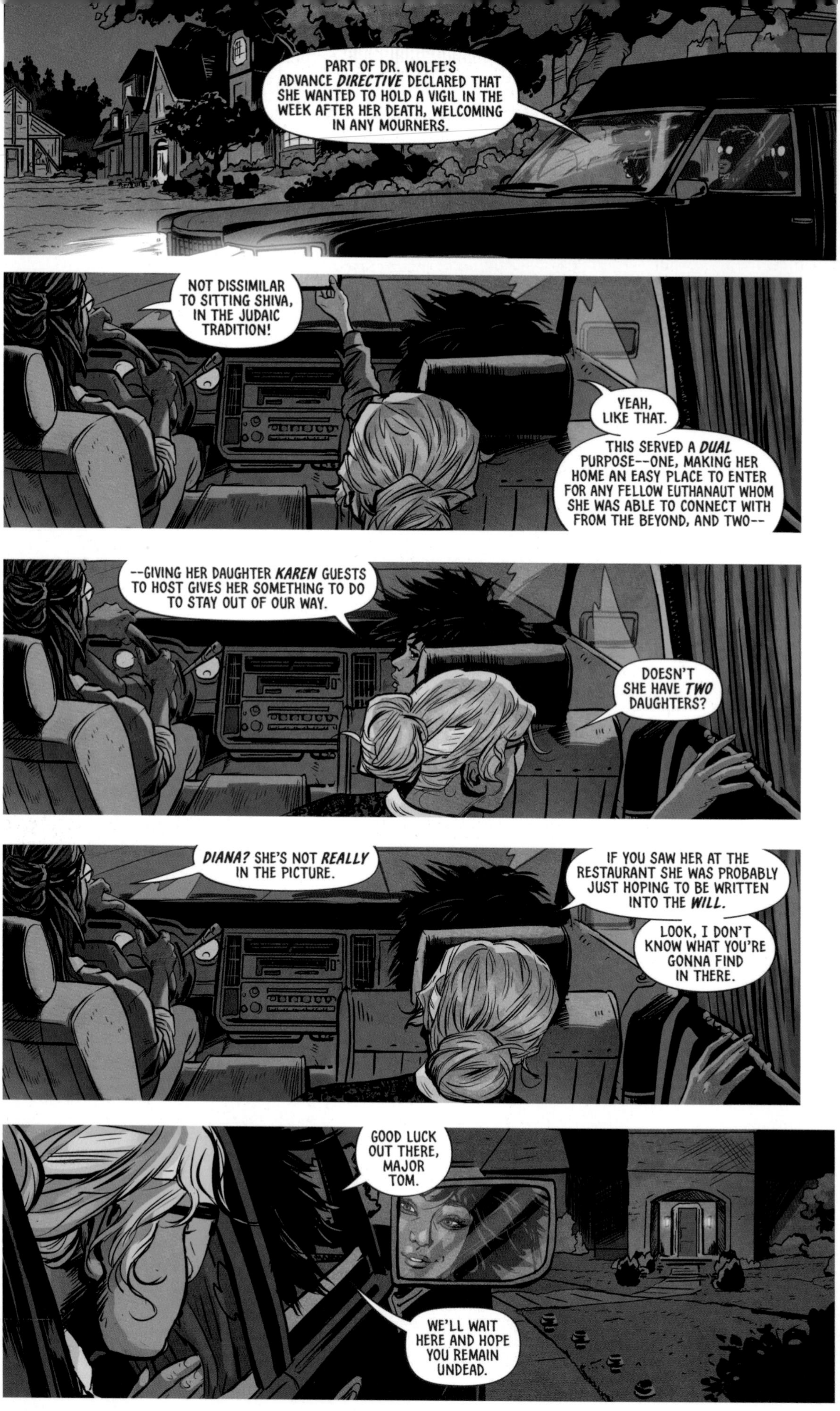
PART OF DR. WOLFE'S ADVANCE DIRECTIVE DECLARED THAT SHE WANTED TO HOLD A VIGIL IN THE WEEK AFTER HER DEATH, WELCOMING IN ANY MOURNERS.
NOT DISSIMILAR TO SITTING SHIVA, IN THE JUDAIC TRADITION!
YEAH, LIKE THAT.
THIS SERVED A DUAL PURPOSE--ONE, MAKING HER HOME AN EASY PLACE TO ENTER FOR ANY FELLOW EUTHANAUT WHOM SHE WAS ABLE TO CONNECT WITH FROM THE BEYOND, AND TWO--
--GIVING HER DAUGHTER KAREN GUESTS TO HOST GIVES HER SOMETHING TO DO TO STAY OUT OF OUR WAY.
DOESN'T SHE HAVE TWO DAUGHTERS?
DIANA? SHE'S NOT REALLY IN THE PICTURE.
IF YOU SAW HER AT THE RESTAURANT SHE WAS PROBABLY JUST HOPING TO BE WRITTEN INTO THE WILL.
LOOK, I DON'T KNOW WHAT YOU'RE GONNA FIND IN THERE.
GOOD LUCK OUT THERE, MAJOR TOM.
WE'LL WAIT HERE AND HOPE YOU REMAIN UNDEAD.

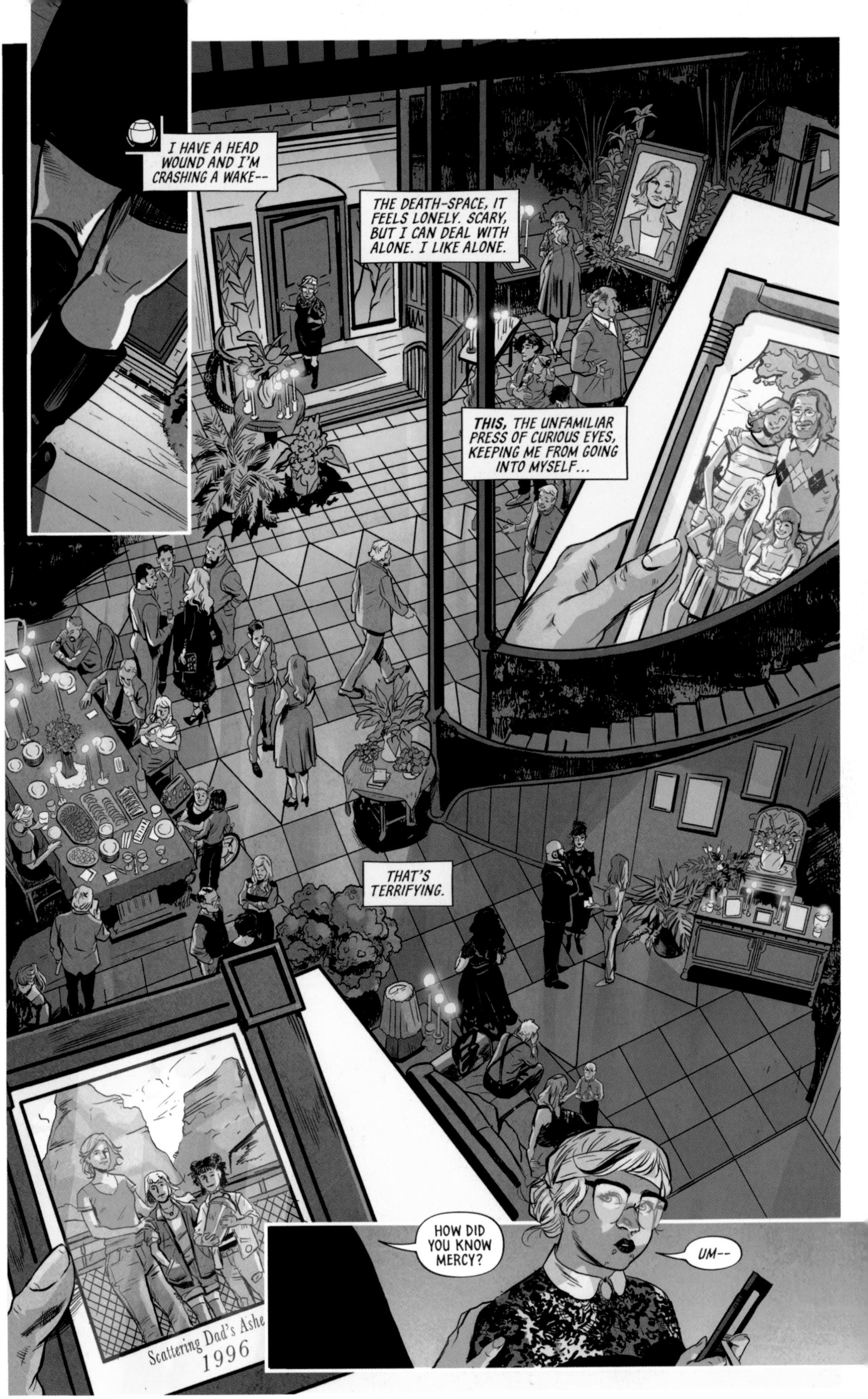
I HAVE A HEAD WOUND AND I'M CRASHING A WAKE--
THE DEATH-SPACE, IT FEELS LONELY. SCARY, BUT I CAN DEAL WITH ALONE. I LIKE ALONE.
THIS, THE UNFAMILIAR PRESS OF CURIOUS EYES, KEEPING ME FROM GOING INTO MYSELF...
THAT'S TERRIFYING.
Scattering Dad's Ashe
1996
HOW DID YOU KNOW MERCY?
UM--

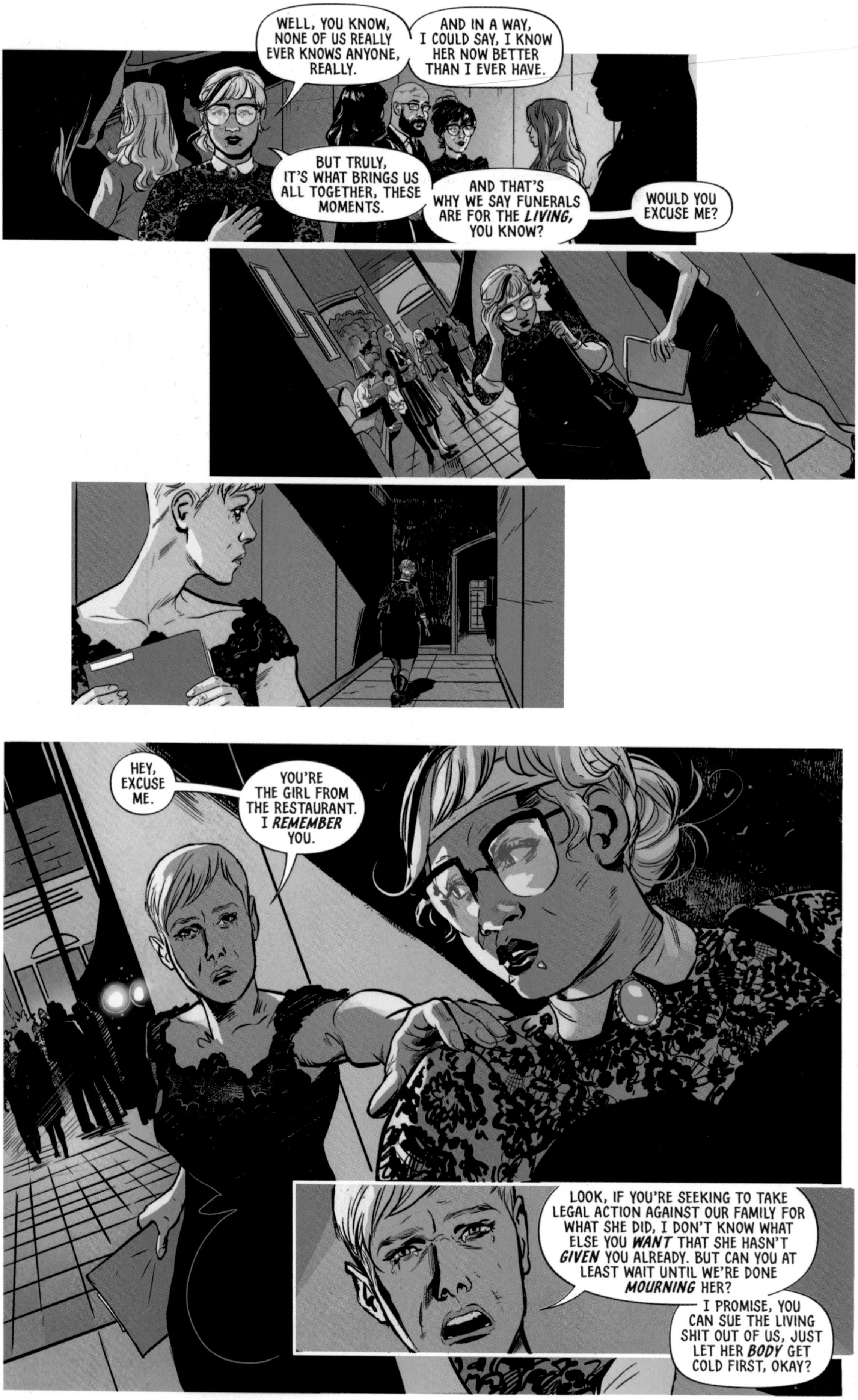

WELL, YOU KNOW, NONE OF US REALLY EVER KNOWS ANYONE, REALLY.
AND IN A WAY, I COULD SAY, I KNOW HER NOW BETTER THAN I EVER HAVE.
BUT TRULY, IT'S WHAT BRINGS US ALL TOGETHER, THESE MOMENTS.
AND THAT'S WHY WE SAY FUNERALS ARE FOR THE *LIVING,* YOU KNOW?
WOULD YOU EXCUSE ME?
HEY, EXCUSE ME.
YOU'RE THE GIRL FROM THE RESTAURANT. I *REMEMBER* YOU.
LOOK, IF YOU'RE SEEKING TO TAKE LEGAL ACTION AGAINST OUR FAMILY FOR WHAT SHE DID, I DON'T KNOW WHAT ELSE YOU *WANT* THAT SHE HASN'T *GIVEN* YOU ALREADY. BUT CAN YOU AT LEAST WAIT UNTIL WE'RE DONE *MOURNING* HER?
I PROMISE, YOU CAN SUE THE LIVING SHIT OUT OF US, JUST LET HER *BODY* GET COLD FIRST, OKAY?

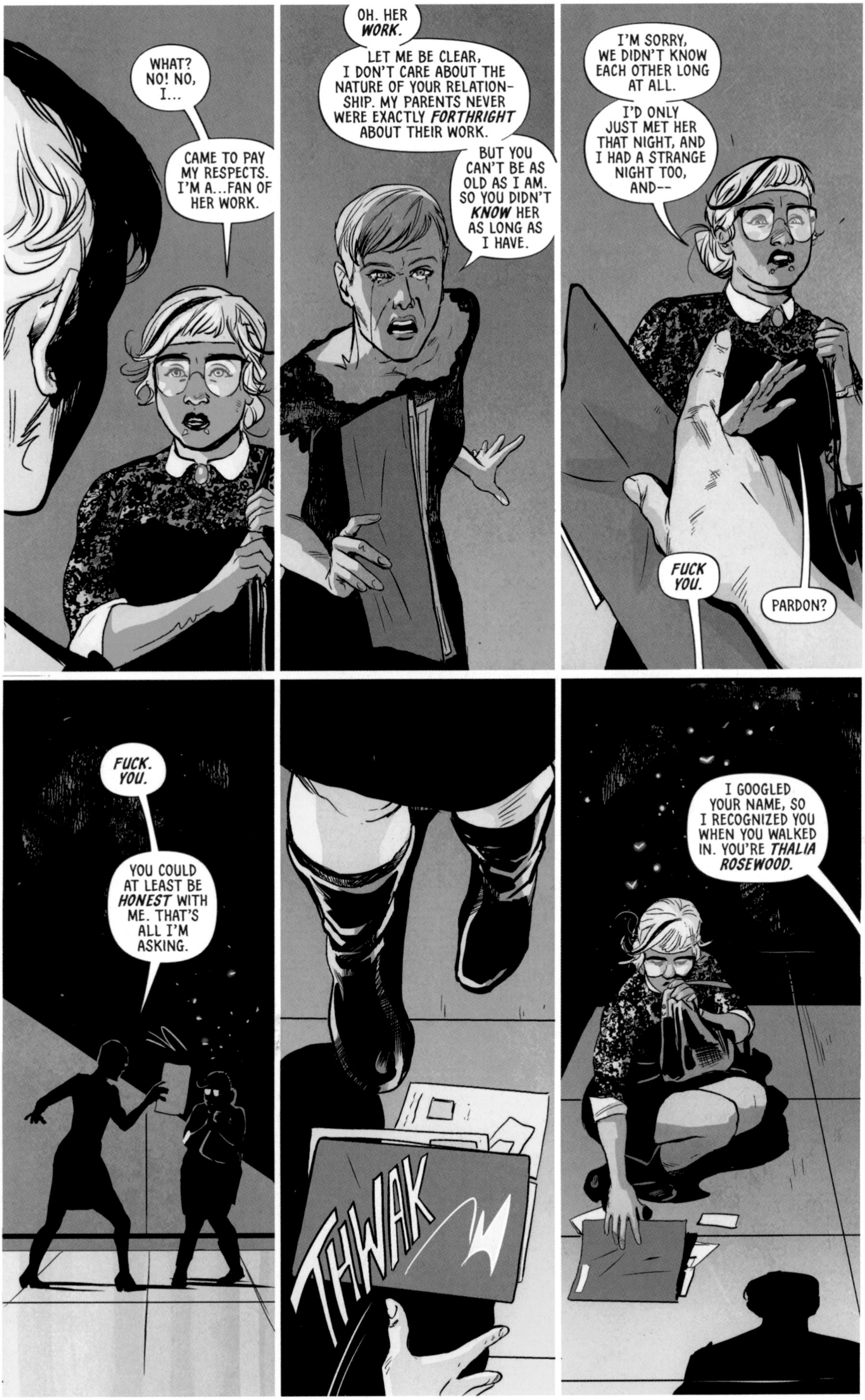
WHAT? NO! NO, I...
CAME TO PAY MY RESPECTS. I'M A...FAN OF HER WORK.
OH. HER WORK.
LET ME BE CLEAR, I DON'T CARE ABOUT THE NATURE OF YOUR RELATION-SHIP. MY PARENTS NEVER WERE EXACTLY FORTHRIGHT ABOUT THEIR WORK.
BUT YOU CAN'T BE AS OLD AS I AM. SO YOU DIDN'T KNOW HER AS LONG AS I HAVE.
I'M SORRY, WE DIDN'T KNOW EACH OTHER LONG AT ALL.
I'D ONLY JUST MET HER THAT NIGHT, AND I HAD A STRANGE NIGHT TOO, AND--
FUCK YOU.
PARDON?
FUCK. YOU.
YOU COULD AT LEAST BE HONEST WITH ME. THAT'S ALL I'M ASKING.
THWAK
I GOOGLED YOUR NAME, SO I RECOGNIZED YOU WHEN YOU WALKED IN. YOU'RE THALIA ROSEWOOD.

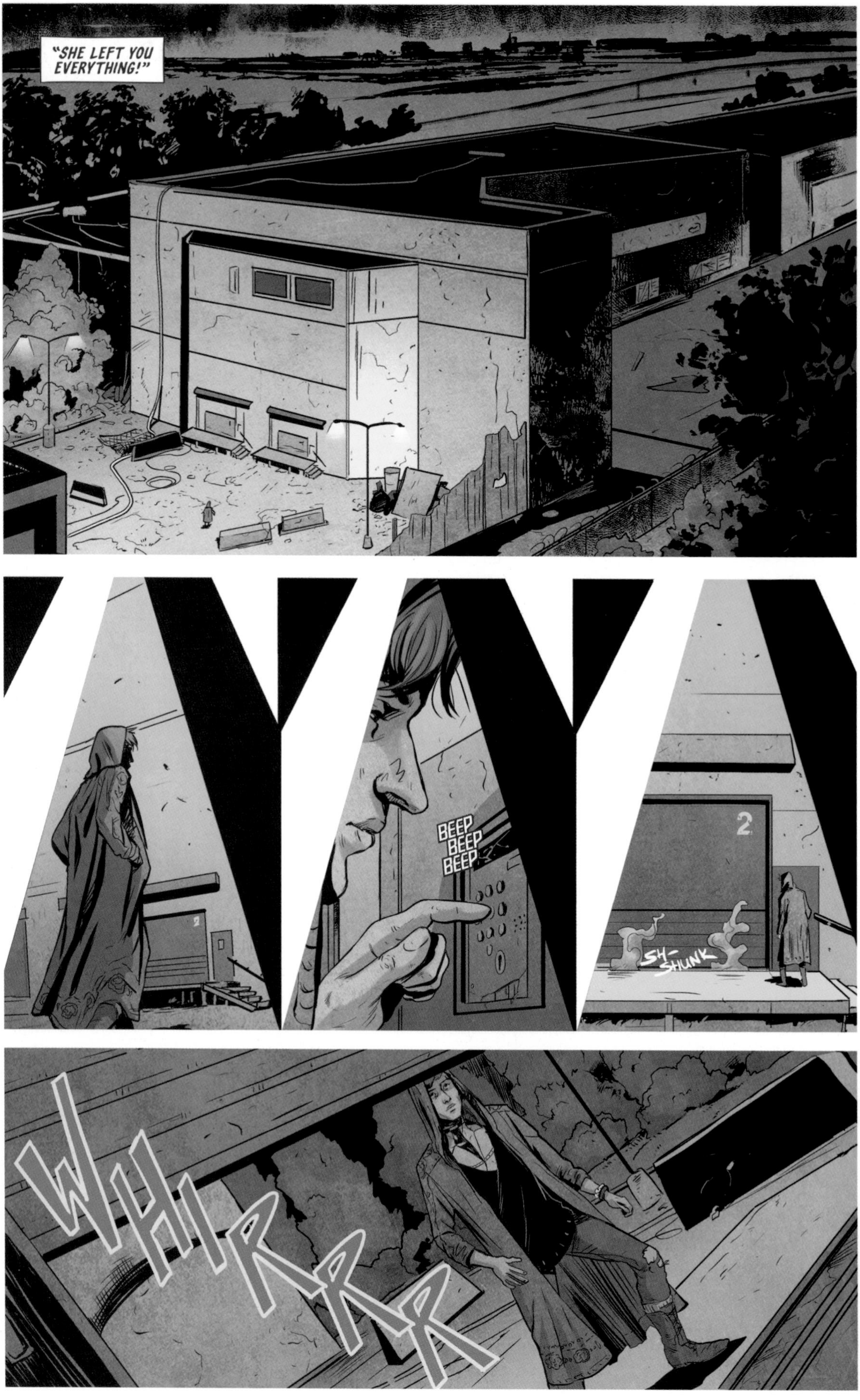
"SHE LEFT YOU EVERYTHING!"
BEEP BEEP BEEP
SH-SHUNK
WHIRRR

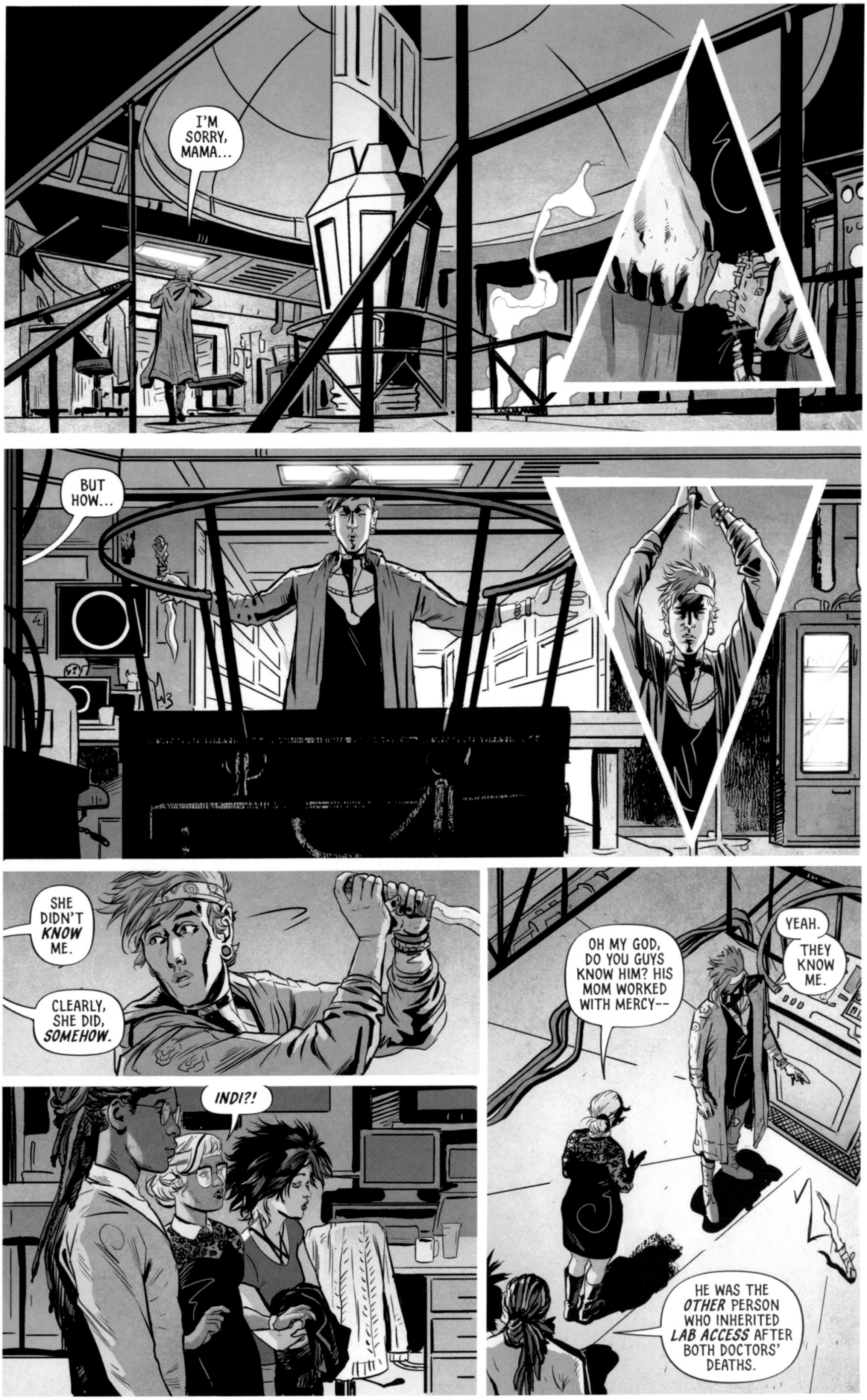
I'M SORRY, MAMA...
BUT HOW...
SHE DIDN'T *KNOW* ME.
CLEARLY, SHE DID, *SOMEHOW*.
INDI?!
OH MY GOD, DO YOU GUYS KNOW HIM? HIS MOM WORKED WITH MERCY--
YEAH.
THEY KNOW ME.
HE WAS THE *OTHER* PERSON WHO INHERITED *LAB ACCESS* AFTER BOTH DOCTORS' DEATHS.

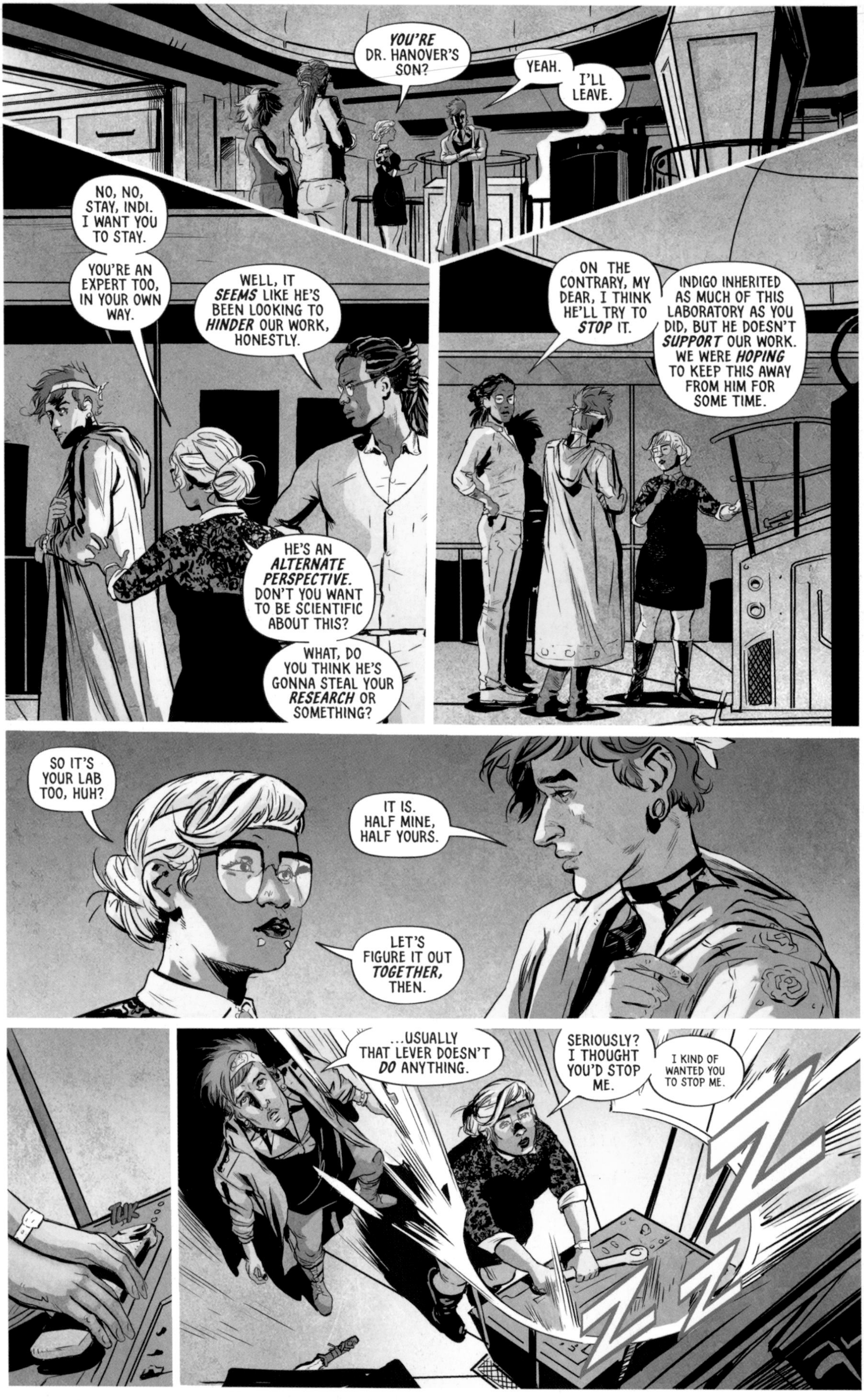
YOU'RE DR. HANOVER'S SON?
YEAH.
I'LL LEAVE.
NO, NO, STAY, INDI. I WANT YOU TO STAY.
YOU'RE AN EXPERT TOO, IN YOUR OWN WAY.
WELL, IT SEEMS LIKE HE'S BEEN LOOKING TO HINDER OUR WORK, HONESTLY.
HE'S AN ALTERNATE PERSPECTIVE. DON'T YOU WANT TO BE SCIENTIFIC ABOUT THIS?
WHAT, DO YOU THINK HE'S GONNA STEAL YOUR RESEARCH OR SOMETHING?
ON THE CONTRARY, MY DEAR, I THINK HE'LL TRY TO STOP IT.
INDIGO INHERITED AS MUCH OF THIS LABORATORY AS YOU DID, BUT HE DOESN'T SUPPORT OUR WORK. WE WERE HOPING TO KEEP THIS AWAY FROM HIM FOR SOME TIME.
SO IT'S YOUR LAB TOO, HUH?
IT IS. HALF MINE, HALF YOURS.
LET'S FIGURE IT OUT TOGETHER, THEN.
TUK
...USUALLY THAT LEVER DOESN'T DO ANYTHING.
SERIOUSLY? I THOUGHT YOU'D STOP ME.
I KIND OF WANTED YOU TO STOP ME.

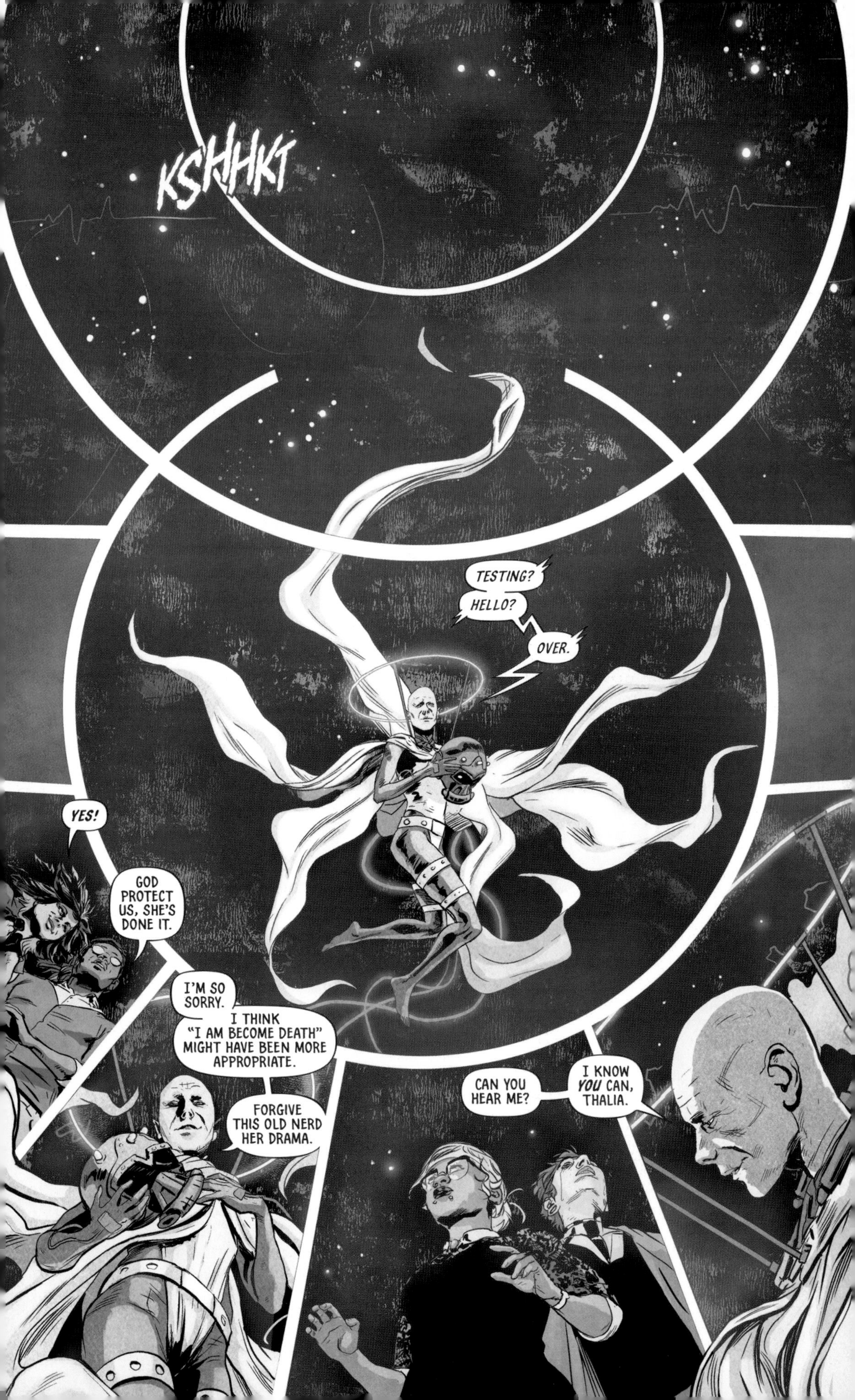
KSHHKT
TESTING?
HELLO?
OVER.
YES!
GOD PROTECT US, SHE'S DONE IT.
I'M SO SORRY.
I THINK "I AM BECOME DEATH" MIGHT HAVE BEEN MORE APPROPRIATE.
FORGIVE THIS OLD NERD HER DRAMA.
CAN YOU HEAR ME?
I KNOW YOU CAN, THALIA.

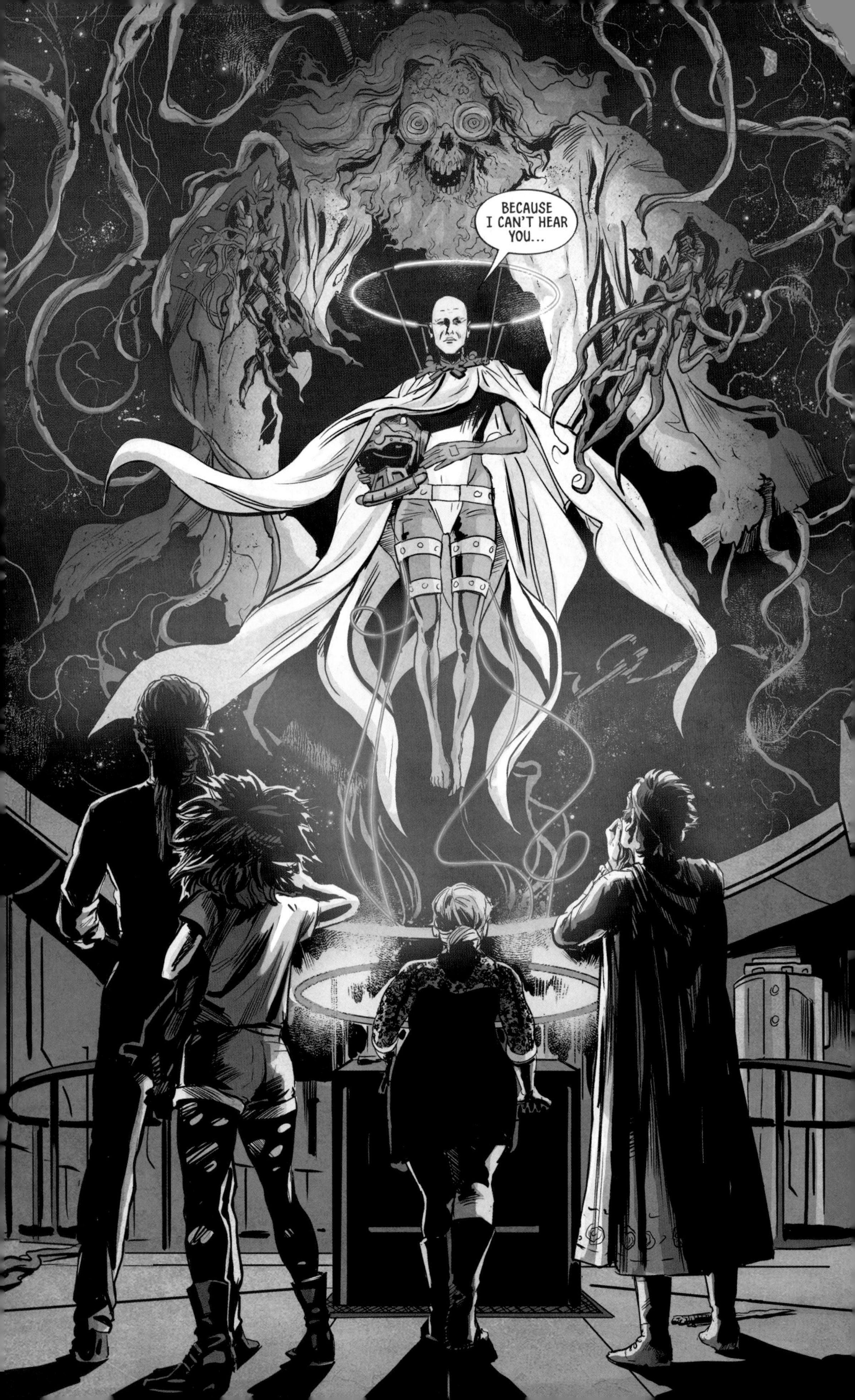
BECAUSE I CAN'T HEAR YOU...

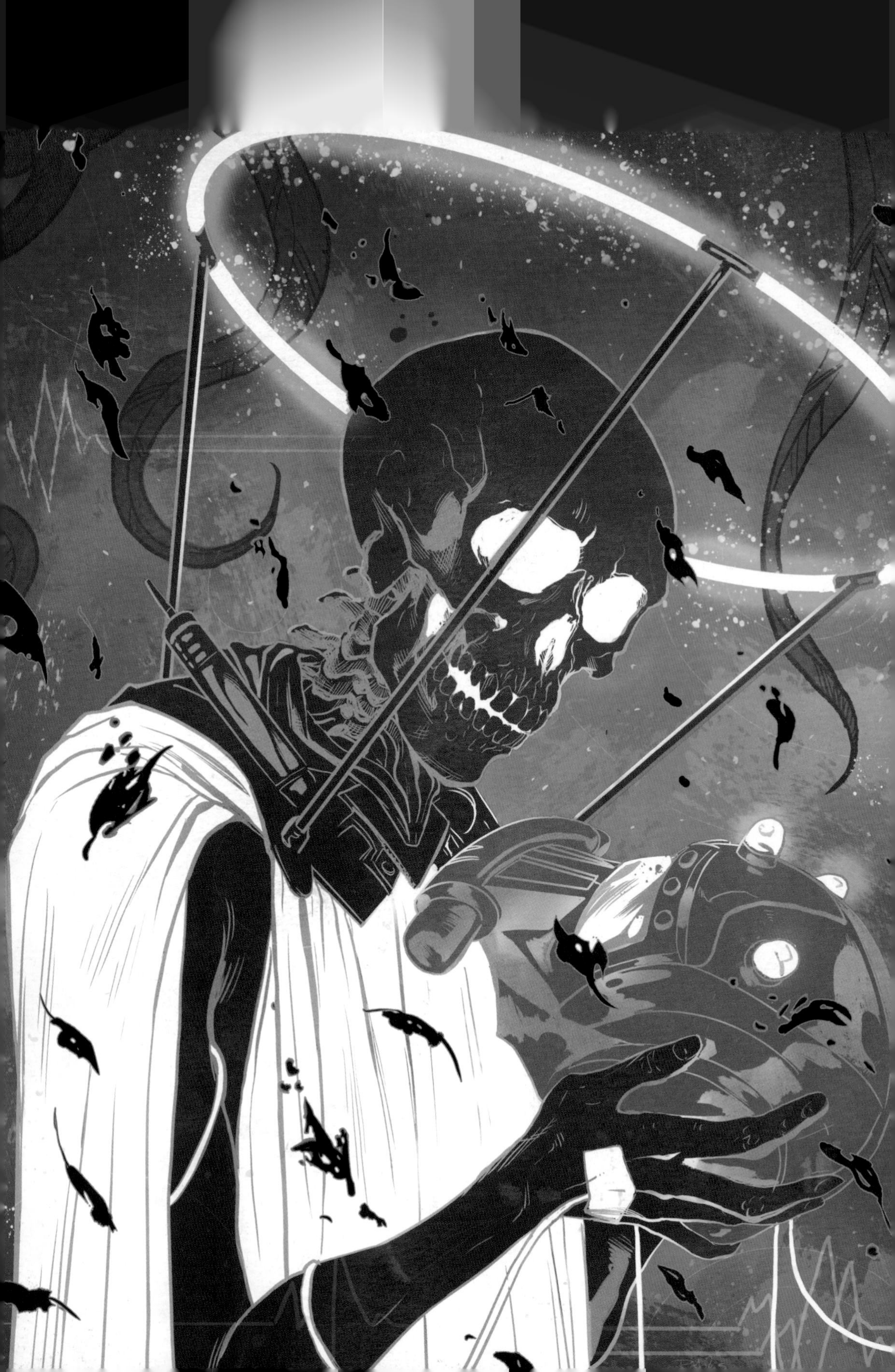

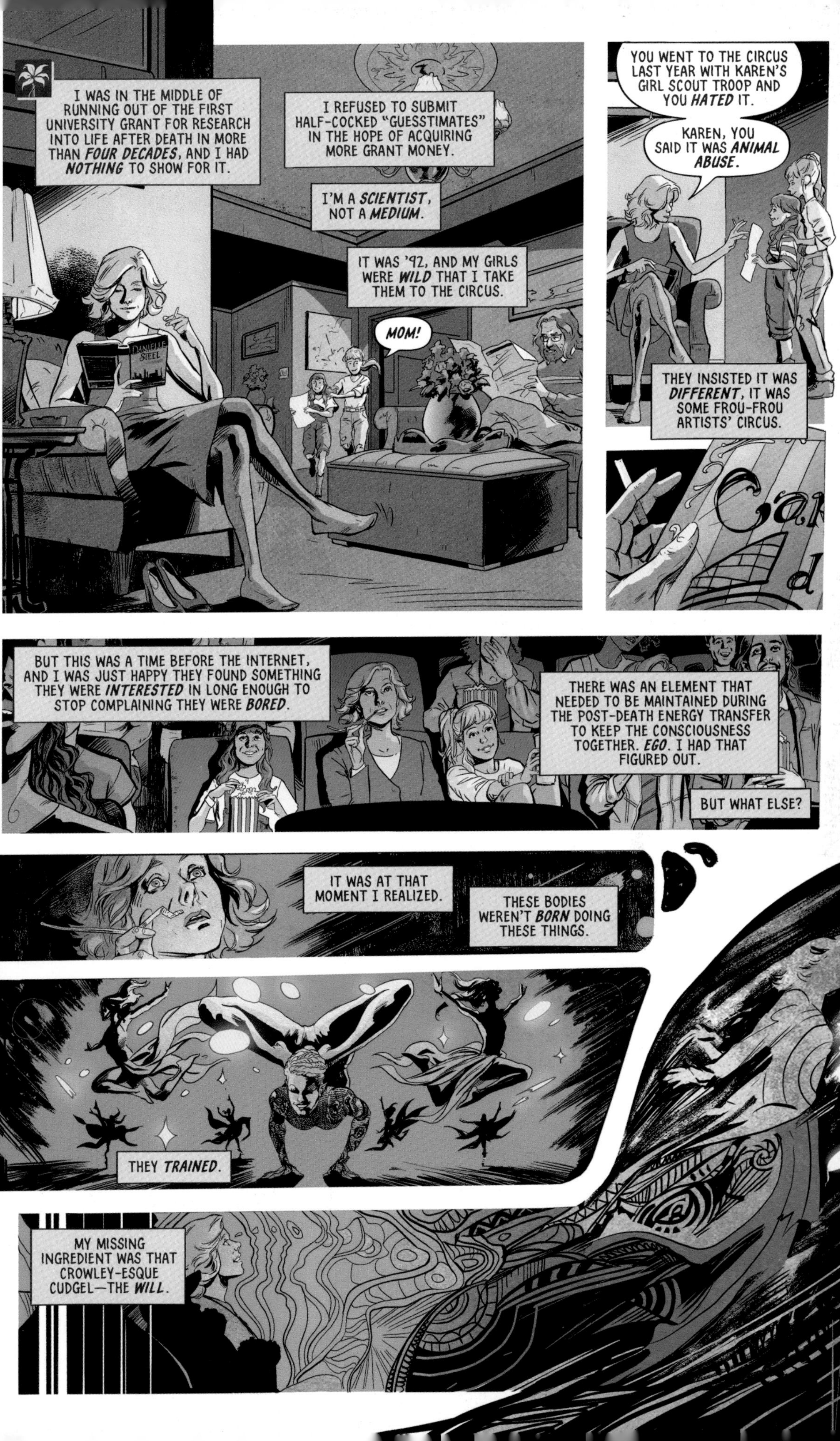
I WAS IN THE MIDDLE OF RUNNING OUT OF THE FIRST UNIVERSITY GRANT FOR RESEARCH INTO LIFE AFTER DEATH IN MORE THAN FOUR DECADES, AND I HAD NOTHING TO SHOW FOR IT.
I REFUSED TO SUBMIT HALF-COCKED "GUESSTIMATES" IN THE HOPE OF ACQUIRING MORE GRANT MONEY.
I'M A SCIENTIST, NOT A MEDIUM.
IT WAS '92, AND MY GIRLS WERE WILD THAT I TAKE THEM TO THE CIRCUS.
MOM!
DANIELLE STEEL
YOU WENT TO THE CIRCUS LAST YEAR WITH KAREN'S GIRL SCOUT TROOP AND YOU HATED IT.
KAREN, YOU SAID IT WAS ANIMAL ABUSE.
THEY INSISTED IT WAS DIFFERENT, IT WAS SOME FROU-FROU ARTISTS' CIRCUS.
BUT THIS WAS A TIME BEFORE THE INTERNET, AND I WAS JUST HAPPY THEY FOUND SOMETHING THEY WERE INTERESTED IN LONG ENOUGH TO STOP COMPLAINING THEY WERE BORED.
THERE WAS AN ELEMENT THAT NEEDED TO BE MAINTAINED DURING THE POST-DEATH ENERGY TRANSFER TO KEEP THE CONSCIOUSNESS TOGETHER. EGO. I HAD THAT FIGURED OUT.
BUT WHAT ELSE?
IT WAS AT THAT MOMENT I REALIZED.
THESE BODIES WEREN'T BORN DOING THESE THINGS.
THEY TRAINED.
MY MISSING INGREDIENT WAS THAT CROWLEY-ESQUE CUDGEL—THE WILL.

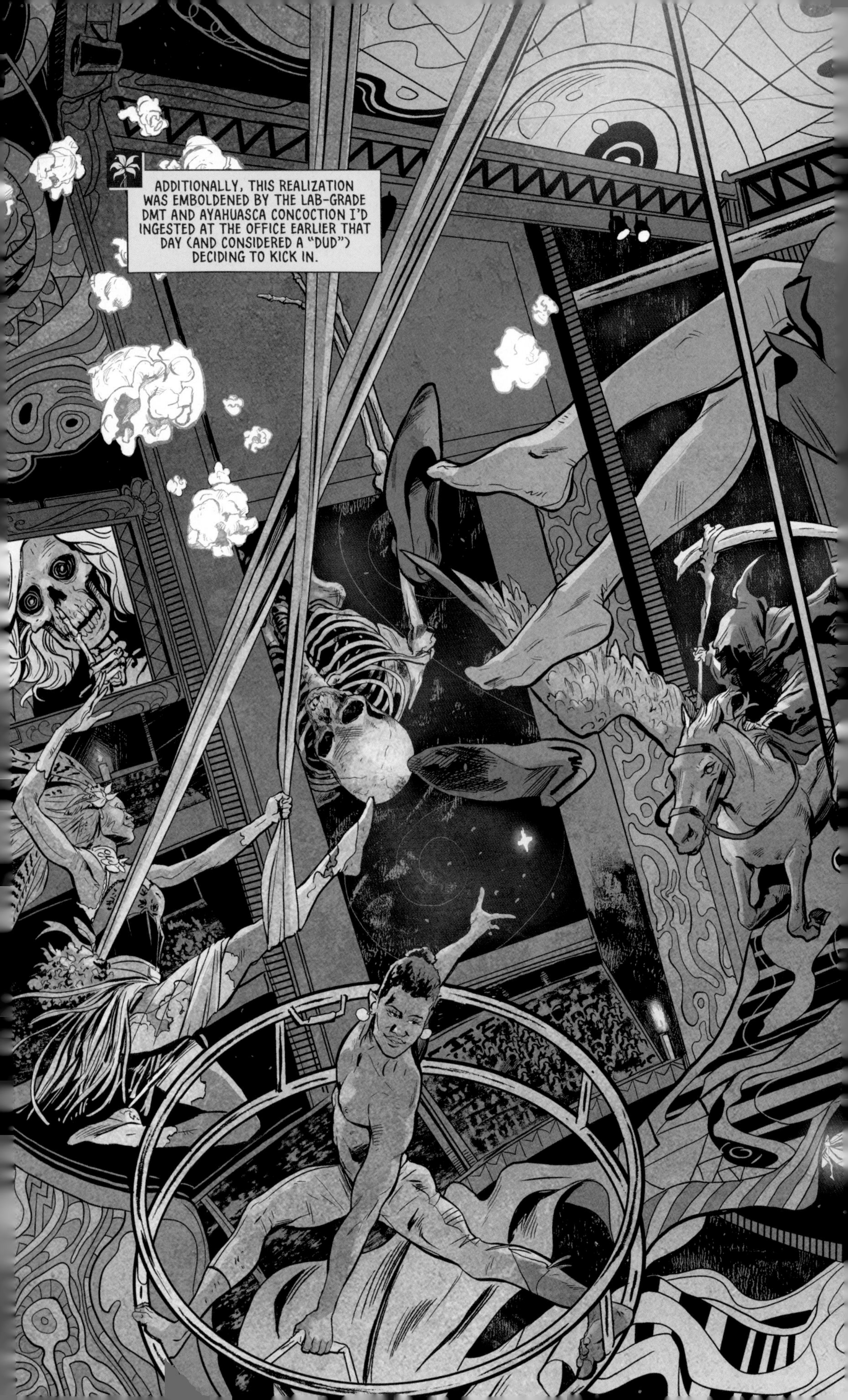
ADDITIONALLY, THIS REALIZATION WAS EMBOLDENED BY THE LAB-GRADE DMT AND AYAHUASCA CONCOCTION I'D INGESTED AT THE OFFICE EARLIER THAT DAY (AND CONSIDERED A "DUD") DECIDING TO KICK IN.

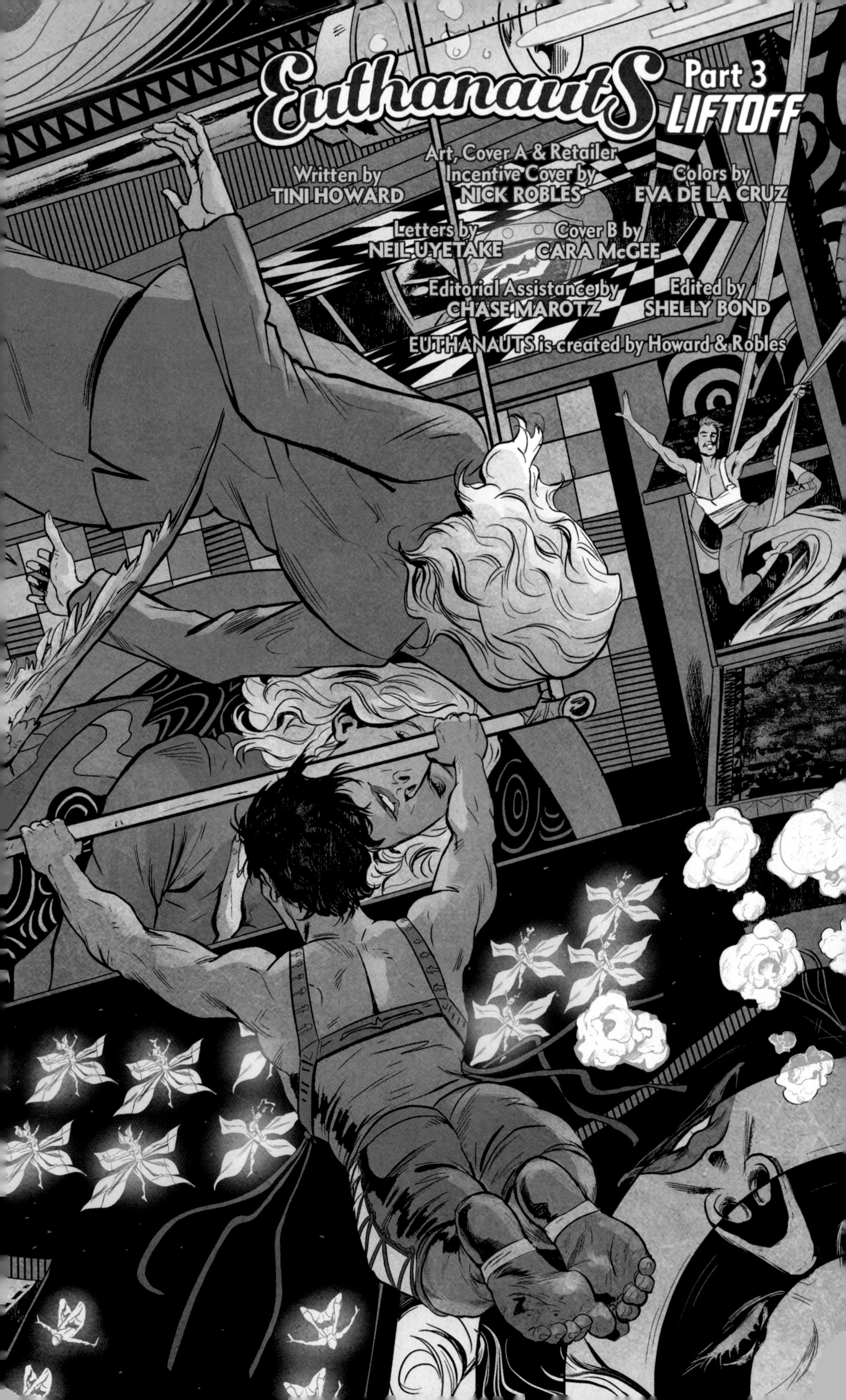
EuthanautS
Part 3
LIFTOFF
Written by
TINI HOWARD
Art, Cover A & Retailer Incentive Cover by
NICK ROBLES
Colors by
EVA DE LA CRUZ
Letters by
NEIL UYETAKE
Cover B by
CARA McGEE
Editorial Assistance by
CHASE MAROTZ
Edited by
SHELLY BOND
EUTHANAUTS is created by Howard & Robles

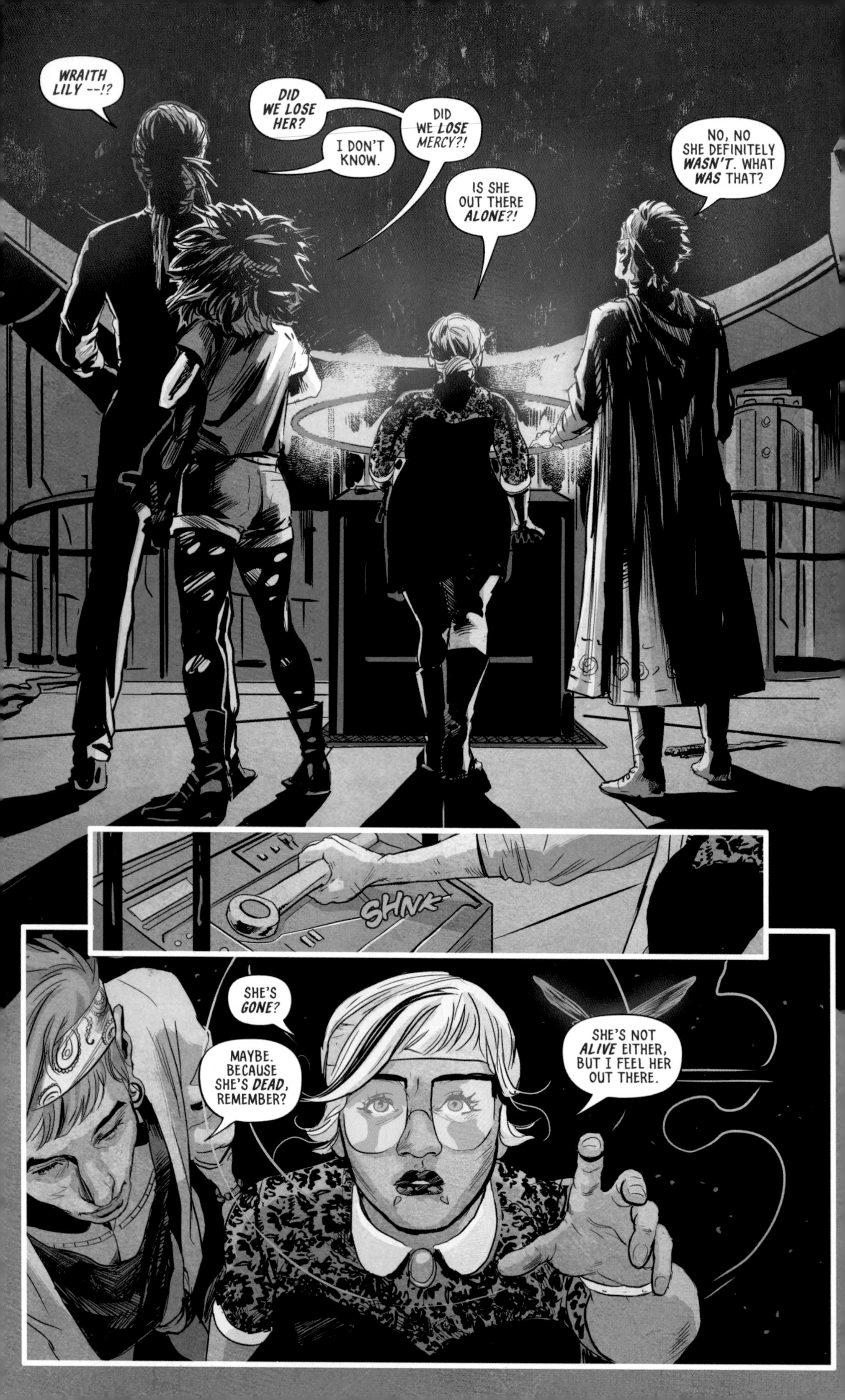
WRAITH LILY --!?
DID WE LOSE HER?
I DON'T KNOW.
DID WE LOSE MERCY?!
IS SHE OUT THERE ALONE?!
NO, NO SHE DEFINITELY WASN'T. WHAT WAS THAT?
SHNK
SHE'S GONE?
MAYBE. BECAUSE SHE'S DEAD, REMEMBER?
SHE'S NOT ALIVE EITHER, BUT I FEEL HER OUT THERE.

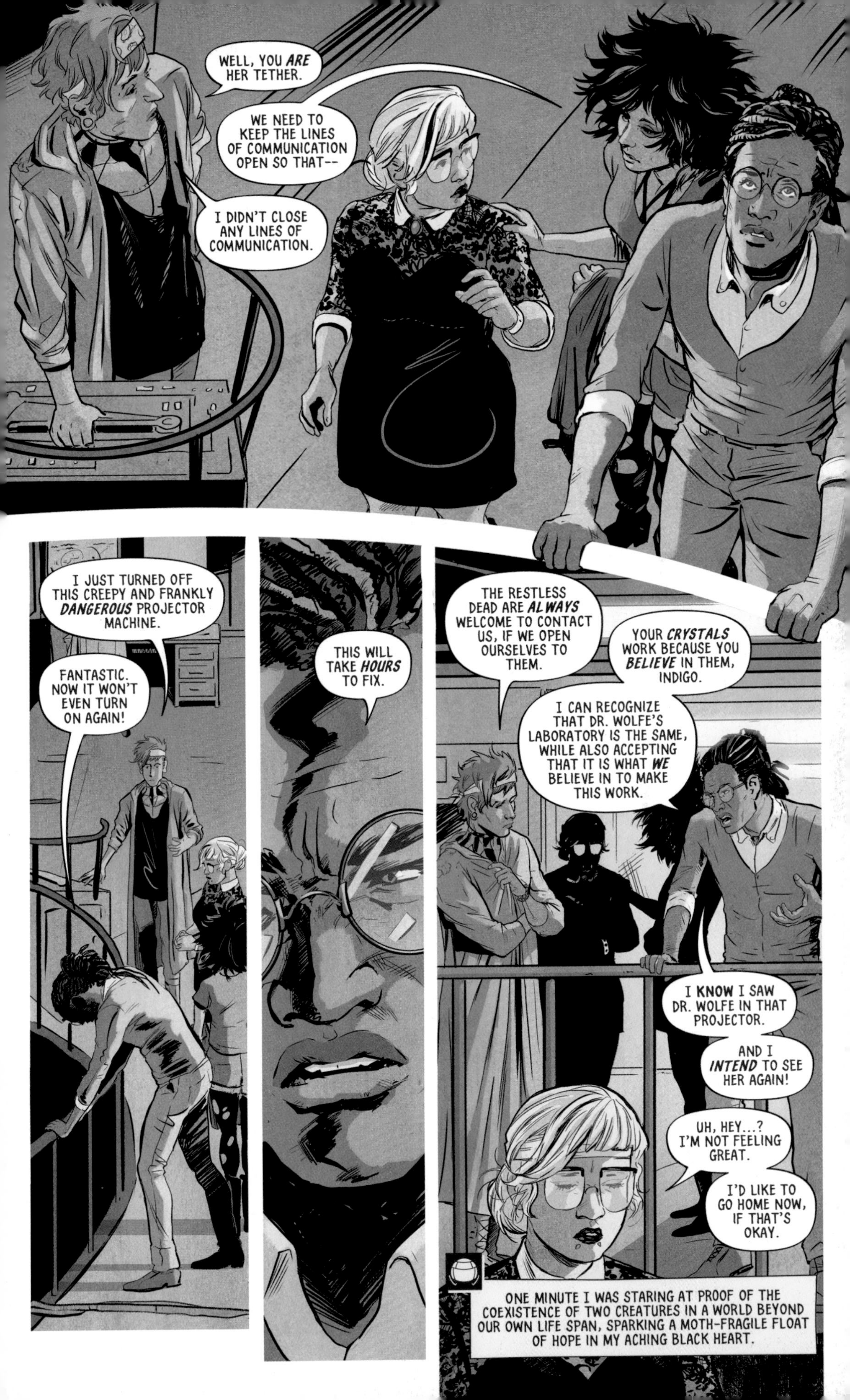

WELL, YOU *ARE* HER TETHER.
WE NEED TO KEEP THE LINES OF COMMUNICATION OPEN SO THAT--
I DIDN'T CLOSE ANY LINES OF COMMUNICATION.
I JUST TURNED OFF THIS CREEPY AND FRANKLY *DANGEROUS* PROJECTOR MACHINE.
FANTASTIC. NOW IT WON'T EVEN TURN ON AGAIN!
THIS WILL TAKE *HOURS* TO FIX.
THE RESTLESS DEAD ARE *ALWAYS* WELCOME TO CONTACT US, IF WE OPEN OURSELVES TO THEM.
YOUR *CRYSTALS* WORK BECAUSE YOU *BELIEVE* IN THEM, INDIGO.
I CAN RECOGNIZE THAT DR. WOLFE'S LABORATORY IS THE SAME, WHILE ALSO ACCEPTING THAT IT IS WHAT *WE* BELIEVE IN TO MAKE THIS WORK.
I **KNOW** I SAW DR. WOLFE IN THAT PROJECTOR.
AND I *INTEND* TO SEE HER AGAIN!
UH, HEY...? I'M NOT FEELING GREAT.
I'D LIKE TO GO HOME NOW, IF THAT'S OKAY.
ONE MINUTE I WAS STARING AT PROOF OF THE COEXISTENCE OF TWO CREATURES IN A WORLD BEYOND OUR OWN LIFE SPAN, SPARKING A MOTH-FRAGILE FLOAT OF HOPE IN MY ACHING BLACK HEART.

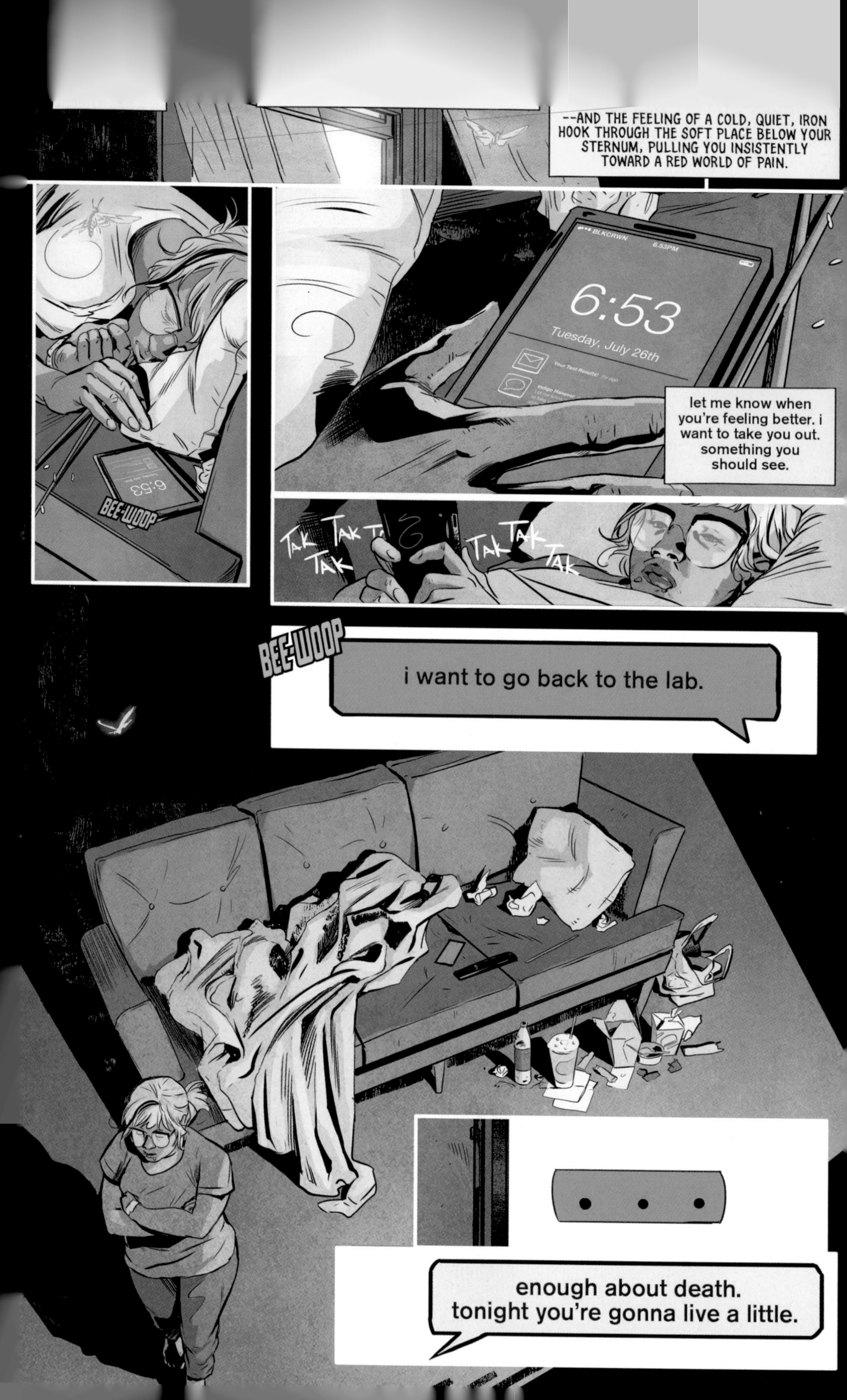

--AND THE FEELING OF A COLD, QUIET, IRON HOOK THROUGH THE SOFT PLACE BELOW YOUR STERNUM, PULLING YOU INSISTENTLY TOWARD A RED WORLD OF PAIN.
BEE-WOOP
BLKCRWN
6:53PM
6:53
Tuesday, July 26th
Your Test Results!
let me know when you're feeling better. i want to take you out. something you should see.
TAK TAK TAK TAK TAK TAK TAK
BEE-WOOP
i want to go back to the lab.
. . .
enough about death.
tonight you're gonna live a little.

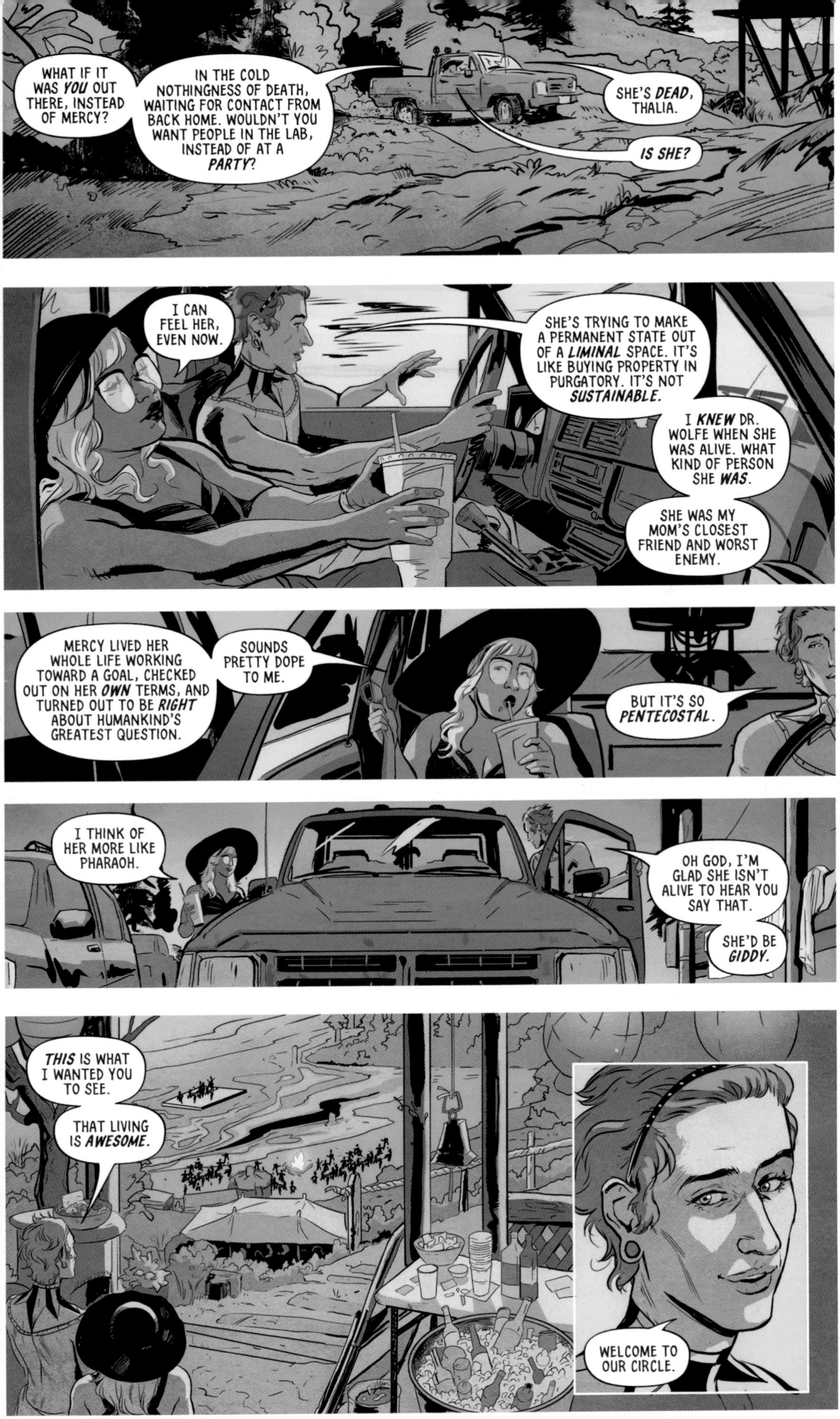
WHAT IF IT WAS *YOU* OUT THERE, INSTEAD OF MERCY?
IN THE COLD NOTHINGNESS OF DEATH, WAITING FOR CONTACT FROM BACK HOME. WOULDN'T YOU WANT PEOPLE IN THE LAB, INSTEAD OF AT A *PARTY*?
SHE'S *DEAD*, THALIA.
IS SHE?
I CAN FEEL HER, EVEN NOW.
SHE'S TRYING TO MAKE A PERMANENT STATE OUT OF A *LIMINAL* SPACE. IT'S LIKE BUYING PROPERTY IN PURGATORY. IT'S NOT *SUSTAINABLE.*
I *KNEW* DR. WOLFE WHEN SHE WAS ALIVE. WHAT KIND OF PERSON SHE *WAS*.
SHE WAS MY MOM'S CLOSEST FRIEND AND WORST ENEMY.
MERCY LIVED HER WHOLE LIFE WORKING TOWARD A GOAL, CHECKED OUT ON HER *OWN* TERMS, AND TURNED OUT TO BE *RIGHT* ABOUT HUMANKIND'S GREATEST QUESTION.
SOUNDS PRETTY DOPE TO ME.
BUT IT'S SO *PENTECOSTAL*.
I THINK OF HER MORE LIKE PHARAOH.
OH GOD, I'M GLAD SHE ISN'T ALIVE TO HEAR YOU SAY THAT.
SHE'D BE *GIDDY*.
THIS IS WHAT I WANTED YOU TO SEE.
THAT LIVING IS *AWESOME*.
WELCOME TO OUR CIRCLE.

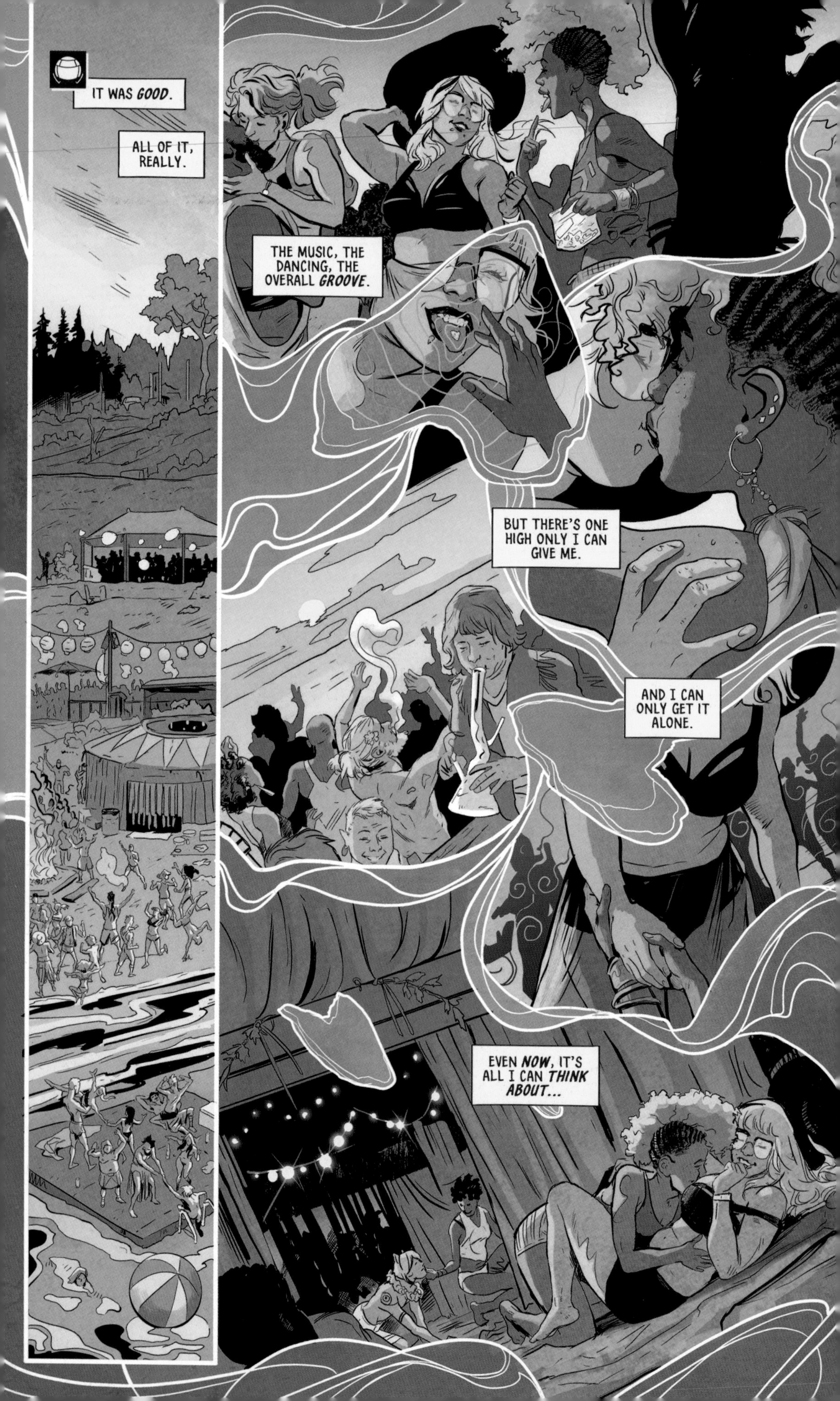
IT WAS *GOOD*.
ALL OF IT, REALLY.
THE MUSIC, THE DANCING, THE OVERALL *GROOVE*.
BUT THERE'S ONE HIGH ONLY I CAN GIVE ME.
AND I CAN ONLY GET IT ALONE.
EVEN *NOW*, IT'S ALL I CAN *THINK ABOUT*...

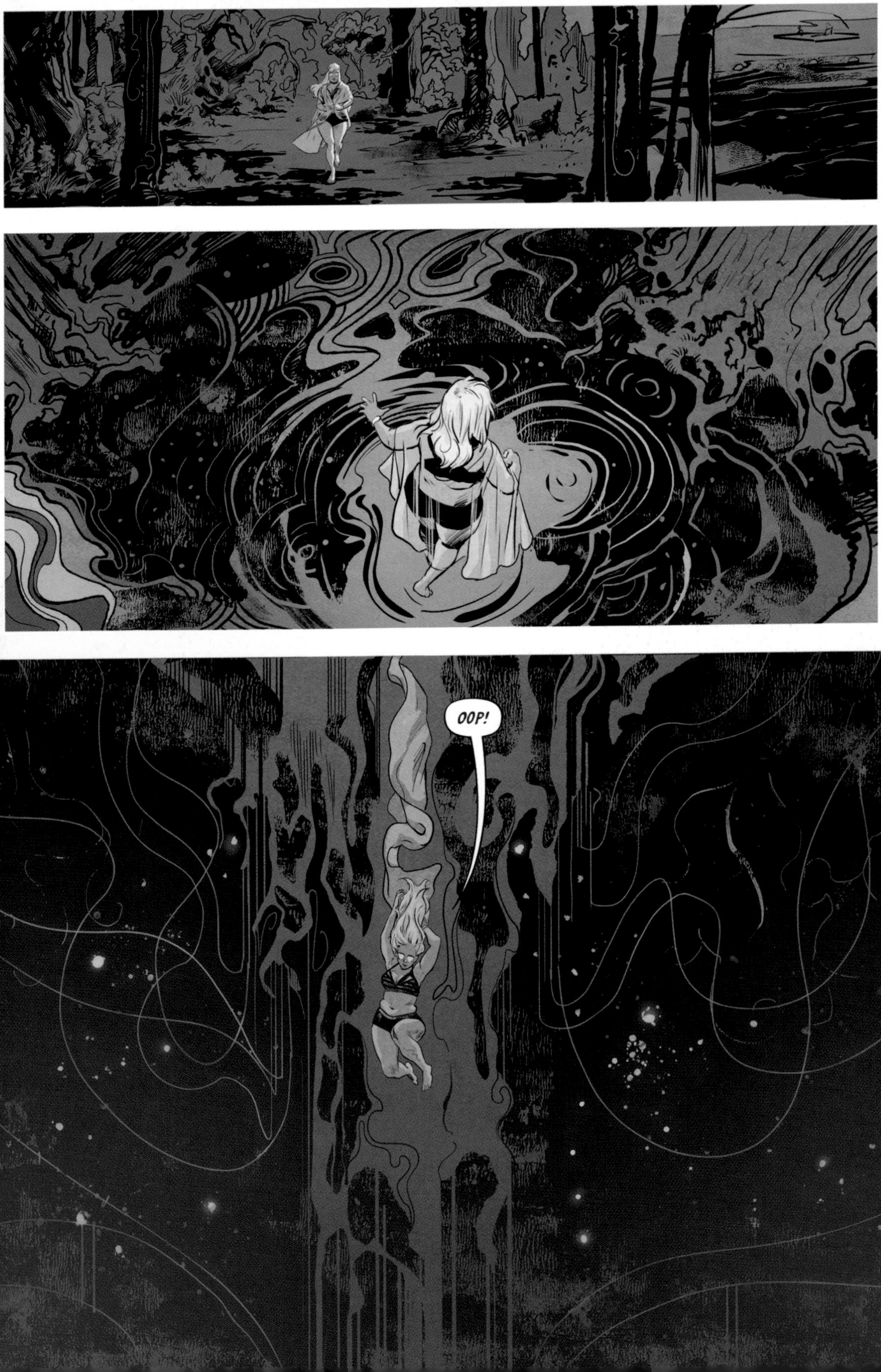
OOP!

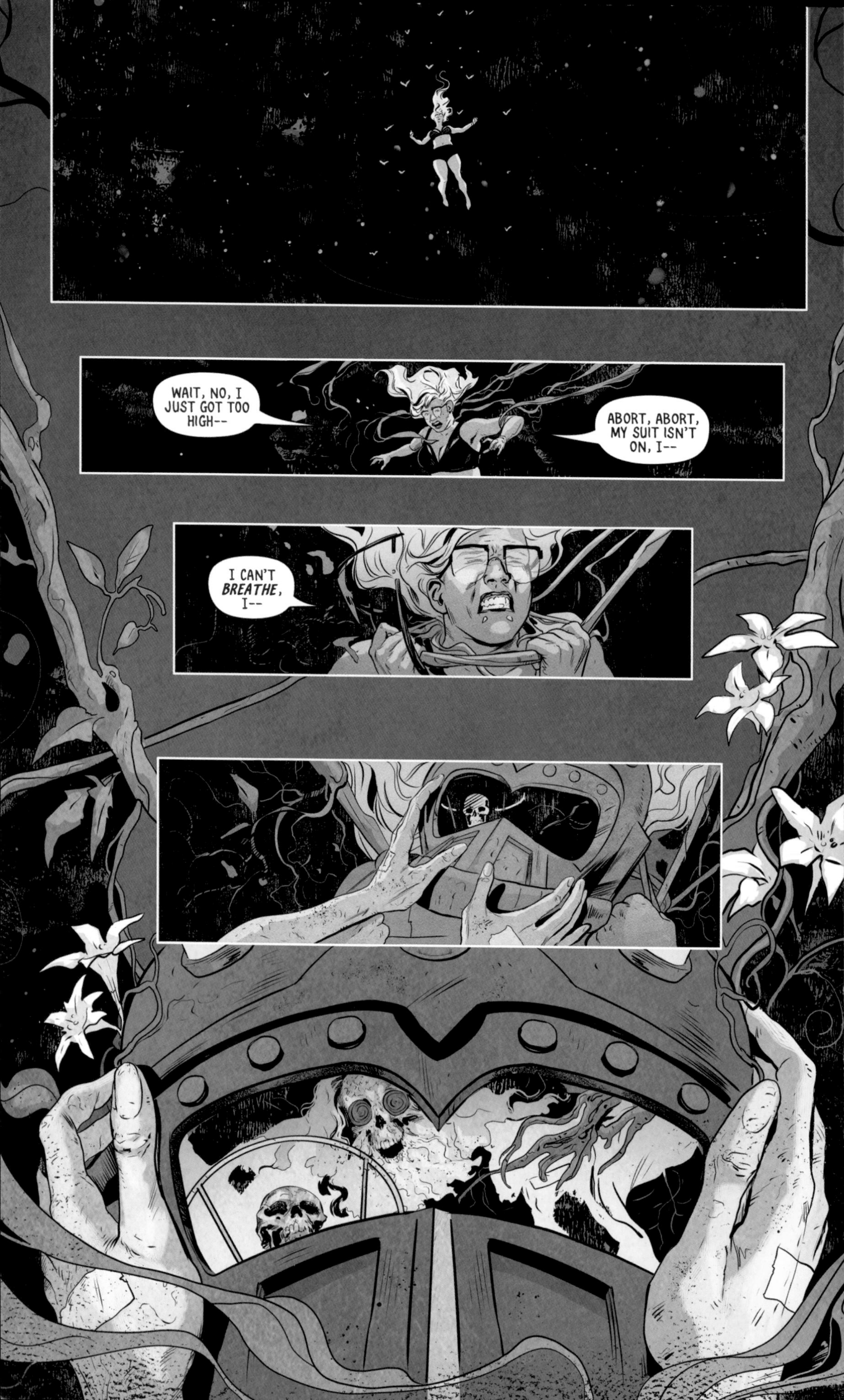
WAIT, NO, I JUST GOT TOO HIGH--
ABORT, ABORT, MY SUIT ISN'T ON, I--
I CAN'T *BREATHE*, I--

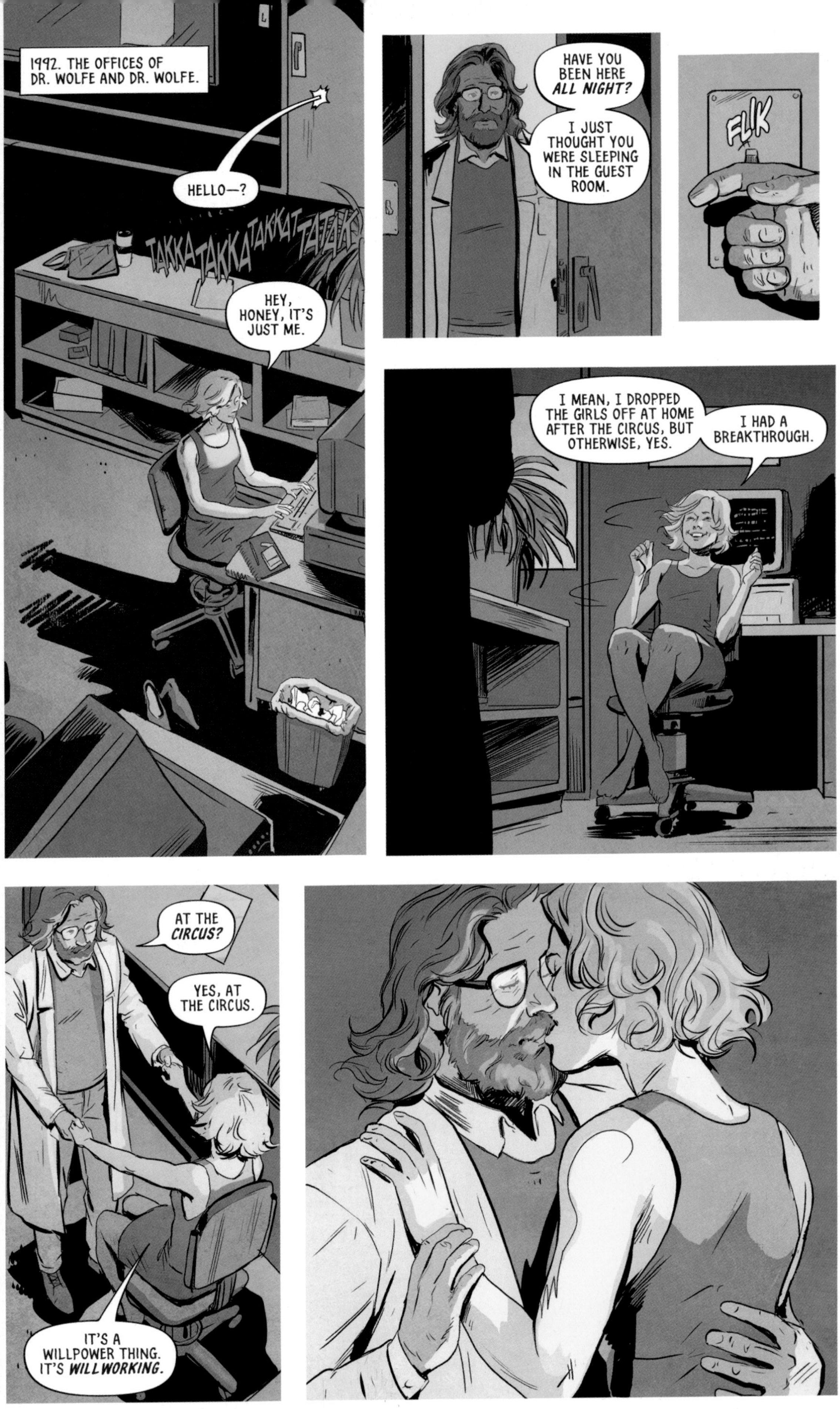
1992. THE OFFICES OF DR. WOLFE AND DR. WOLFE.
HELLO—?
TAKKA TAKKA TAKKAT TATAK
HEY, HONEY, IT'S JUST ME.
HAVE YOU BEEN HERE *ALL NIGHT?*
I JUST THOUGHT YOU WERE SLEEPING IN THE GUEST ROOM.
FLIK
I MEAN, I DROPPED THE GIRLS OFF AT HOME AFTER THE CIRCUS, BUT OTHERWISE, YES.
I HAD A BREAKTHROUGH.
AT THE *CIRCUS?*
YES, AT THE CIRCUS.
IT'S A WILLPOWER THING. IT'S *WILLWORKING.*

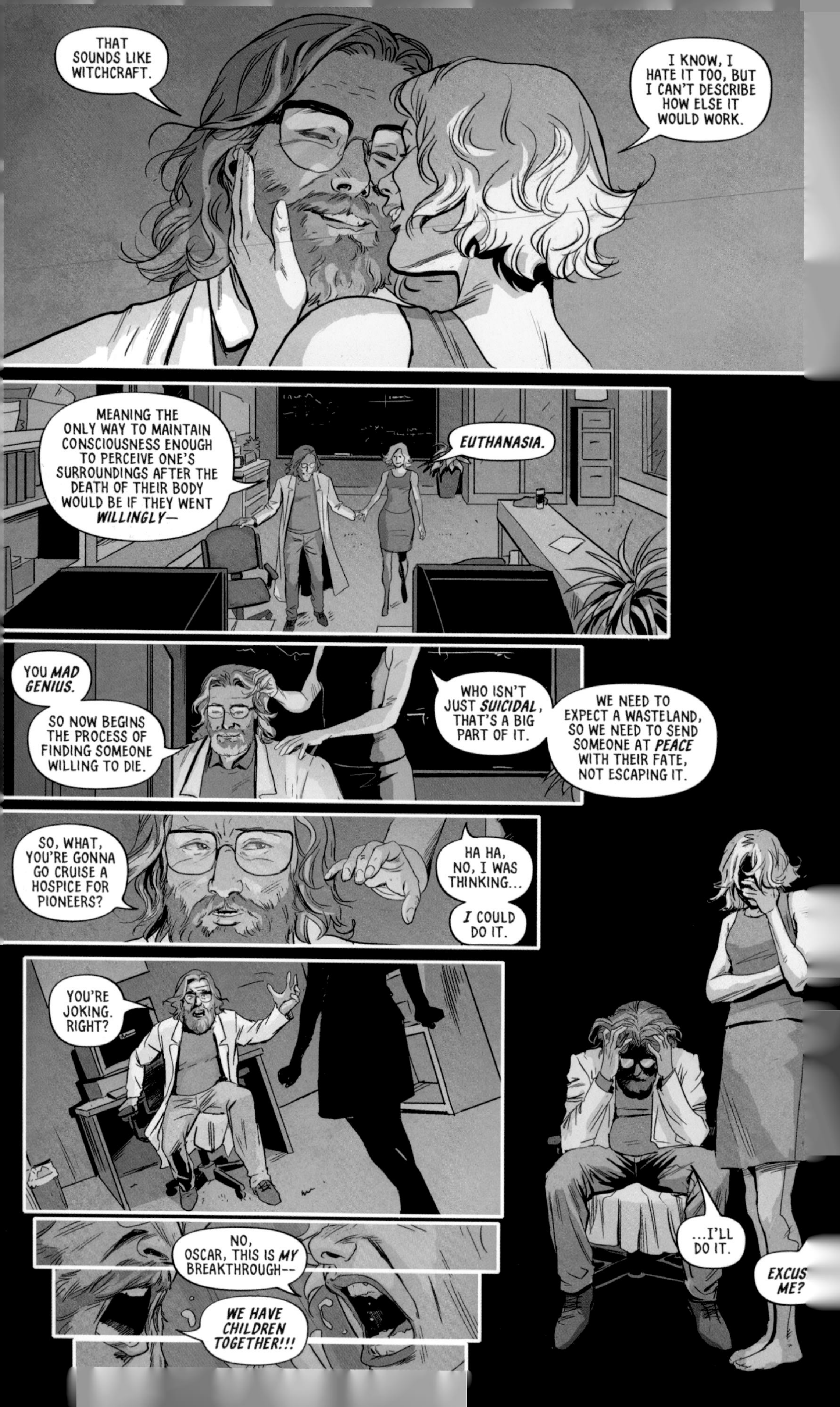
THAT SOUNDS LIKE WITCHCRAFT.
I KNOW, I HATE IT TOO, BUT I CAN'T DESCRIBE HOW ELSE IT WOULD WORK.
MEANING THE ONLY WAY TO MAINTAIN CONSCIOUSNESS ENOUGH TO PERCEIVE ONE'S SURROUNDINGS AFTER THE DEATH OF THEIR BODY WOULD BE IF THEY WENT WILLINGLY—
EUTHANASIA.
YOU MAD GENIUS.
SO NOW BEGINS THE PROCESS OF FINDING SOMEONE WILLING TO DIE.
WHO ISN'T JUST SUICIDAL, THAT'S A BIG PART OF IT.
WE NEED TO EXPECT A WASTELAND, SO WE NEED TO SEND SOMEONE AT PEACE WITH THEIR FATE, NOT ESCAPING IT.
SO, WHAT, YOU'RE GONNA GO CRUISE A HOSPICE FOR PIONEERS?
HA HA, NO, I WAS THINKING...
I COULD DO IT.
YOU'RE JOKING. RIGHT?
NO, OSCAR, THIS IS MY BREAKTHROUGH--
WE HAVE CHILDREN TOGETHER!!!
...I'LL DO IT.
EXCUS ME?

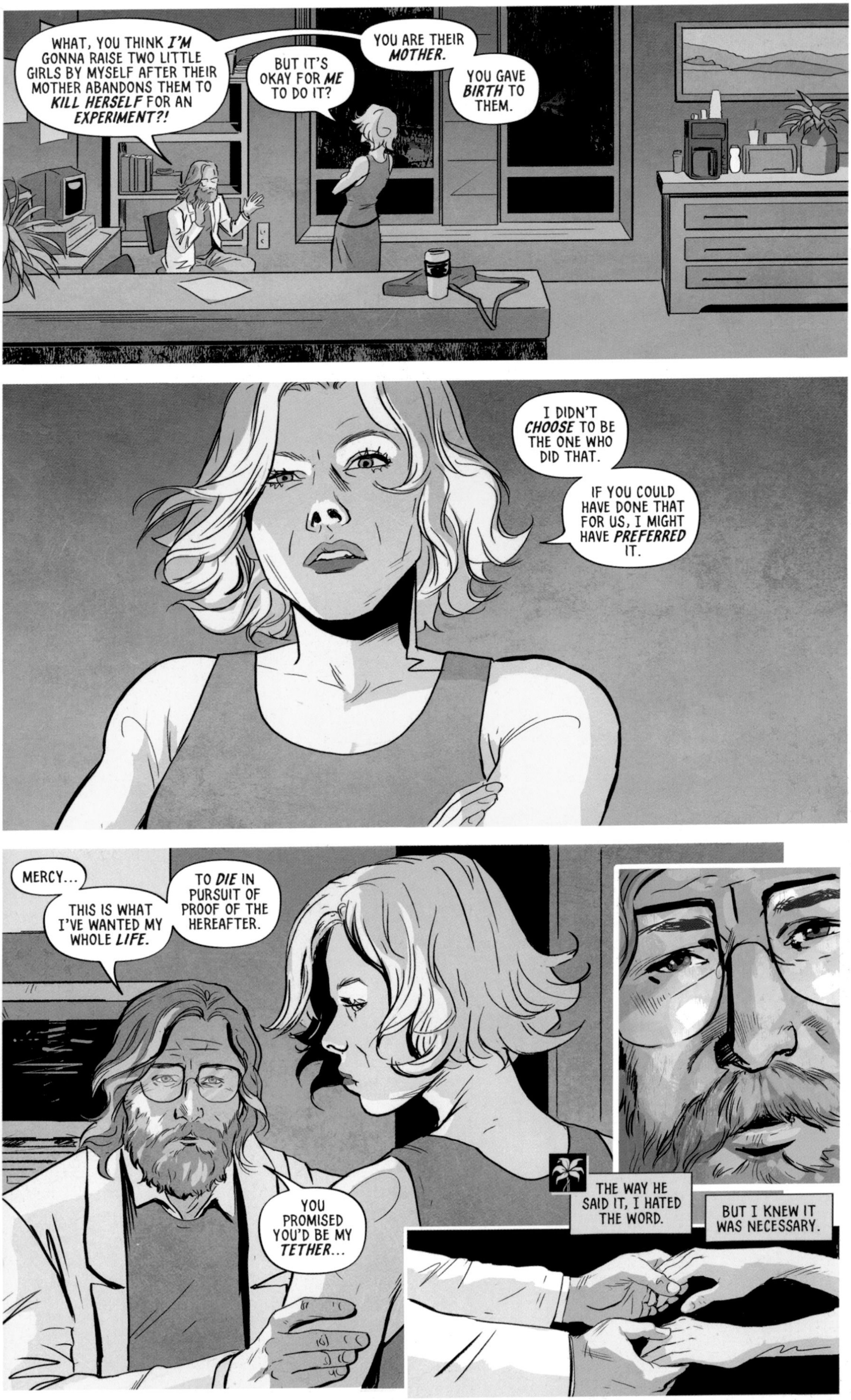

WHAT, YOU THINK I'M GONNA RAISE TWO LITTLE GIRLS BY MYSELF AFTER THEIR MOTHER ABANDONS THEM TO KILL HERSELF FOR AN EXPERIMENT?!
YOU ARE THEIR MOTHER.
BUT IT'S OKAY FOR ME TO DO IT?
YOU GAVE BIRTH TO THEM.
I DIDN'T CHOOSE TO BE THE ONE WHO DID THAT.
IF YOU COULD HAVE DONE THAT FOR US, I MIGHT HAVE PREFERRED IT.
MERCY...
THIS IS WHAT I'VE WANTED MY WHOLE LIFE.
TO DIE IN PURSUIT OF PROOF OF THE HEREAFTER.
YOU PROMISED YOU'D BE MY TETHER...
THE WAY HE SAID IT, I HATED THE WORD.
BUT I KNEW IT WAS NECESSARY.

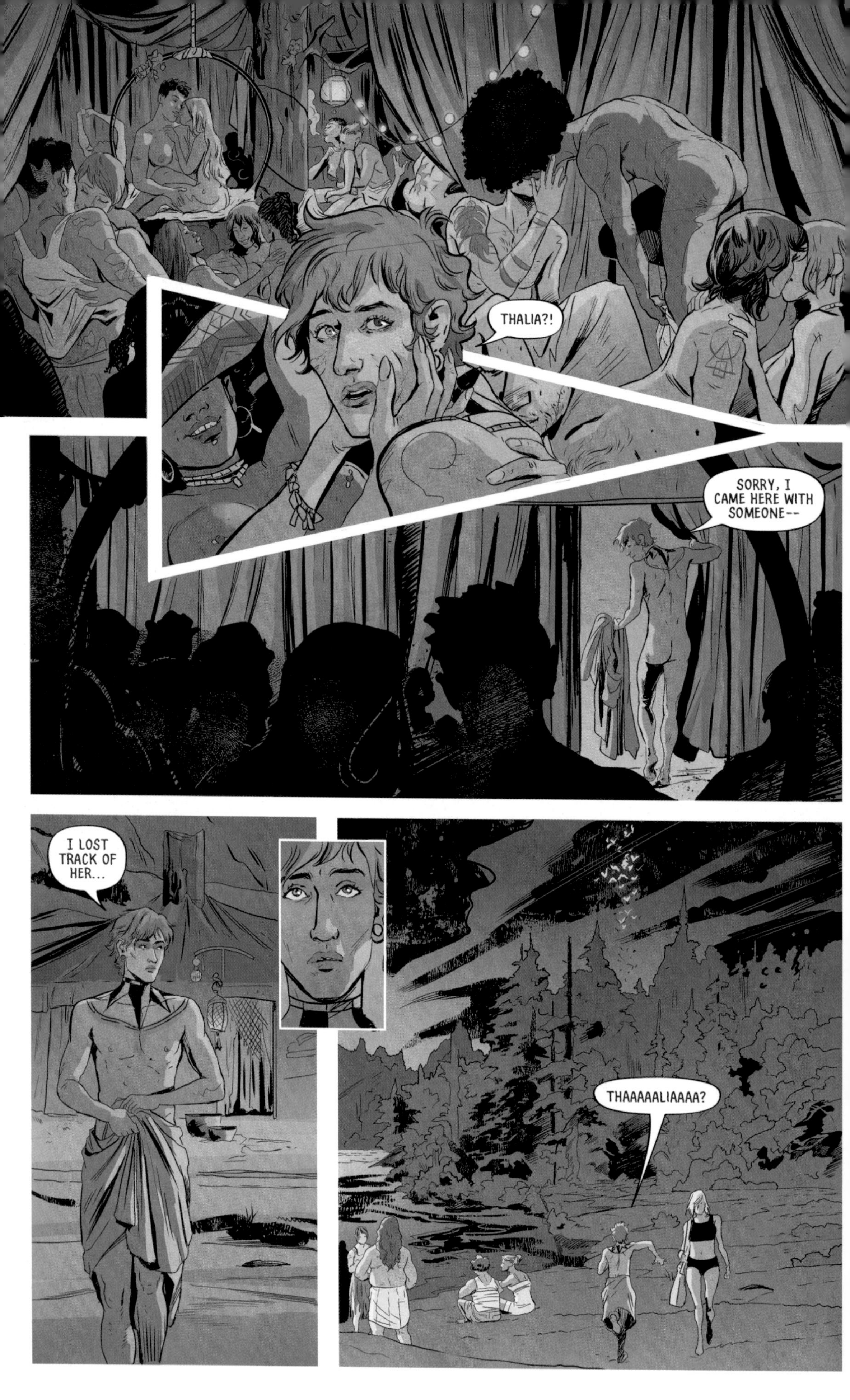
THALIA?!
SORRY, I CAME HERE WITH SOMEONE--
I LOST TRACK OF HER...
THAAAAALIAAAA?

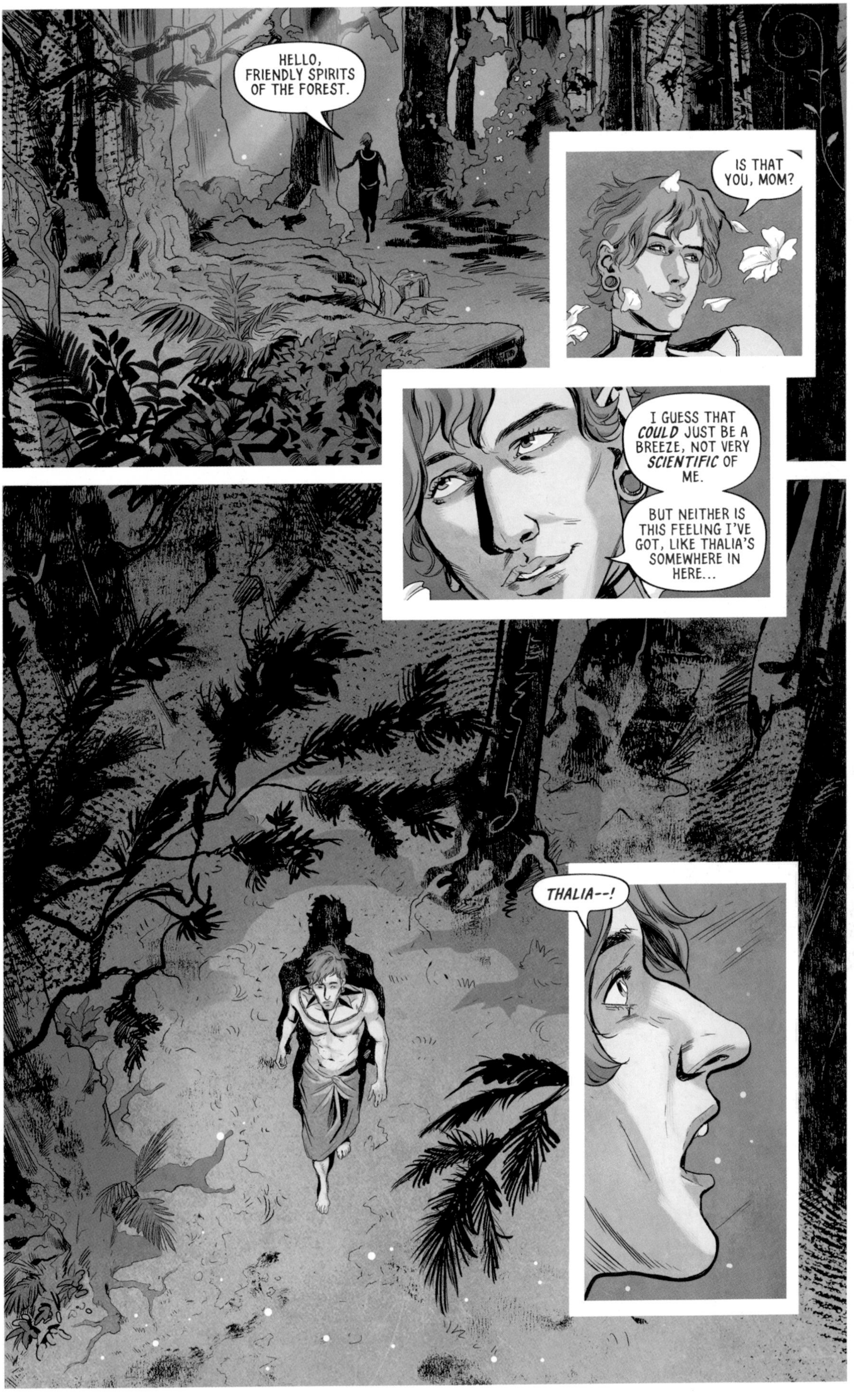
HELLO, FRIENDLY SPIRITS OF THE FOREST.
IS THAT YOU, MOM?
I GUESS THAT *COULD* JUST BE A BREEZE, NOT VERY *SCIENTIFIC* OF ME.
BUT NEITHER IS THIS FEELING I'VE GOT, LIKE THALIA'S SOMEWHERE IN HERE...
THALIA--!

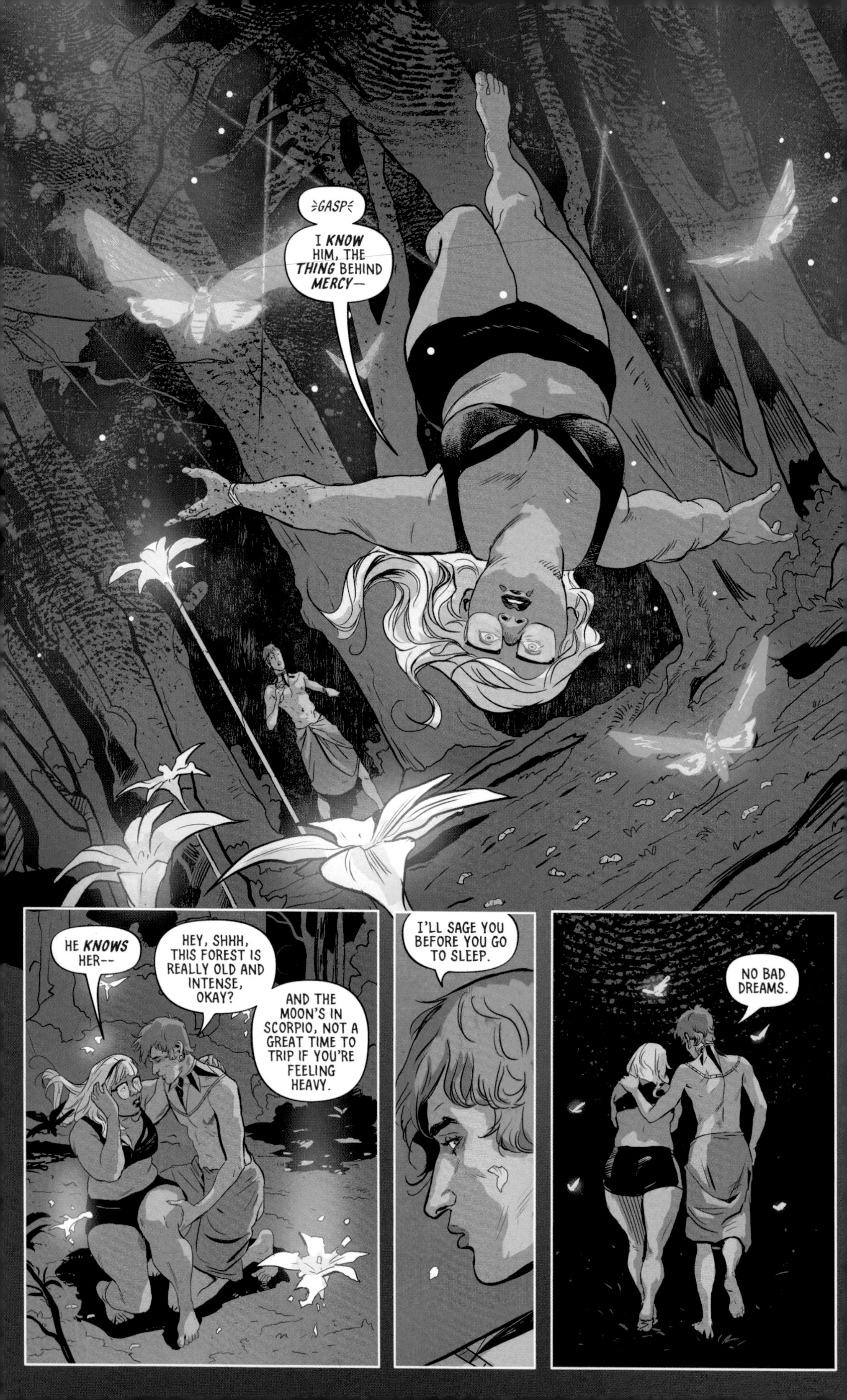

⋟GASP⋞
I KNOW HIM, THE THING BEHIND MERCY—
HE KNOWS HER--
HEY, SHHH, THIS FOREST IS REALLY OLD AND INTENSE, OKAY?
AND THE MOON'S IN SCORPIO, NOT A GREAT TIME TO TRIP IF YOU'RE FEELING HEAVY.
I'LL SAGE YOU BEFORE YOU GO TO SLEEP.
NO BAD DREAMS.

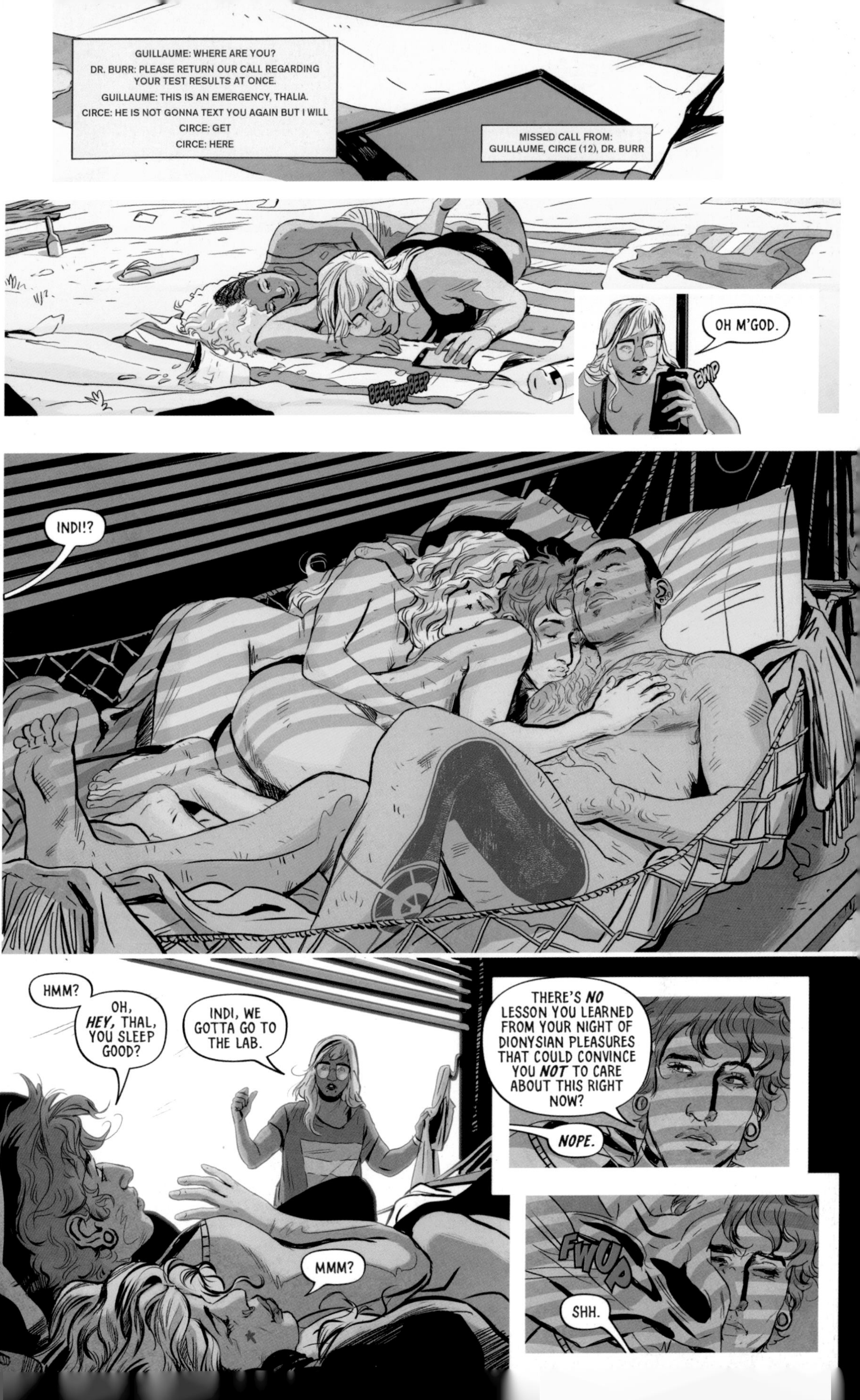
GUILLAUME: WHERE ARE YOU?
DR. BURR: PLEASE RETURN OUR CALL REGARDING YOUR TEST RESULTS AT ONCE.
GUILLAUME: THIS IS AN EMERGENCY, THALIA.
CIRCE: HE IS NOT GONNA TEXT YOU AGAIN BUT I WILL
CIRCE: GET
CIRCE: HERE
MISSED CALL FROM:
GUILLAUME, CIRCE (12), DR. BURR
BEEPBEEPBEEP
OH M'GOD.
BWP
INDI!?
HMM?
OH, HEY, THAL, YOU SLEEP GOOD?
INDI, WE GOTTA GO TO THE LAB.
MMM?
THERE'S NO LESSON YOU LEARNED FROM YOUR NIGHT OF DIONYSIAN PLEASURES THAT COULD CONVINCE YOU NOT TO CARE ABOUT THIS RIGHT NOW?
NOPE.
FWUP
SHH.

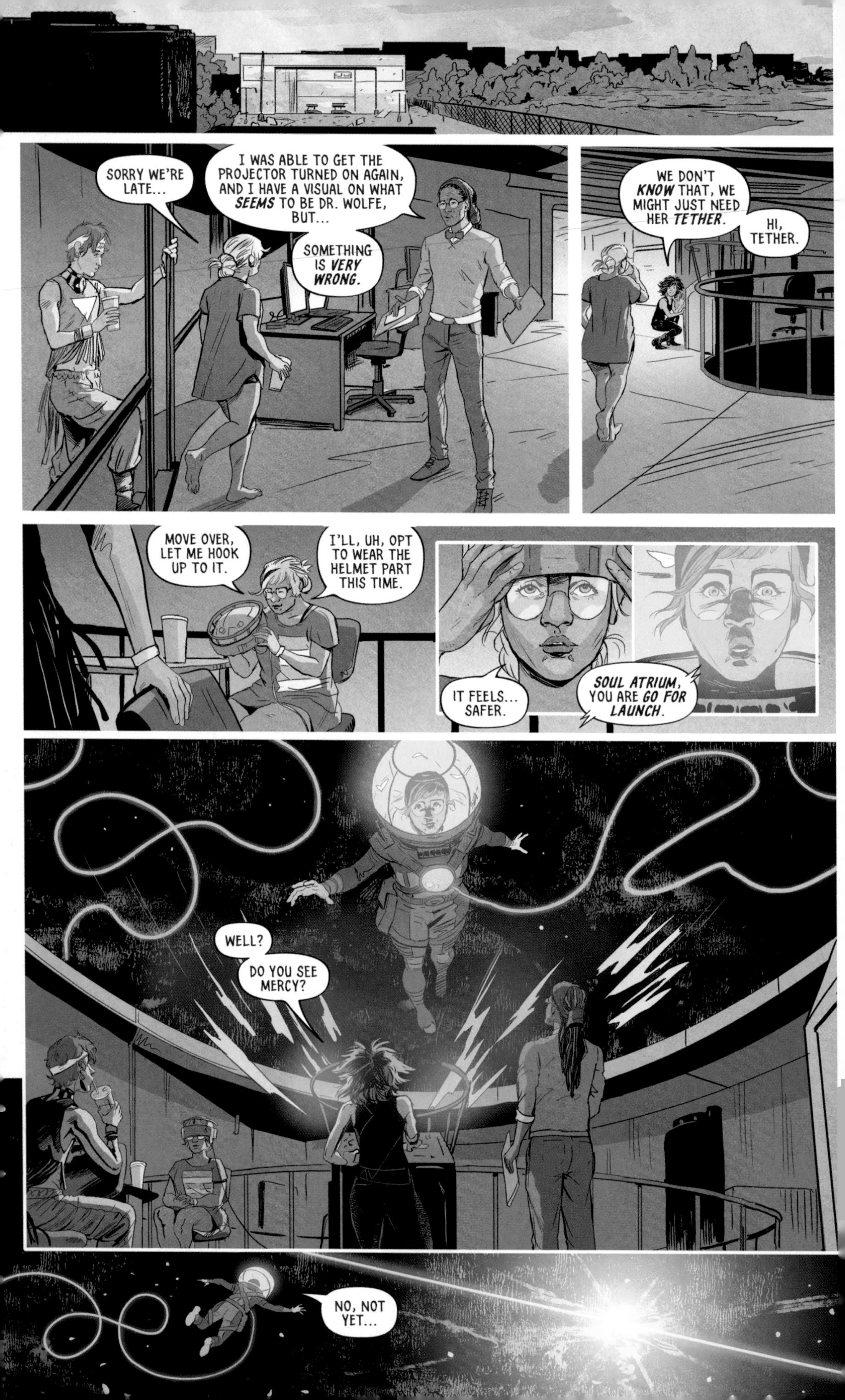
SORRY WE'RE LATE...
I WAS ABLE TO GET THE PROJECTOR TURNED ON AGAIN, AND I HAVE A VISUAL ON WHAT SEEMS TO BE DR. WOLFE, BUT...
SOMETHING IS VERY WRONG.
WE DON'T KNOW THAT, WE MIGHT JUST NEED HER TETHER.
HI, TETHER.
MOVE OVER, LET ME HOOK UP TO IT.
I'LL, UH, OPT TO WEAR THE HELMET PART THIS TIME.
IT FEELS... SAFER.
SOUL ATRIUM, YOU ARE GO FOR LAUNCH.
WELL?
DO YOU SEE MERCY?
NO, NOT YET...

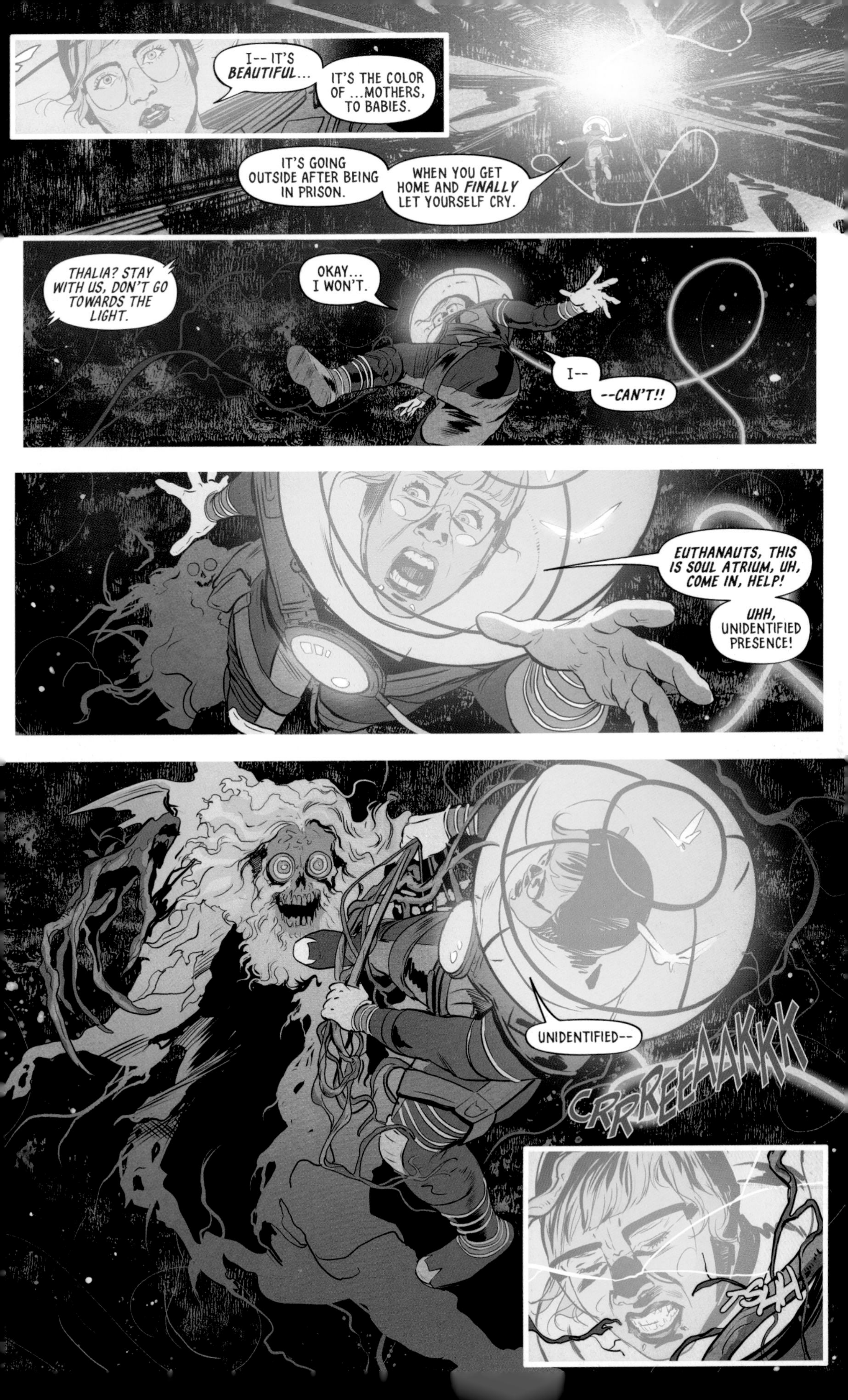
I-- IT'S BEAUTIFUL...
IT'S THE COLOR OF ...MOTHERS, TO BABIES.
IT'S GOING OUTSIDE AFTER BEING IN PRISON.
WHEN YOU GET HOME AND FINALLY LET YOURSELF CRY.
THALIA? STAY WITH US, DON'T GO TOWARDS THE LIGHT.
OKAY... I WON'T.
I--
--CAN'T!!
EUTHANAUTS, THIS IS SOUL ATRIUM, UH, COME IN, HELP!
UHH, UNIDENTIFIED PRESENCE!
UNIDENTIFIED--
CRRREEAAKKK
TSLH

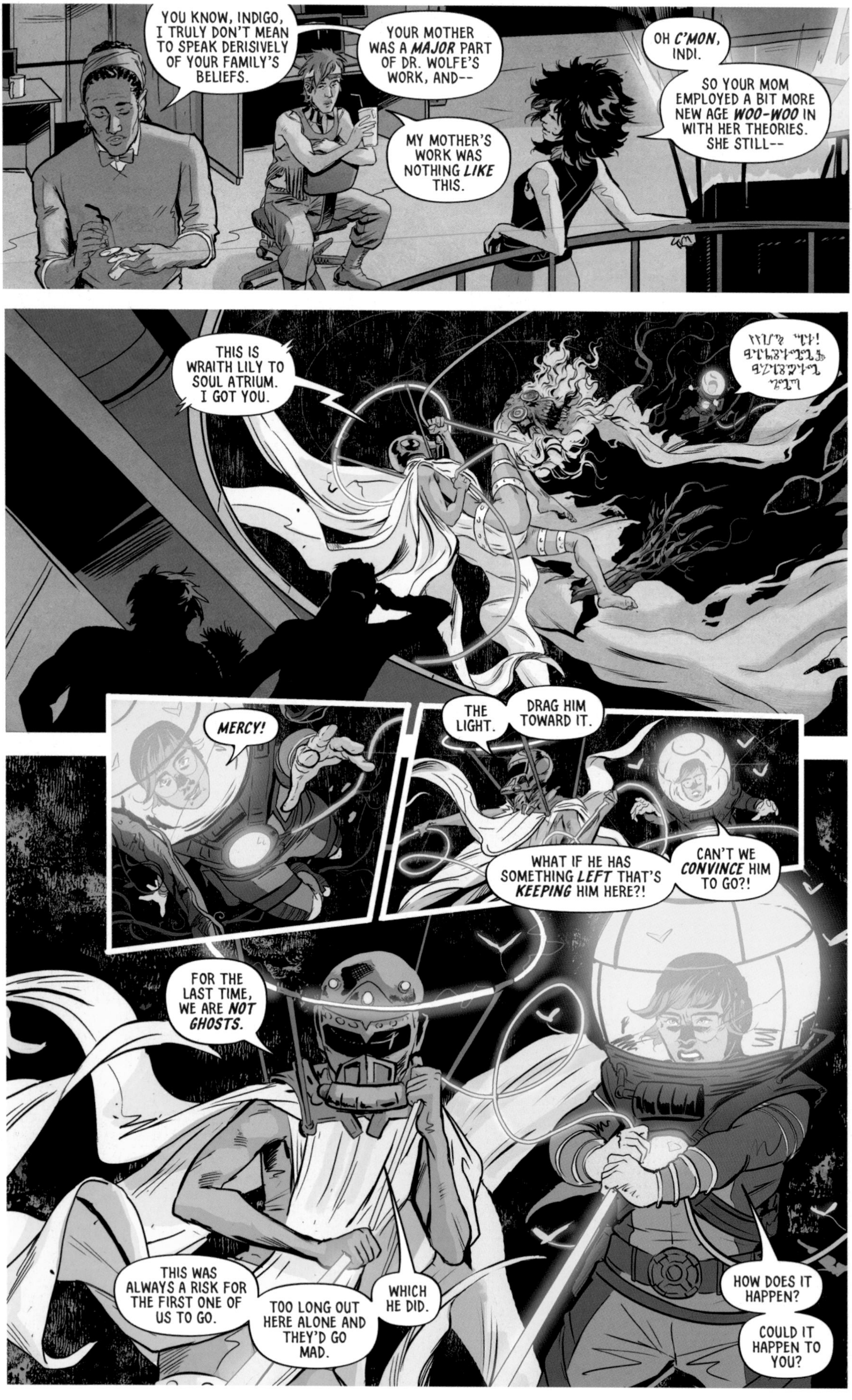
YOU KNOW, INDIGO, I TRULY DON'T MEAN TO SPEAK DERISIVELY OF YOUR FAMILY'S BELIEFS.
YOUR MOTHER WAS A MAJOR PART OF DR. WOLFE'S WORK, AND--
MY MOTHER'S WORK WAS NOTHING LIKE THIS.
OH C'MON, INDI.
SO YOUR MOM EMPLOYED A BIT MORE NEW AGE WOO-WOO IN WITH HER THEORIES. SHE STILL--
THIS IS WRAITH LILY TO SOUL ATRIUM. I GOT YOU.
MERCY!
THE LIGHT.
DRAG HIM TOWARD IT.
WHAT IF HE HAS SOMETHING LEFT THAT'S KEEPING HIM HERE?!
CAN'T WE CONVINCE HIM TO GO?!
FOR THE LAST TIME, WE ARE NOT GHOSTS.
THIS WAS ALWAYS A RISK FOR THE FIRST ONE OF US TO GO.
TOO LONG OUT HERE ALONE AND THEY'D GO MAD.
WHICH HE DID.
HOW DOES IT HAPPEN?
COULD IT HAPPEN TO YOU?

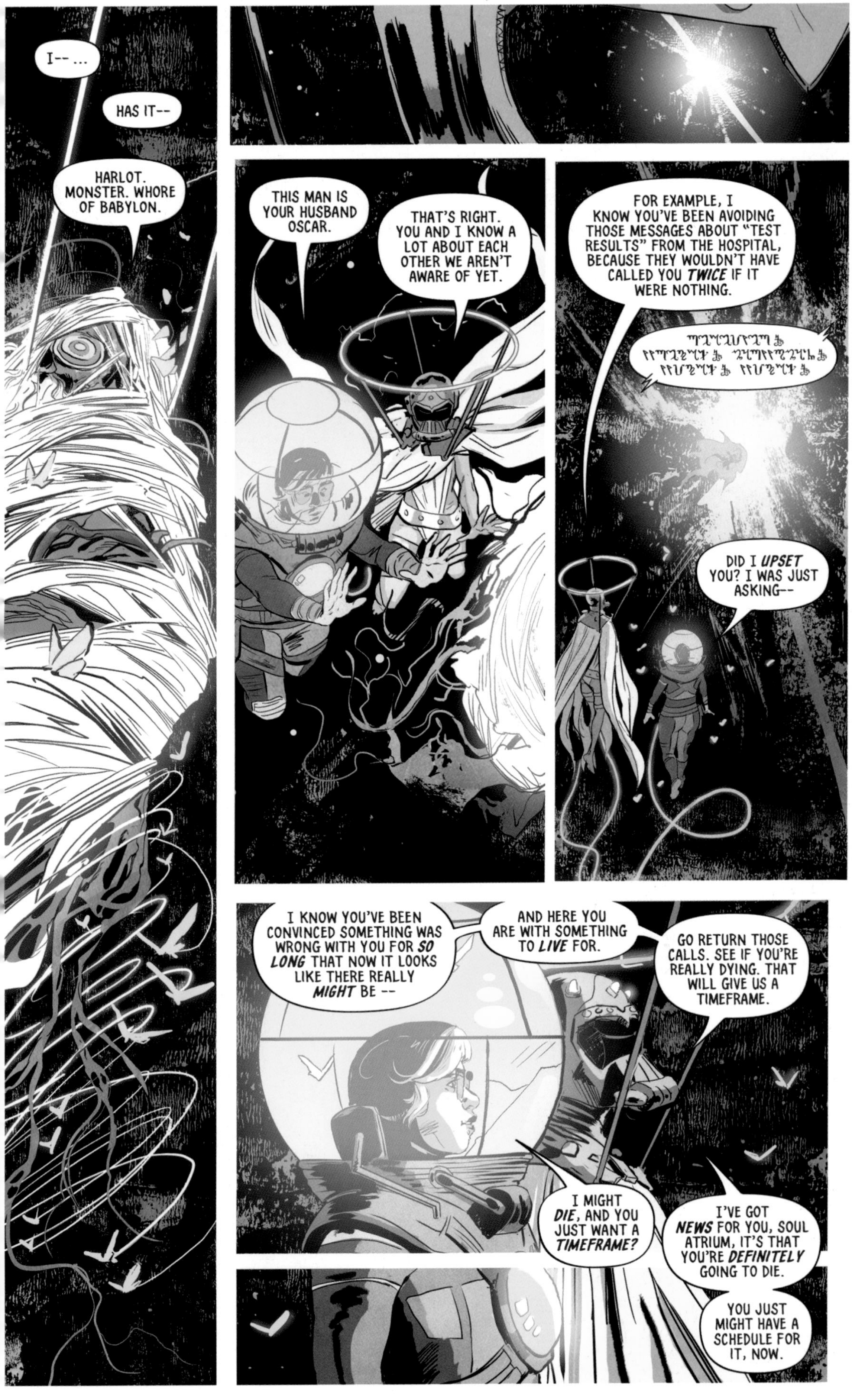

I-- ...
HAS IT--
HARLOT. MONSTER. WHORE OF BABYLON.
THIS MAN IS YOUR HUSBAND OSCAR.
THAT'S RIGHT. YOU AND I KNOW A LOT ABOUT EACH OTHER WE AREN'T AWARE OF YET.
FOR EXAMPLE, I KNOW YOU'VE BEEN AVOIDING THOSE MESSAGES ABOUT "TEST RESULTS" FROM THE HOSPITAL, BECAUSE THEY WOULDN'T HAVE CALLED YOU TWICE IF IT WERE NOTHING.
DID I UPSET YOU? I WAS JUST ASKING--
I KNOW YOU'VE BEEN CONVINCED SOMETHING WAS WRONG WITH YOU FOR SO LONG THAT NOW IT LOOKS LIKE THERE REALLY MIGHT BE --
AND HERE YOU ARE WITH SOMETHING TO LIVE FOR.
GO RETURN THOSE CALLS. SEE IF YOU'RE REALLY DYING. THAT WILL GIVE US A TIMEFRAME.
I MIGHT DIE, AND YOU JUST WANT A TIMEFRAME?
I'VE GOT NEWS FOR YOU, SOUL ATRIUM, IT'S THAT YOU'RE DEFINITELY GOING TO DIE.
YOU JUST MIGHT HAVE A SCHEDULE FOR IT, NOW.

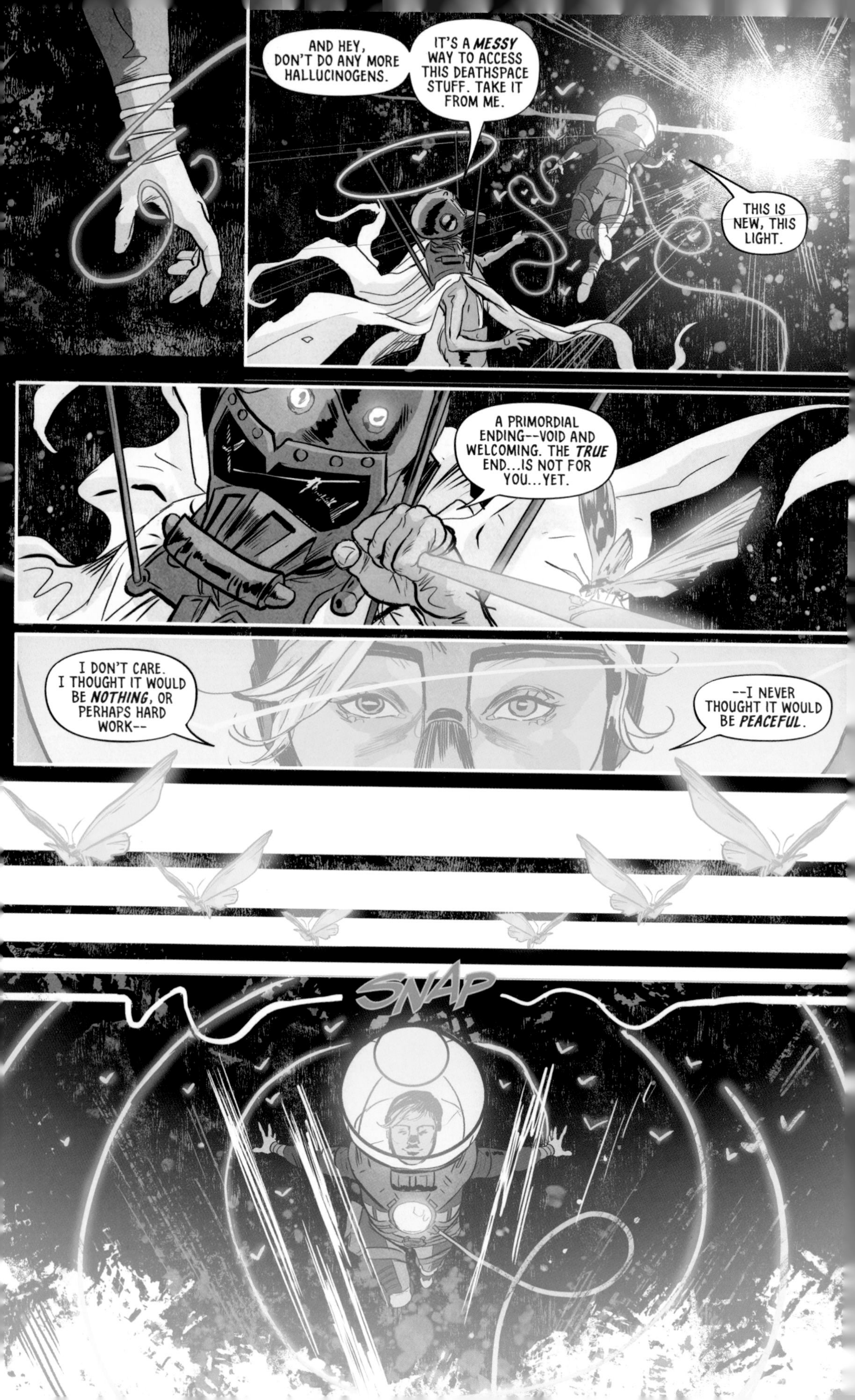
AND HEY, DON'T DO ANY MORE HALLUCINOGENS.
IT'S A MESSY WAY TO ACCESS THIS DEATHSPACE STUFF. TAKE IT FROM ME.
THIS IS NEW, THIS LIGHT.
A PRIMORDIAL ENDING--VOID AND WELCOMING. THE TRUE END...IS NOT FOR YOU...YET.
I DON'T CARE. I THOUGHT IT WOULD BE NOTHING, OR PERHAPS HARD WORK--
--I NEVER THOUGHT IT WOULD BE PEACEFUL.
SNAP

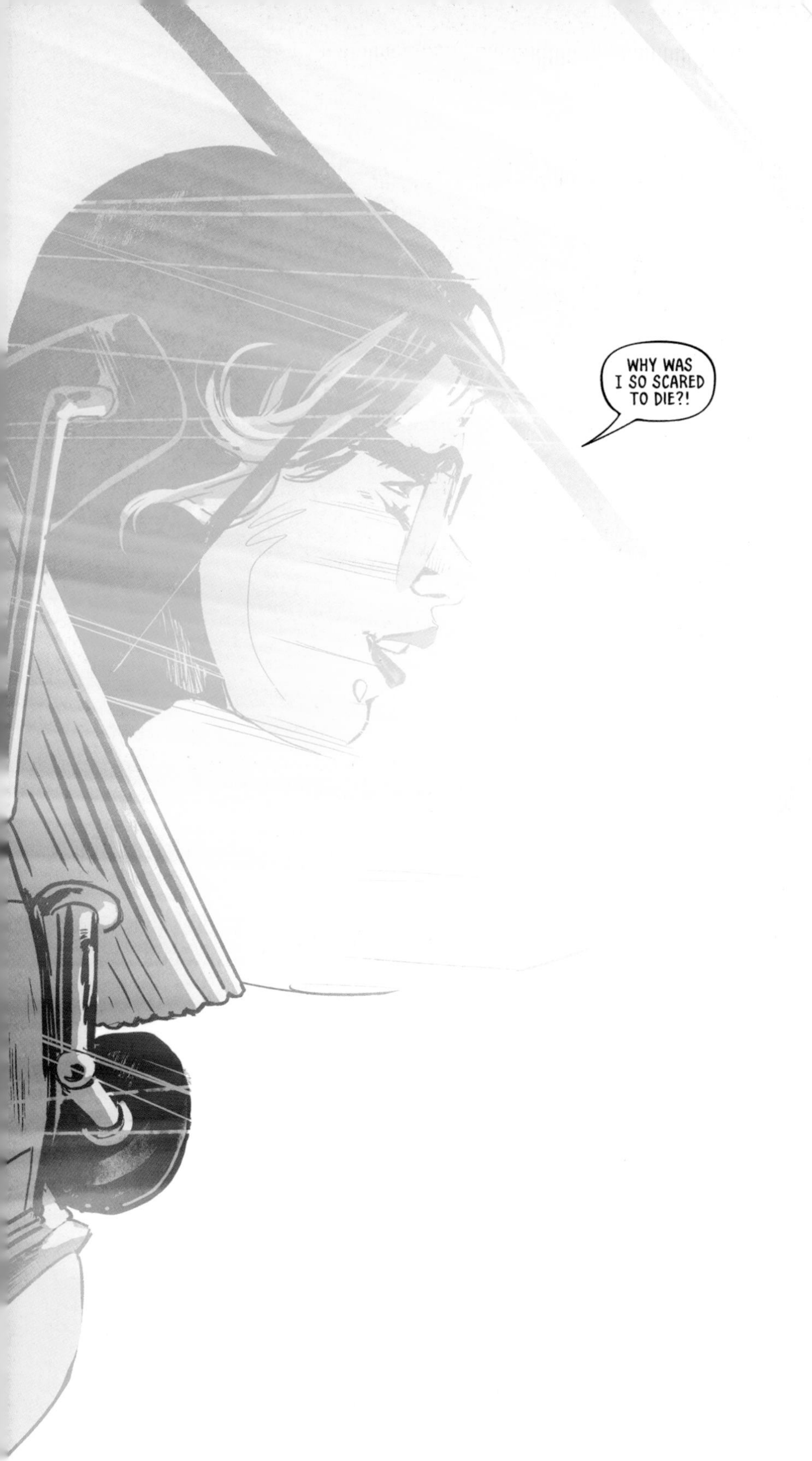
WHY WAS I SO SCARED TO DIE?!

"THIS IS DANGEROUS,
FOR THE RECORD."

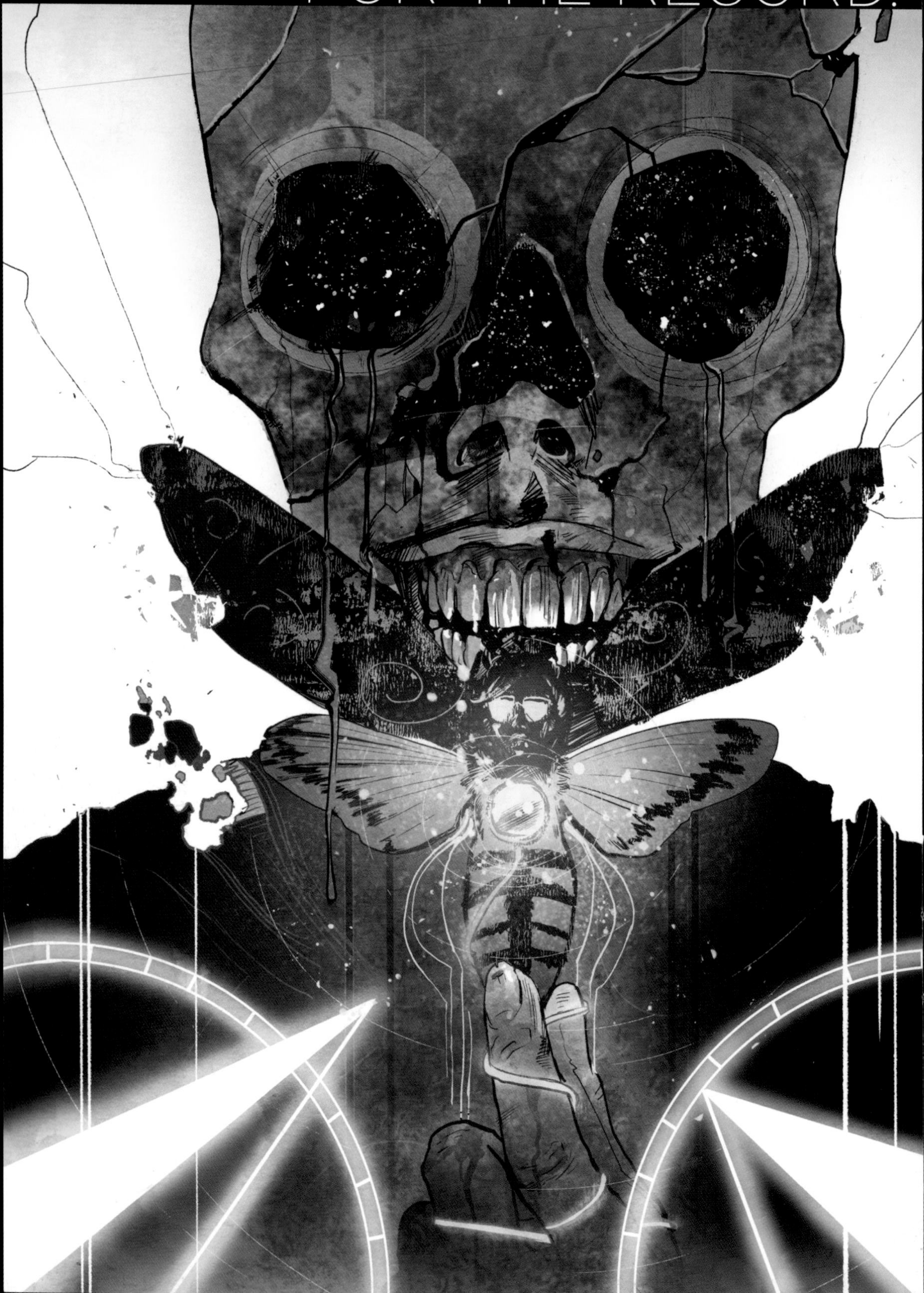

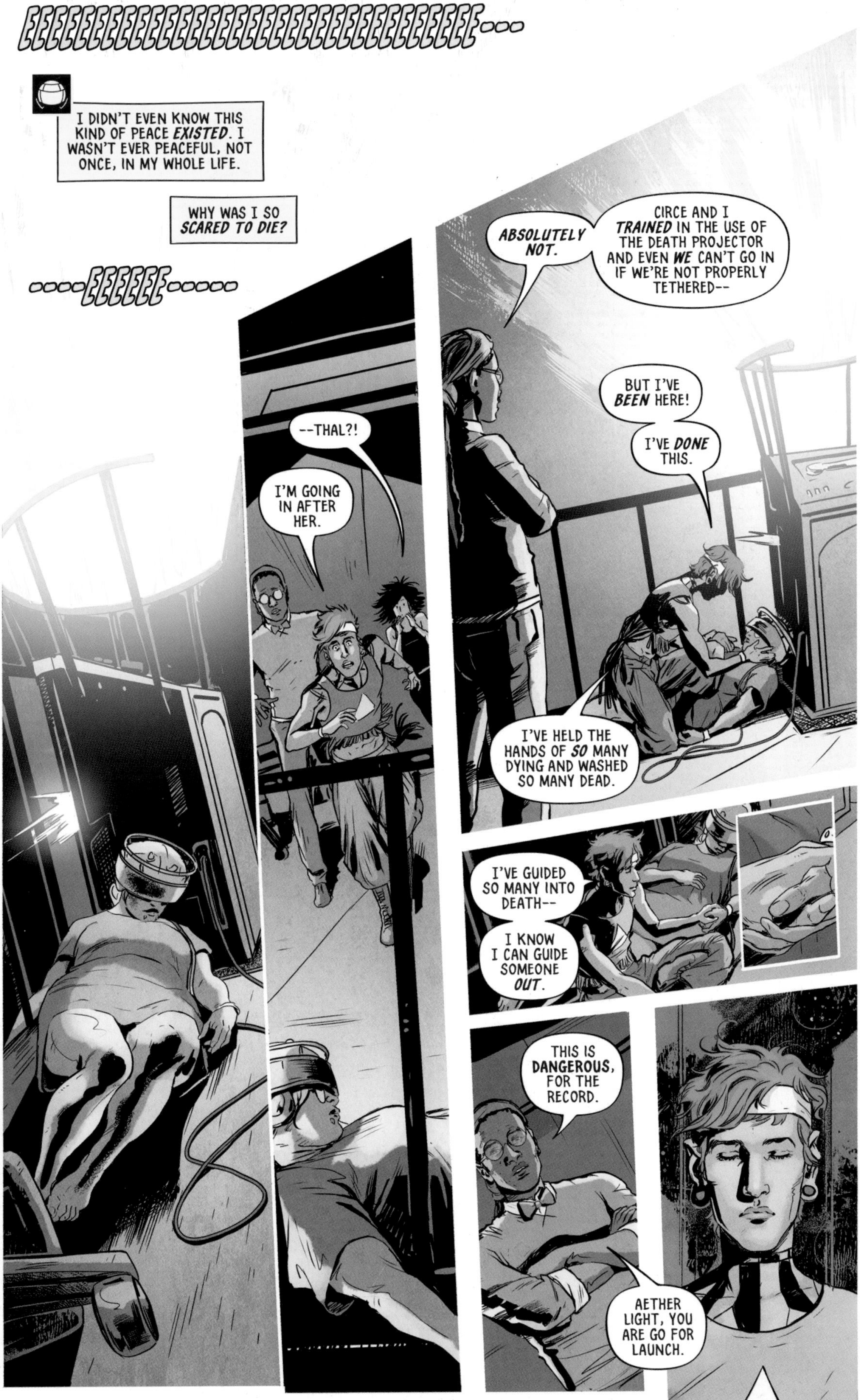
EEEEEEEEEEEEEEEEEEEEEEEEEEEEEEEEEE---
I DIDN'T EVEN KNOW THIS KIND OF PEACE EXISTED. I WASN'T EVER PEACEFUL, NOT ONCE, IN MY WHOLE LIFE.
WHY WAS I SO SCARED TO DIE?
----EEEEEE-----
--THAL?!
I'M GOING IN AFTER HER.
ABSOLUTELY NOT.
CIRCE AND I TRAINED IN THE USE OF THE DEATH PROJECTOR AND EVEN WE CAN'T GO IN IF WE'RE NOT PROPERLY TETHERED--
BUT I'VE BEEN HERE!
I'VE DONE THIS.
I'VE HELD THE HANDS OF SO MANY DYING AND WASHED SO MANY DEAD.
I'VE GUIDED SO MANY INTO DEATH--
I KNOW I CAN GUIDE SOMEONE OUT.
THIS IS DANGEROUS, FOR THE RECORD.
AETHER LIGHT, YOU ARE GO FOR LAUNCH.

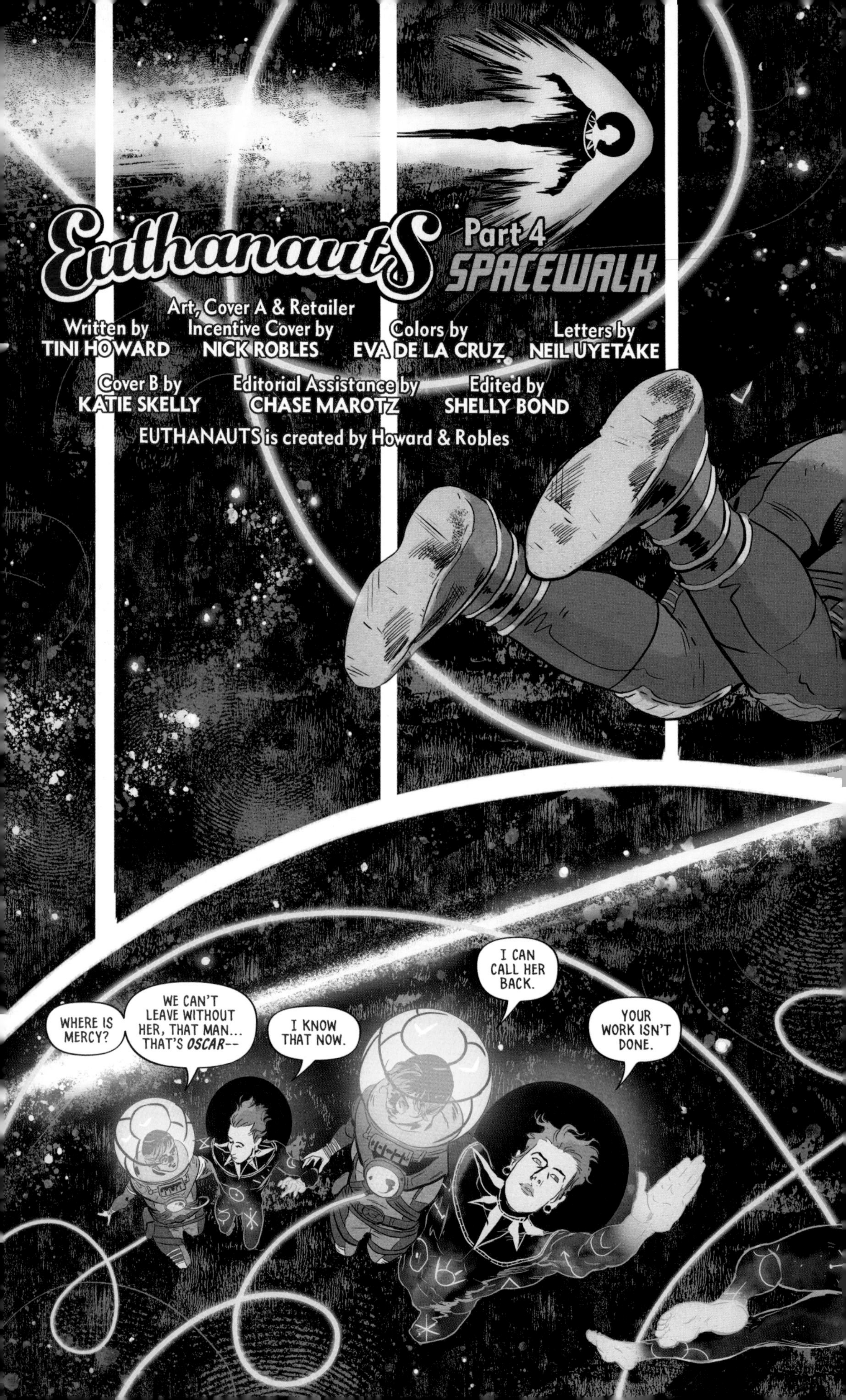

Euthanauts
Part 4
SPACEWALK
Written by
TINI HOWARD
Art, Cover A & Retailer Incentive Cover by
NICK ROBLES
Colors by
EVA DE LA CRUZ
Letters by
NEIL UYETAKE
Cover B by
KATIE SKELLY
Editorial Assistance by
CHASE MAROTZ
Edited by
SHELLY BOND
EUTHANAUTS is created by Howard & Robles
WHERE IS MERCY?
WE CAN'T LEAVE WITHOUT HER, THAT MAN... THAT'S OSCAR--
I KNOW THAT NOW.
I CAN CALL HER BACK.
YOUR WORK ISN'T DONE.

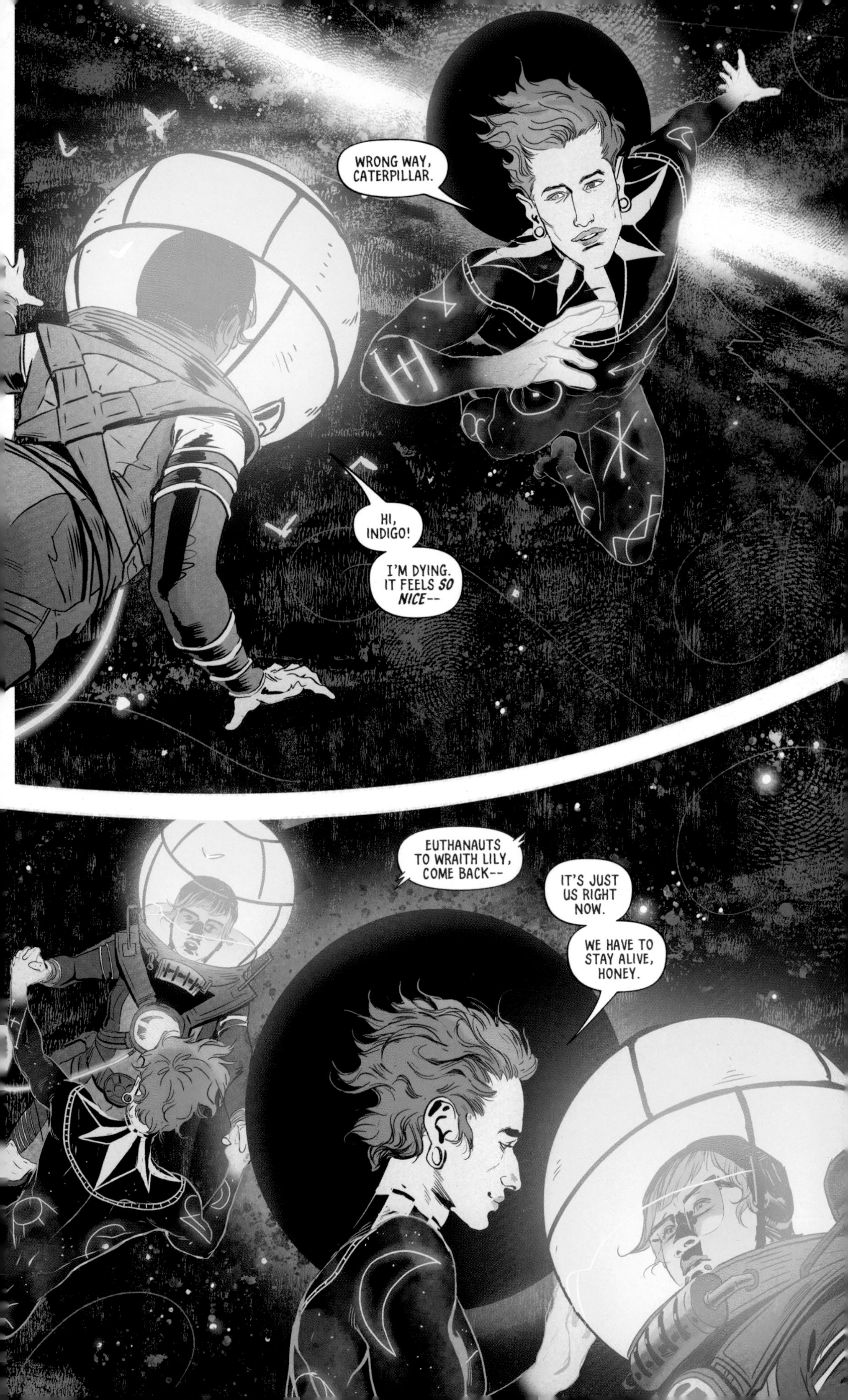
WRONG WAY, CATERPILLAR.
HI, INDIGO!
I'M DYING. IT FEELS SO NICE--
EUTHANAUTS TO WRAITH LILY, COME BACK--
IT'S JUST US RIGHT NOW.
WE HAVE TO STAY ALIVE, HONEY.

ELSEWHERE. IN THE FLESH-SPACE.

FLIK BBUBUBUBUBUBUBUBUBUBUB

CREEAAAK

...D'YOU HEAR SOMETHING?

ZZ... Z...

...DADDY?

...OH, OH, AND MOM!

ZZ... Z...

CLIK

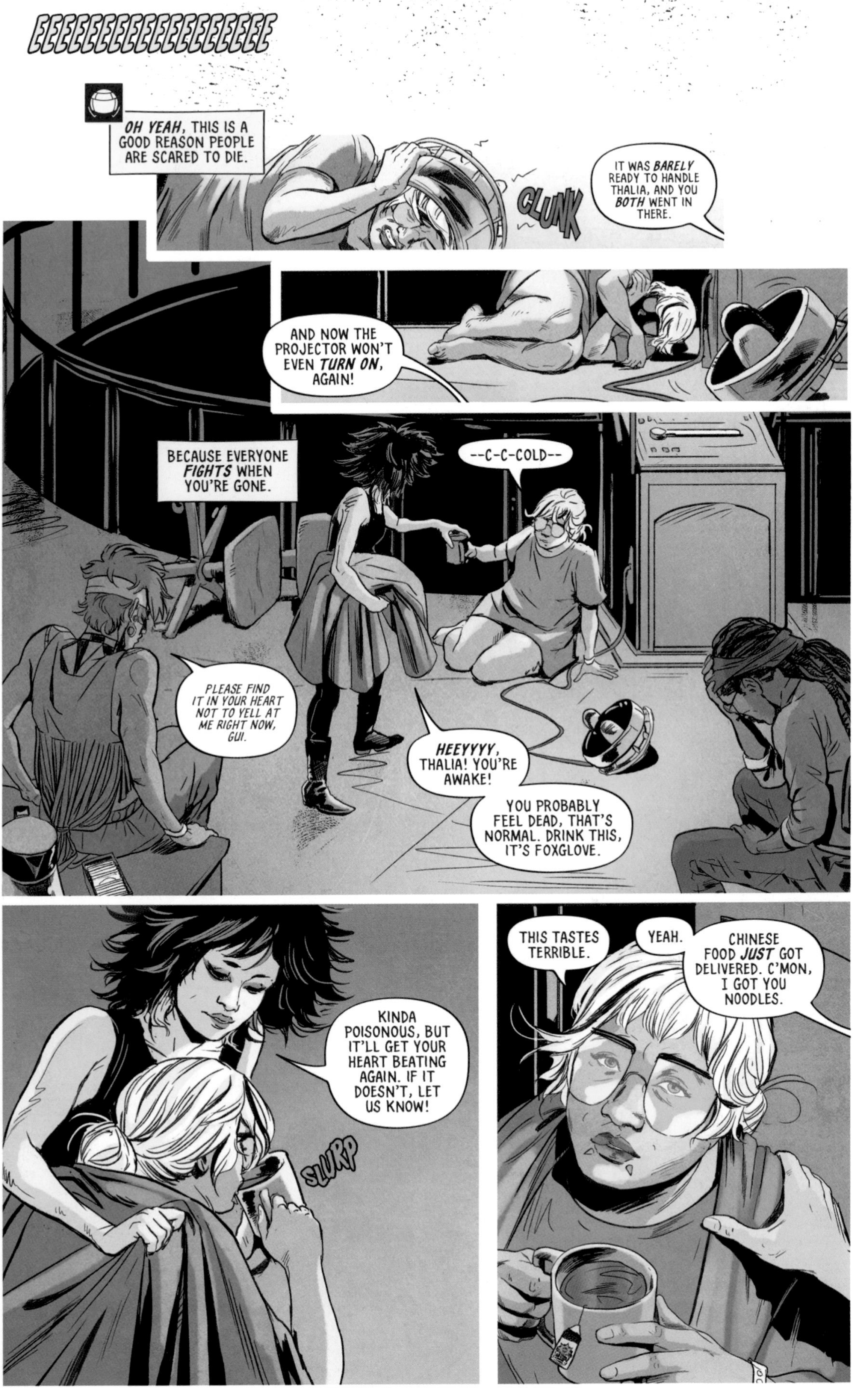
EEEEEEEEEEEEEEEEEEE
OH YEAH, THIS IS A GOOD REASON PEOPLE ARE SCARED TO DIE.
CLUNK
IT WAS BARELY READY TO HANDLE THALIA, AND YOU BOTH WENT IN THERE.
AND NOW THE PROJECTOR WON'T EVEN TURN ON, AGAIN!
BECAUSE EVERYONE FIGHTS WHEN YOU'RE GONE.
--C-C-COLD--
PLEASE FIND IT IN YOUR HEART NOT TO YELL AT ME RIGHT NOW, GUI.
HEEYYYY, THALIA! YOU'RE AWAKE!
YOU PROBABLY FEEL DEAD, THAT'S NORMAL. DRINK THIS, IT'S FOXGLOVE.
KINDA POISONOUS, BUT IT'LL GET YOUR HEART BEATING AGAIN. IF IT DOESN'T, LET US KNOW!
SLURP
THIS TASTES TERRIBLE.
YEAH.
CHINESE FOOD JUST GOT DELIVERED. C'MON, I GOT YOU NOODLES.

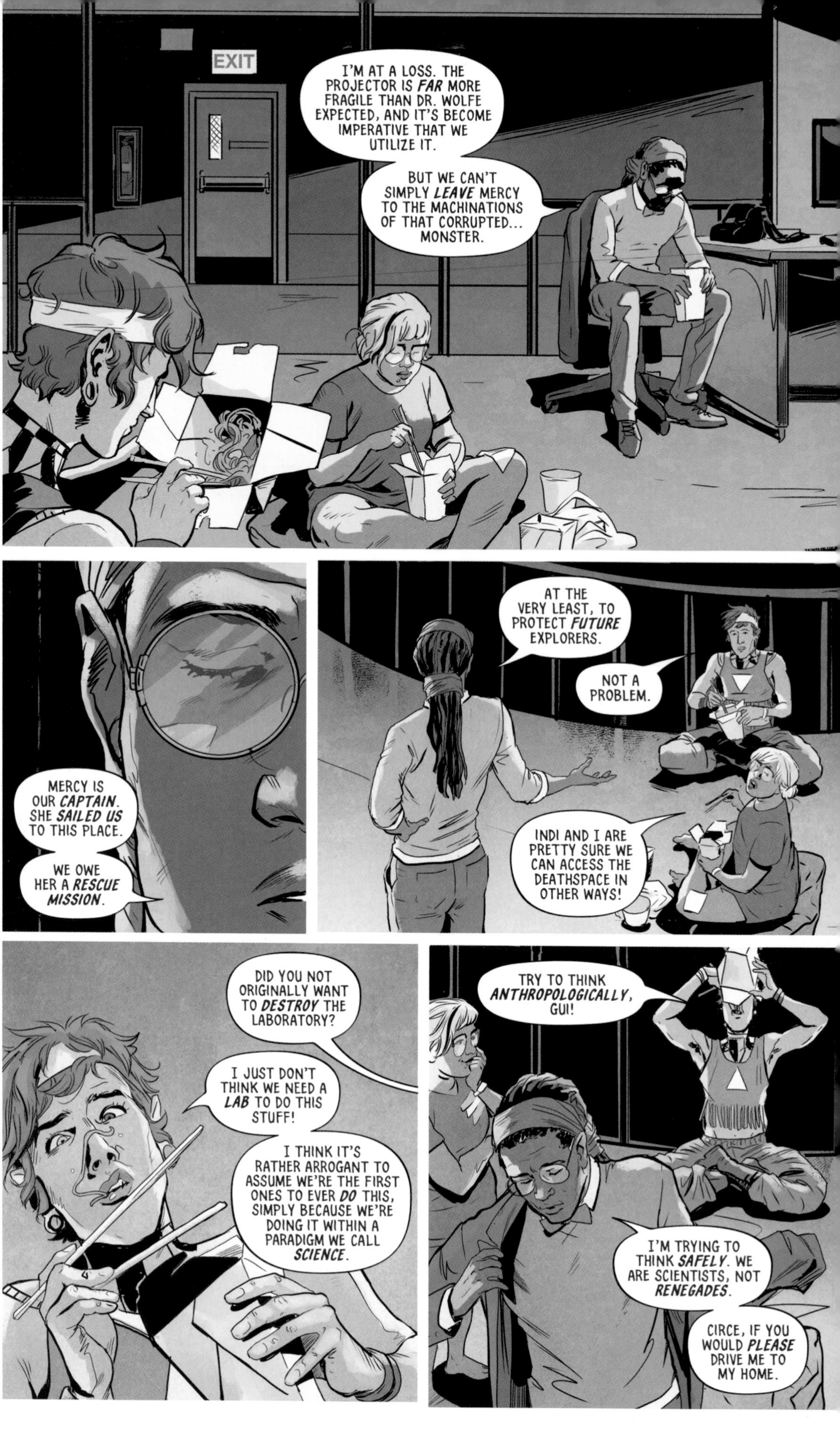

EXIT
I'M AT A LOSS. THE PROJECTOR IS *FAR* MORE FRAGILE THAN DR. WOLFE EXPECTED, AND IT'S BECOME IMPERATIVE THAT WE UTILIZE IT.
BUT WE CAN'T SIMPLY *LEAVE* MERCY TO THE MACHINATIONS OF THAT CORRUPTED... MONSTER.
MERCY IS OUR *CAPTAIN*. SHE *SAILED US* TO THIS PLACE.
WE OWE HER A *RESCUE MISSION*.
AT THE VERY LEAST, TO PROTECT *FUTURE* EXPLORERS.
NOT A PROBLEM.
INDI AND I ARE PRETTY SURE WE CAN ACCESS THE DEATHSPACE IN OTHER WAYS!
DID YOU NOT ORIGINALLY WANT TO *DESTROY* THE LABORATORY?
I JUST DON'T THINK WE NEED A *LAB* TO DO THIS STUFF!
I THINK IT'S RATHER ARROGANT TO ASSUME WE'RE THE FIRST ONES TO EVER *DO* THIS, SIMPLY BECAUSE WE'RE DOING IT WITHIN A PARADIGM WE CALL *SCIENCE*.
TRY TO THINK *ANTHROPOLOGICALLY*, GUI!
I'M TRYING TO THINK *SAFELY*. WE ARE SCIENTISTS, NOT *RENEGADES*.
CIRCE, IF YOU WOULD *PLEASE* DRIVE ME TO MY HOME.

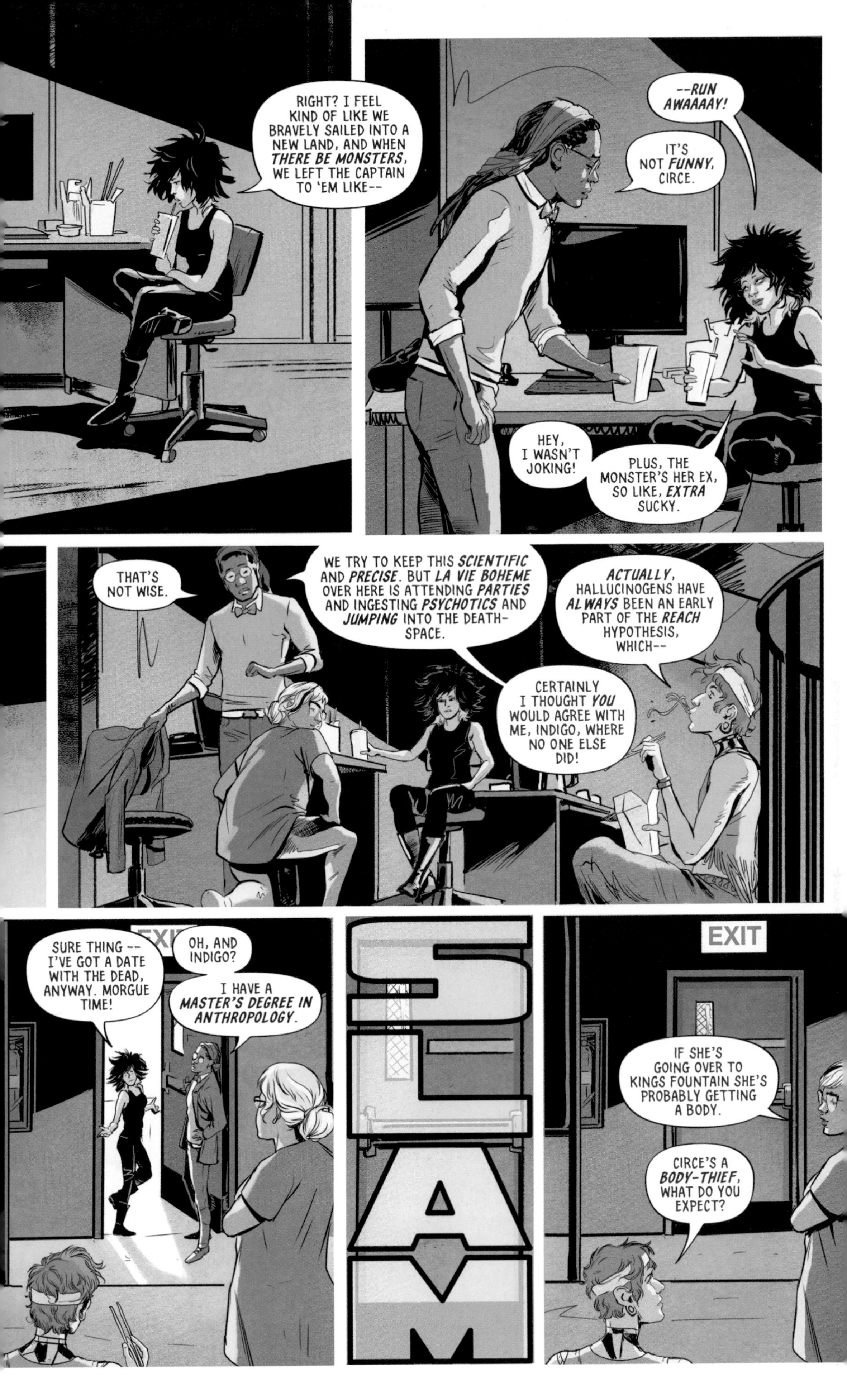
RIGHT? I FEEL KIND OF LIKE WE BRAVELY SAILED INTO A NEW LAND, AND WHEN THERE BE MONSTERS, WE LEFT THE CAPTAIN TO 'EM LIKE--
--RUN AWAAAAY!
IT'S NOT FUNNY, CIRCE.
HEY, I WASN'T JOKING!
PLUS, THE MONSTER'S HER EX, SO LIKE, EXTRA SUCKY.
THAT'S NOT WISE.
WE TRY TO KEEP THIS SCIENTIFIC AND PRECISE. BUT LA VIE BOHEME OVER HERE IS ATTENDING PARTIES AND INGESTING PSYCHOTICS AND JUMPING INTO THE DEATH-SPACE.
ACTUALLY, HALLUCINOGENS HAVE ALWAYS BEEN AN EARLY PART OF THE REACH HYPOTHESIS, WHICH--
CERTAINLY I THOUGHT YOU WOULD AGREE WITH ME, INDIGO, WHERE NO ONE ELSE DID!
SURE THING -- I'VE GOT A DATE WITH THE DEAD, ANYWAY. MORGUE TIME!
OH, AND INDIGO?
I HAVE A MASTER'S DEGREE IN ANTHROPOLOGY.
SLAM
EXIT
IF SHE'S GOING OVER TO KINGS FOUNTAIN SHE'S PROBABLY GETTING A BODY.
CIRCE'S A BODY-THIEF, WHAT DO YOU EXPECT?

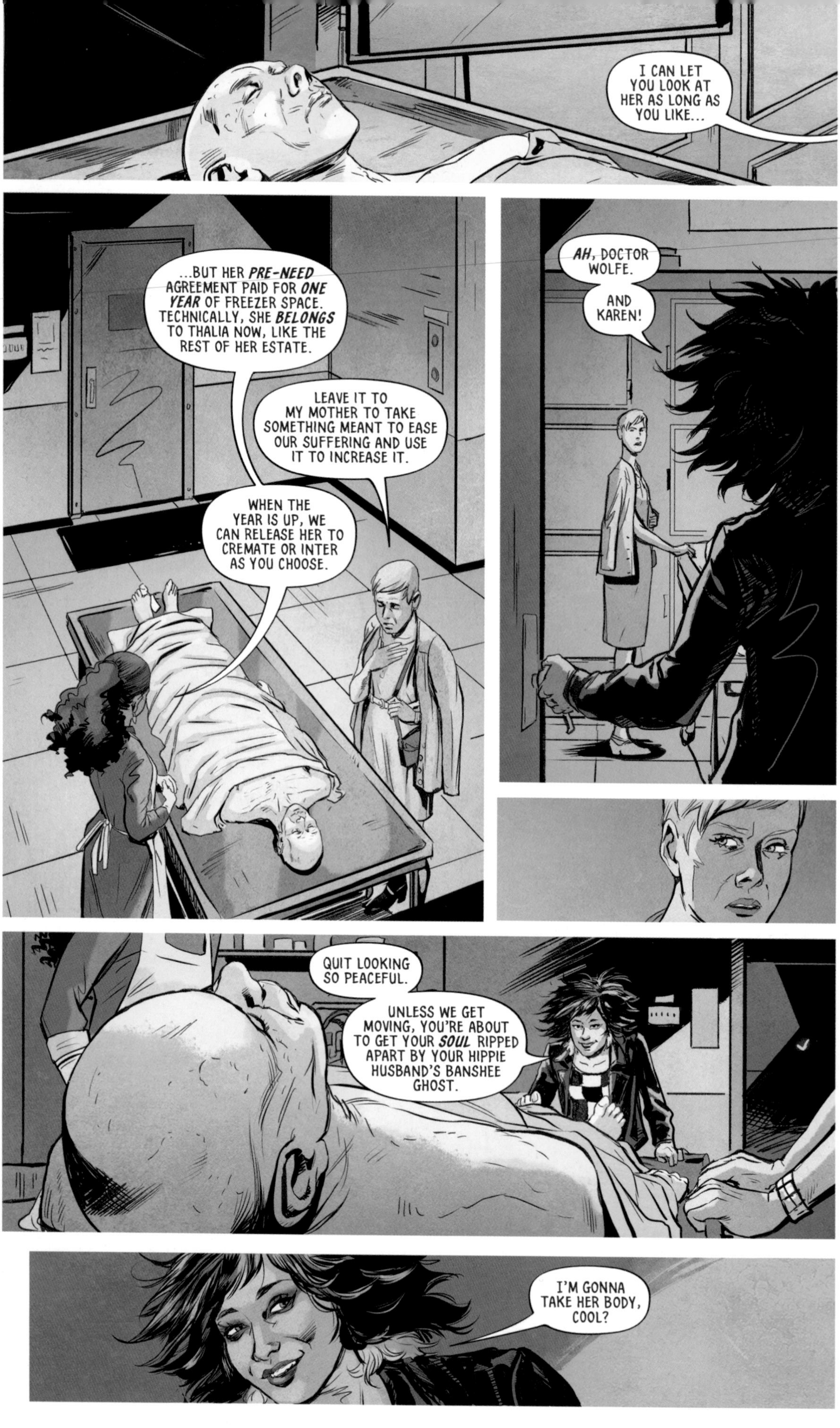
I CAN LET YOU LOOK AT HER AS LONG AS YOU LIKE...
...BUT HER *PRE-NEED* AGREEMENT PAID FOR *ONE YEAR* OF FREEZER SPACE. TECHNICALLY, SHE *BELONGS* TO THALIA NOW, LIKE THE REST OF HER ESTATE.
WHEN THE YEAR IS UP, WE CAN RELEASE HER TO CREMATE OR INTER AS YOU CHOOSE.
LEAVE IT TO MY MOTHER TO TAKE SOMETHING MEANT TO EASE OUR SUFFERING AND USE IT TO INCREASE IT.
AH, DOCTOR WOLFE.
AND KAREN!
QUIT LOOKING SO PEACEFUL.
UNLESS WE GET MOVING, YOU'RE ABOUT TO GET YOUR *SOUL* RIPPED APART BY YOUR HIPPIE HUSBAND'S BANSHEE GHOST.
I'M GONNA TAKE HER BODY, COOL?

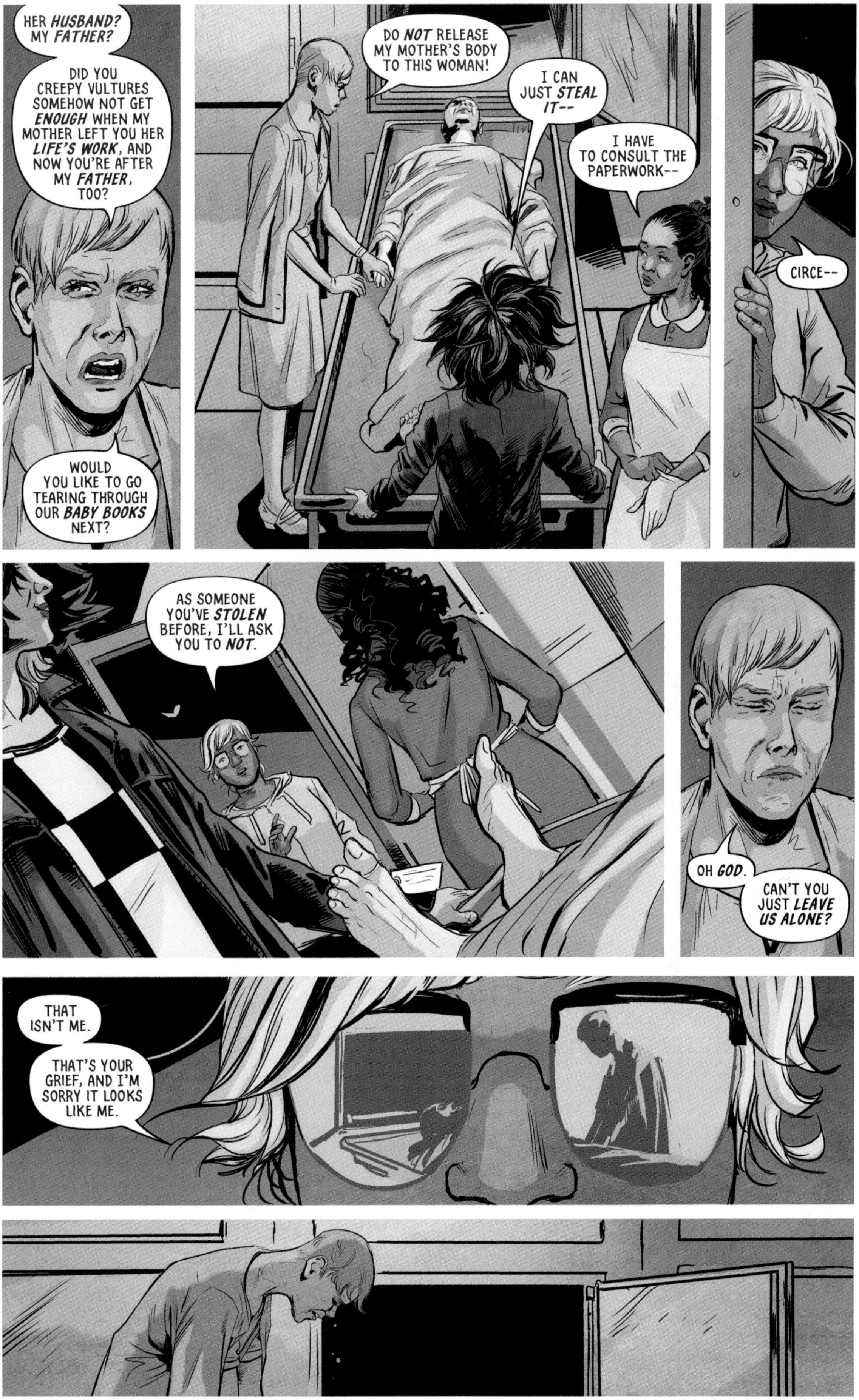
HER HUSBAND? MY FATHER?
DID YOU CREEPY VULTURES SOMEHOW NOT GET ENOUGH WHEN MY MOTHER LEFT YOU HER LIFE'S WORK, AND NOW YOU'RE AFTER MY FATHER, TOO?
WOULD YOU LIKE TO GO TEARING THROUGH OUR BABY BOOKS NEXT?
DO NOT RELEASE MY MOTHER'S BODY TO THIS WOMAN!
I CAN JUST STEAL IT--
I HAVE TO CONSULT THE PAPERWORK--
CIRCE--
AS SOMEONE YOU'VE STOLEN BEFORE, I'LL ASK YOU TO NOT.
OH GOD.
CAN'T YOU JUST LEAVE US ALONE?
THAT ISN'T ME.
THAT'S YOUR GRIEF, AND I'M SORRY IT LOOKS LIKE ME.

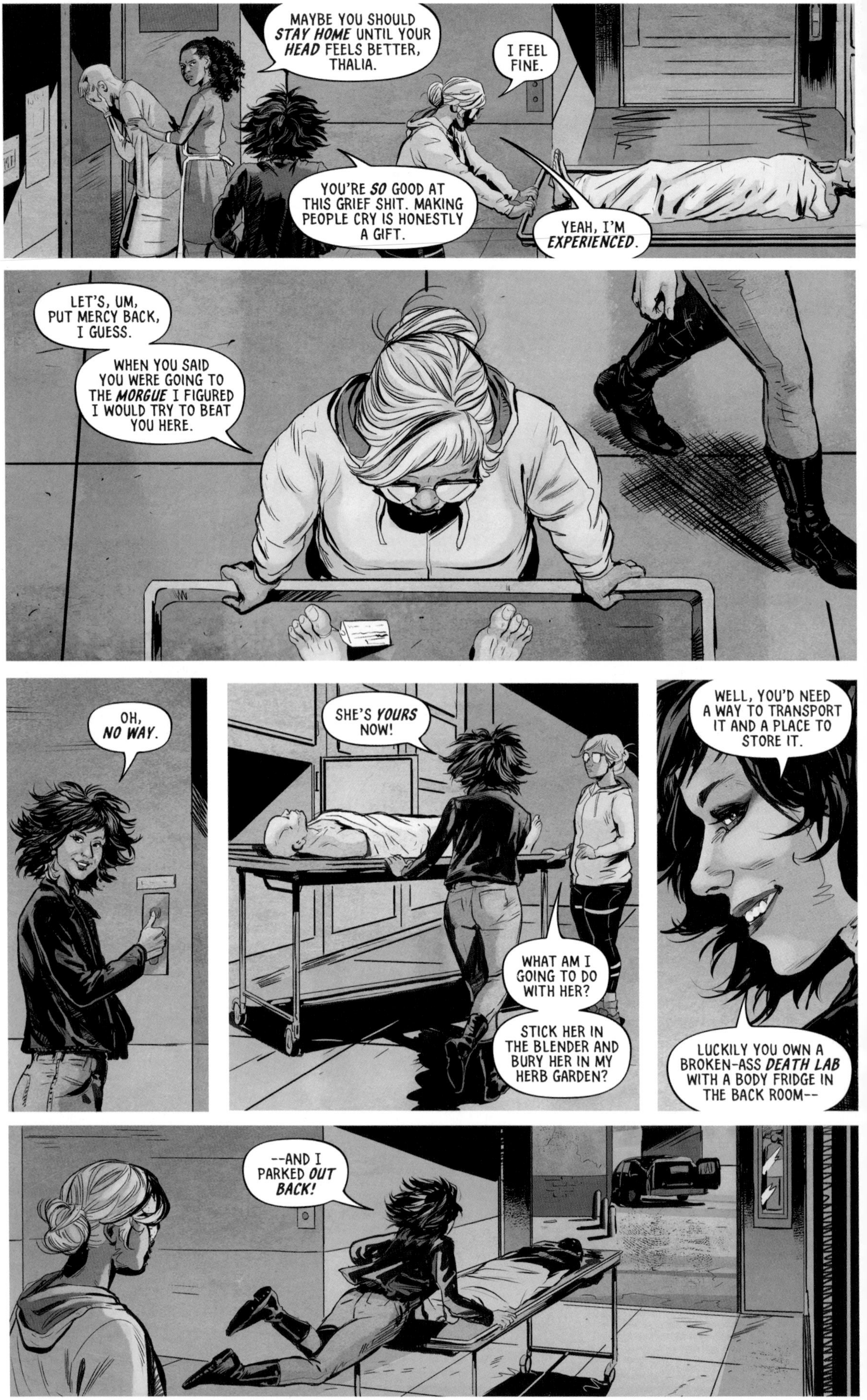
MAYBE YOU SHOULD STAY HOME UNTIL YOUR HEAD FEELS BETTER, THALIA.
I FEEL FINE.
YOU'RE SO GOOD AT THIS GRIEF SHIT. MAKING PEOPLE CRY IS HONESTLY A GIFT.
YEAH, I'M EXPERIENCED.
LET'S, UM, PUT MERCY BACK, I GUESS.
WHEN YOU SAID YOU WERE GOING TO THE MORGUE I FIGURED I WOULD TRY TO BEAT YOU HERE.
OH, NO WAY.
SHE'S YOURS NOW!
WHAT AM I GOING TO DO WITH HER?
STICK HER IN THE BLENDER AND BURY HER IN MY HERB GARDEN?
WELL, YOU'D NEED A WAY TO TRANSPORT IT AND A PLACE TO STORE IT.
LUCKILY YOU OWN A BROKEN-ASS DEATH LAB WITH A BODY FRIDGE IN THE BACK ROOM--
--AND I PARKED OUT BACK!

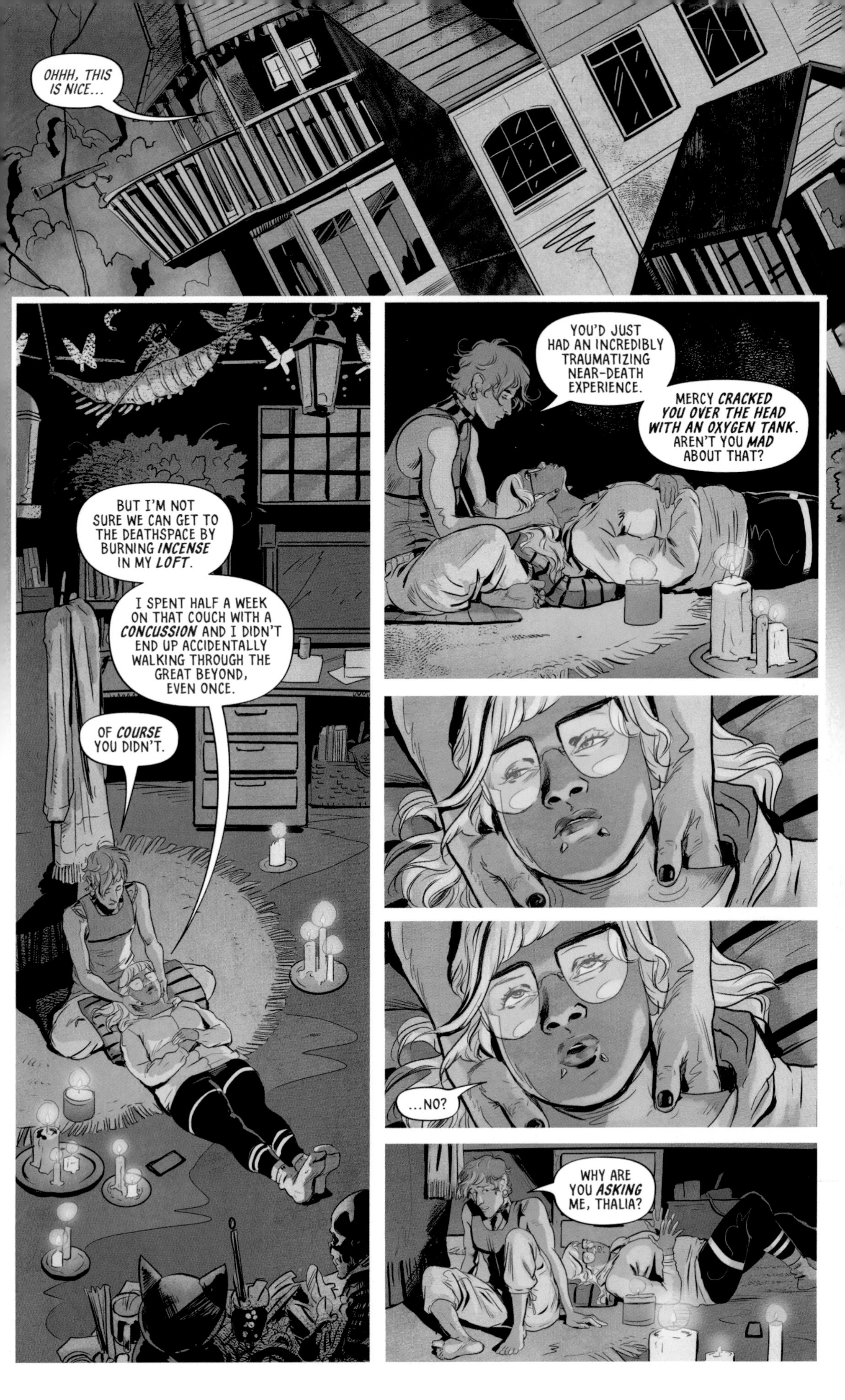
OHHH, THIS IS NICE...
BUT I'M NOT SURE WE CAN GET TO THE DEATHSPACE BY BURNING *INCENSE* IN MY *LOFT*.
I SPENT HALF A WEEK ON THAT COUCH WITH A *CONCUSSION* AND I DIDN'T END UP ACCIDENTALLY WALKING THROUGH THE GREAT BEYOND, EVEN ONCE.
OF *COURSE* YOU DIDN'T.
YOU'D JUST HAD AN INCREDIBLY TRAUMATIZING NEAR-DEATH EXPERIENCE.
MERCY *CRACKED YOU OVER THE HEAD WITH AN OXYGEN TANK.* AREN'T YOU *MAD* ABOUT THAT?
...NO?
WHY ARE YOU *ASKING* ME, THALIA?

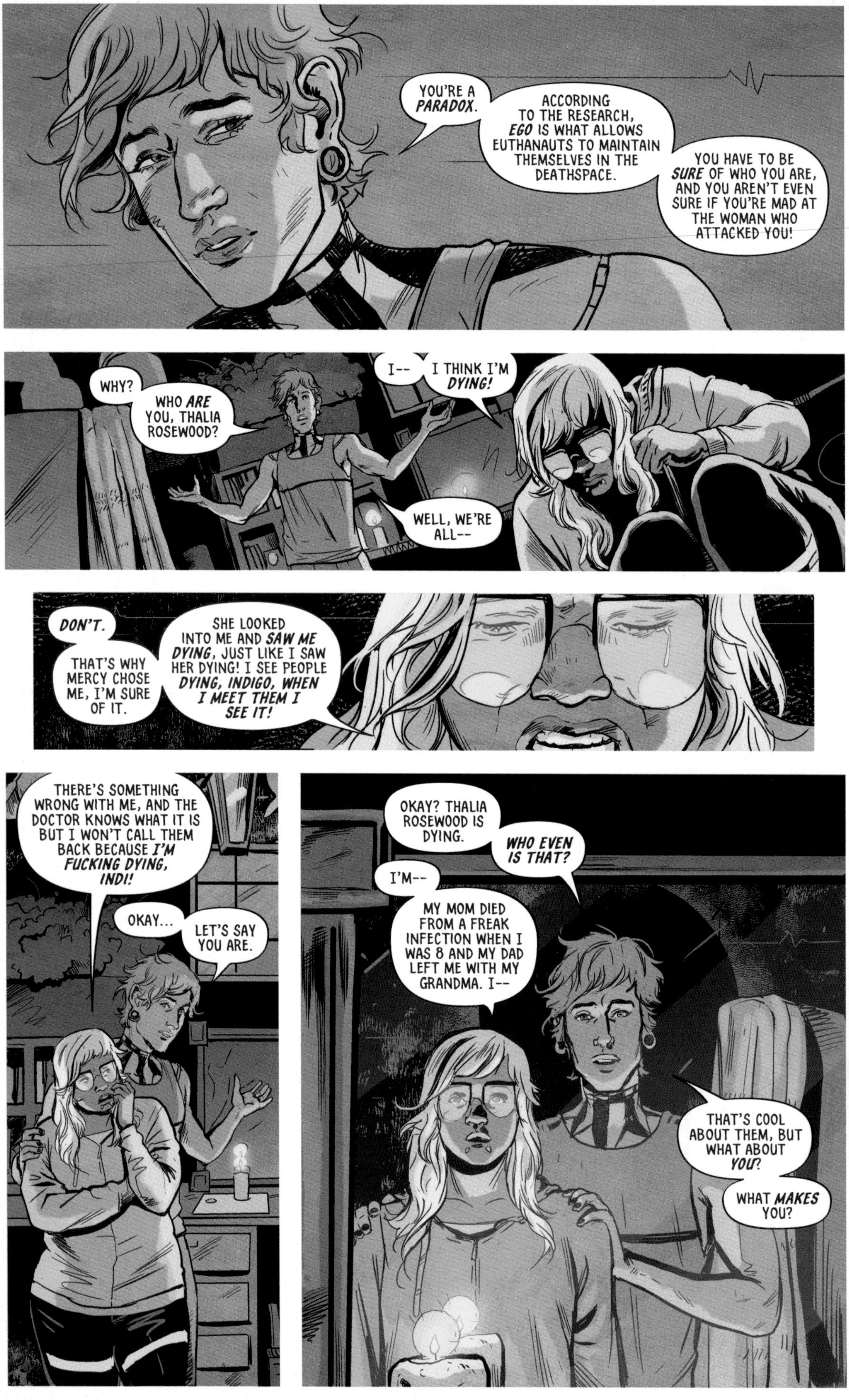
YOU'RE A PARADOX.
ACCORDING TO THE RESEARCH, EGO IS WHAT ALLOWS EUTHANAUTS TO MAINTAIN THEMSELVES IN THE DEATHSPACE.
YOU HAVE TO BE SURE OF WHO YOU ARE, AND YOU AREN'T EVEN SURE IF YOU'RE MAD AT THE WOMAN WHO ATTACKED YOU!
WHY?
WHO ARE YOU, THALIA ROSEWOOD?
I--
I THINK I'M DYING!
WELL, WE'RE ALL--
DON'T.
THAT'S WHY MERCY CHOSE ME, I'M SURE OF IT.
SHE LOOKED INTO ME AND SAW ME DYING, JUST LIKE I SAW HER DYING! I SEE PEOPLE DYING, INDIGO, WHEN I MEET THEM I SEE IT!
THERE'S SOMETHING WRONG WITH ME, AND THE DOCTOR KNOWS WHAT IT IS BUT I WON'T CALL THEM BACK BECAUSE I'M FUCKING DYING, INDI!
OKAY...
LET'S SAY YOU ARE.
OKAY? THALIA ROSEWOOD IS DYING.
WHO EVEN IS THAT?
I'M--
MY MOM DIED FROM A FREAK INFECTION WHEN I WAS 8 AND MY DAD LEFT ME WITH MY GRANDMA. I--
THAT'S COOL ABOUT THEM, BUT WHAT ABOUT YOU?
WHAT MAKES YOU?

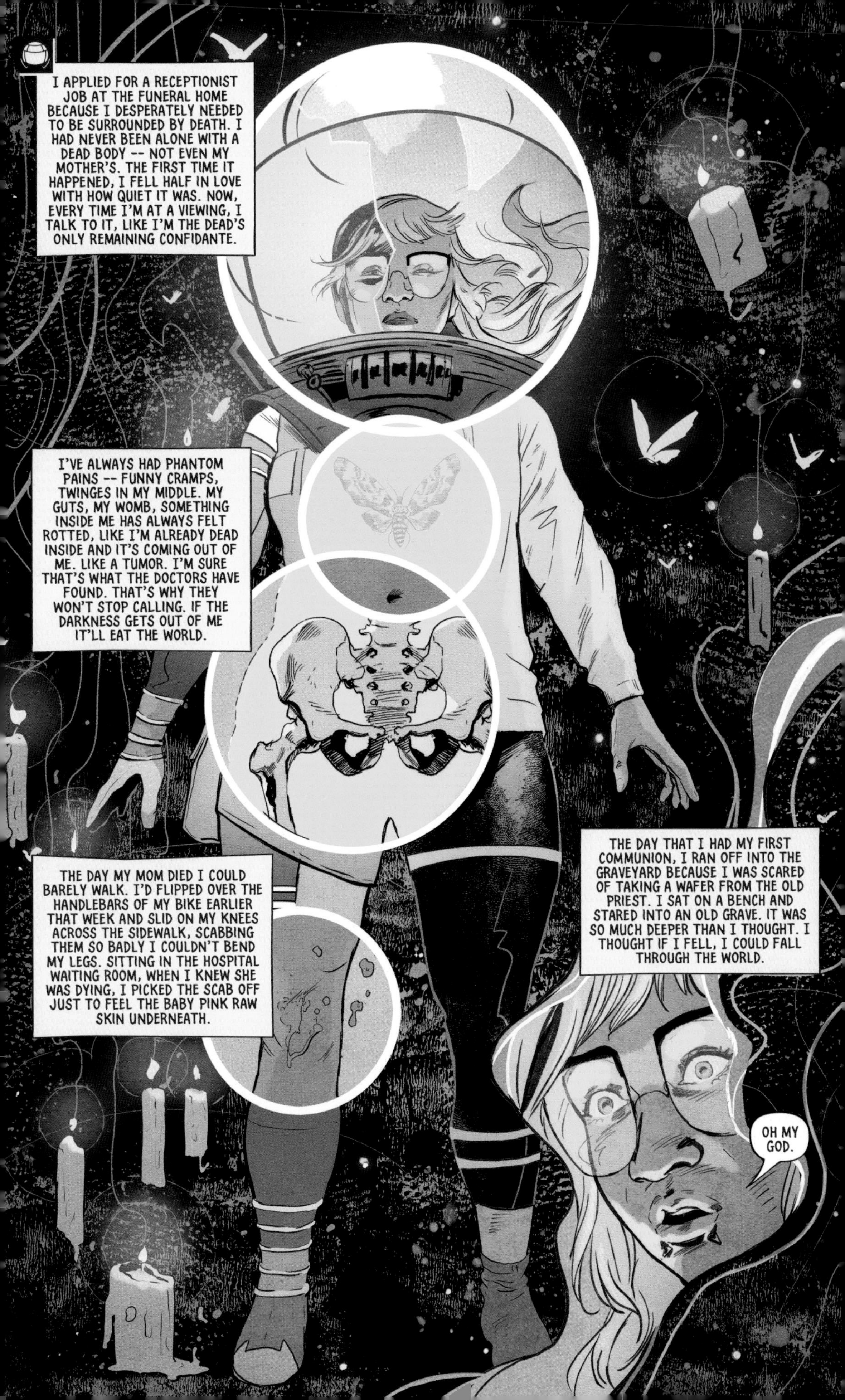
I APPLIED FOR A RECEPTIONIST JOB AT THE FUNERAL HOME BECAUSE I DESPERATELY NEEDED TO BE SURROUNDED BY DEATH. I HAD NEVER BEEN ALONE WITH A DEAD BODY -- NOT EVEN MY MOTHER'S. THE FIRST TIME IT HAPPENED, I FELL HALF IN LOVE WITH HOW QUIET IT WAS. NOW, EVERY TIME I'M AT A VIEWING, I TALK TO IT, LIKE I'M THE DEAD'S ONLY REMAINING CONFIDANTE.
I'VE ALWAYS HAD PHANTOM PAINS -- FUNNY CRAMPS, TWINGES IN MY MIDDLE. MY GUTS, MY WOMB, SOMETHING INSIDE ME HAS ALWAYS FELT ROTTED, LIKE I'M ALREADY DEAD INSIDE AND IT'S COMING OUT OF ME. LIKE A TUMOR. I'M SURE THAT'S WHAT THE DOCTORS HAVE FOUND. THAT'S WHY THEY WON'T STOP CALLING. IF THE DARKNESS GETS OUT OF ME IT'LL EAT THE WORLD.
THE DAY MY MOM DIED I COULD BARELY WALK. I'D FLIPPED OVER THE HANDLEBARS OF MY BIKE EARLIER THAT WEEK AND SLID ON MY KNEES ACROSS THE SIDEWALK, SCABBING THEM SO BADLY I COULDN'T BEND MY LEGS. SITTING IN THE HOSPITAL WAITING ROOM, WHEN I KNEW SHE WAS DYING, I PICKED THE SCAB OFF JUST TO FEEL THE BABY PINK RAW SKIN UNDERNEATH.
THE DAY THAT I HAD MY FIRST COMMUNION, I RAN OFF INTO THE GRAVEYARD BECAUSE I WAS SCARED OF TAKING A WAFER FROM THE OLD PRIEST. I SAT ON A BENCH AND STARED INTO AN OLD GRAVE. IT WAS SO MUCH DEEPER THAN I THOUGHT. I THOUGHT IF I FELL, I COULD FALL THROUGH THE WORLD.
OH MY GOD.

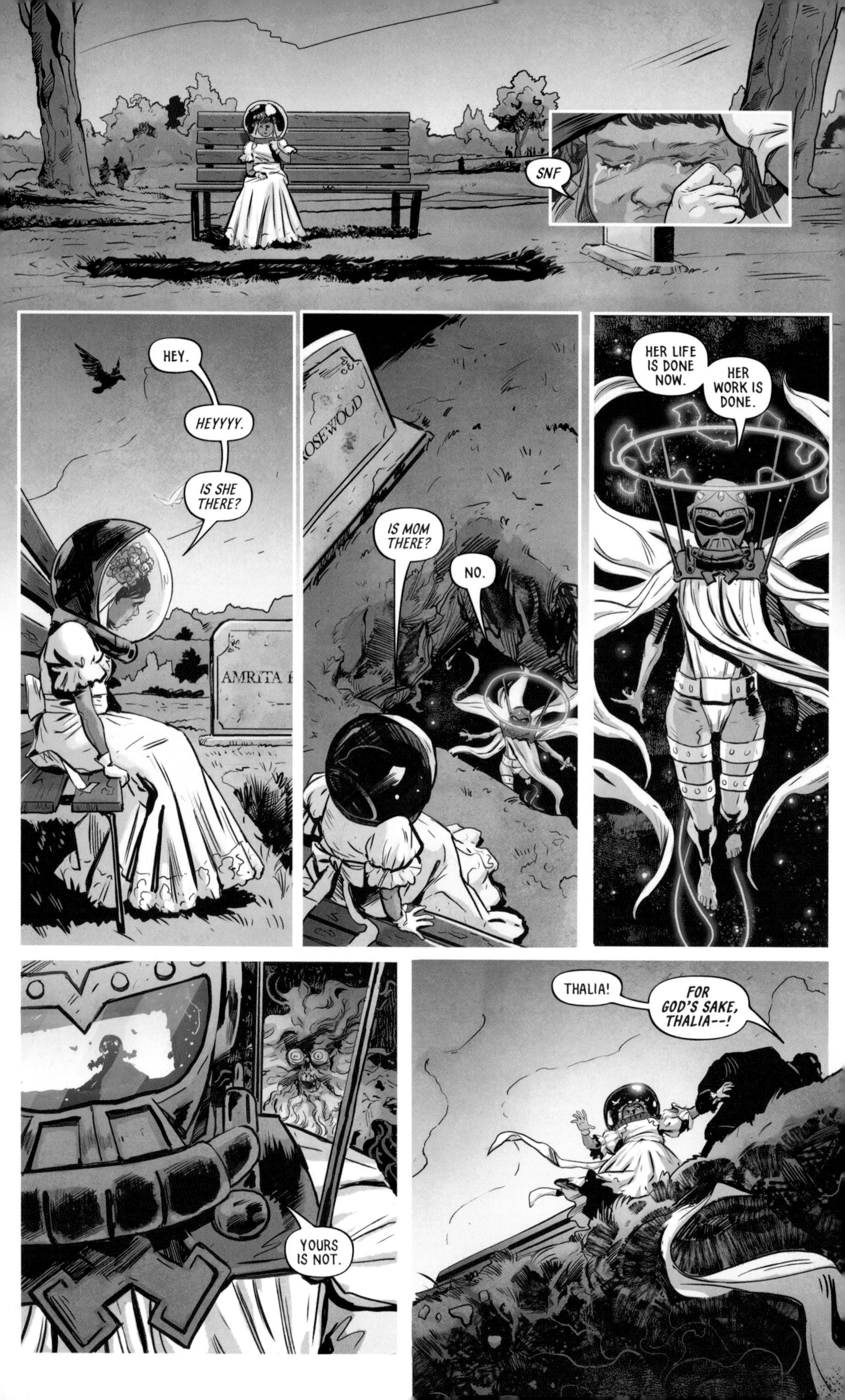
SNF
HEY.
HEYYYY.
IS SHE THERE?
AMRITA
ROSEWOOD
IS MOM THERE?
NO.
HER LIFE IS DONE NOW.
HER WORK IS DONE.
YOURS IS NOT.
THALIA!
FOR GOD'S SAKE, THALIA--!

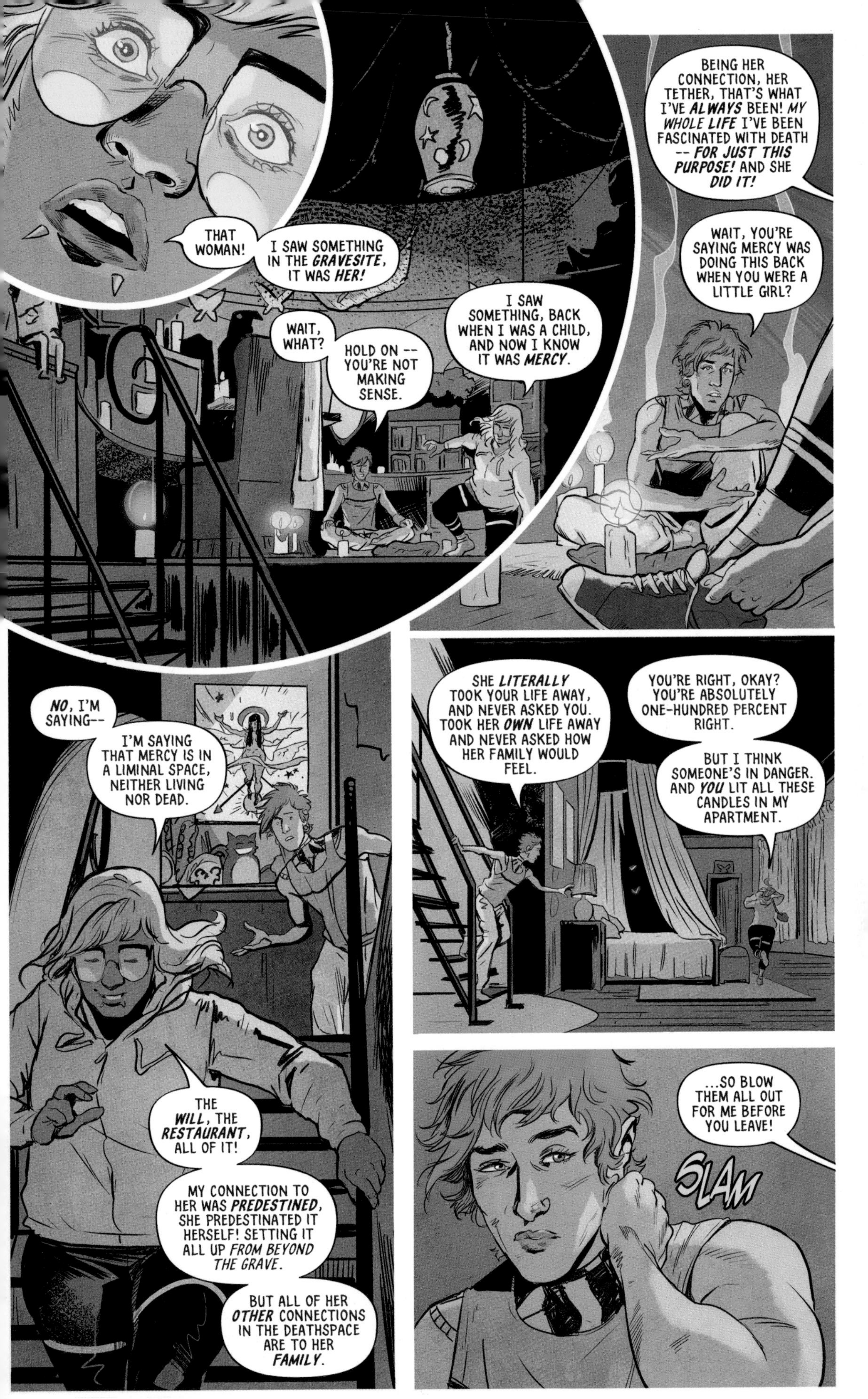

THAT WOMAN!
I SAW SOMETHING IN THE GRAVESITE, IT WAS HER!
WAIT, WHAT?
HOLD ON -- YOU'RE NOT MAKING SENSE.
I SAW SOMETHING, BACK WHEN I WAS A CHILD, AND NOW I KNOW IT WAS MERCY.
BEING HER CONNECTION, HER TETHER, THAT'S WHAT I'VE ALWAYS BEEN! MY WHOLE LIFE I'VE BEEN FASCINATED WITH DEATH -- FOR JUST THIS PURPOSE! AND SHE DID IT!
WAIT, YOU'RE SAYING MERCY WAS DOING THIS BACK WHEN YOU WERE A LITTLE GIRL?
NO, I'M SAYING--
I'M SAYING THAT MERCY IS IN A LIMINAL SPACE, NEITHER LIVING NOR DEAD.
THE WILL, THE RESTAURANT, ALL OF IT!
MY CONNECTION TO HER WAS PREDESTINED, SHE PREDESTINATED IT HERSELF! SETTING IT ALL UP FROM BEYOND THE GRAVE.
BUT ALL OF HER OTHER CONNECTIONS IN THE DEATHSPACE ARE TO HER FAMILY.
SHE LITERALLY TOOK YOUR LIFE AWAY, AND NEVER ASKED YOU. TOOK HER OWN LIFE AWAY AND NEVER ASKED HOW HER FAMILY WOULD FEEL.
YOU'RE RIGHT, OKAY? YOU'RE ABSOLUTELY ONE-HUNDRED PERCENT RIGHT.
BUT I THINK SOMEONE'S IN DANGER. AND YOU LIT ALL THESE CANDLES IN MY APARTMENT.
...SO BLOW THEM ALL OUT FOR ME BEFORE YOU LEAVE!
SLAM

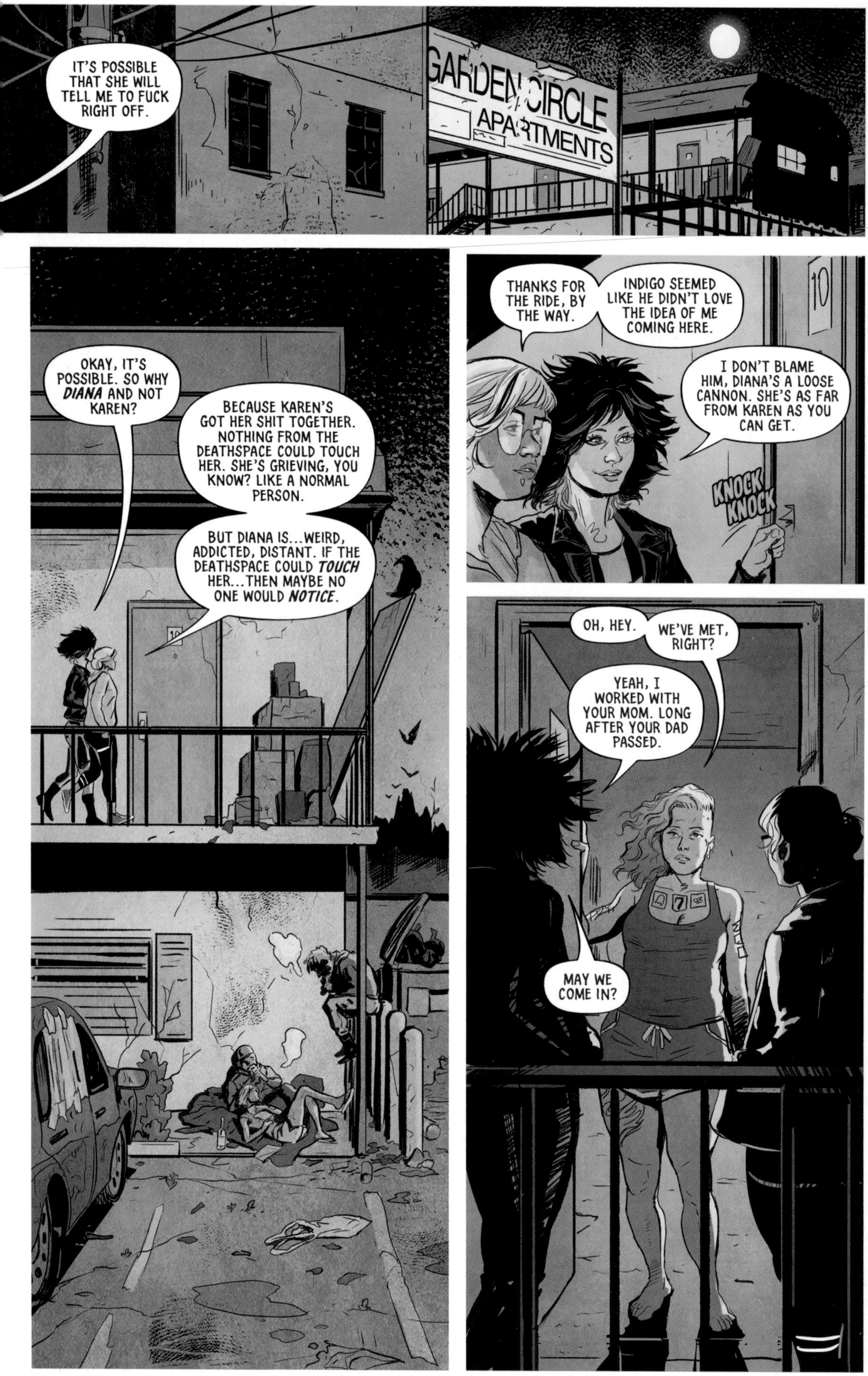
IT'S POSSIBLE THAT SHE WILL TELL ME TO FUCK RIGHT OFF.
GARDEN CIRCLE APARTMENTS
OKAY, IT'S POSSIBLE. SO WHY *DIANA* AND NOT KAREN?
BECAUSE KAREN'S GOT HER SHIT TOGETHER. NOTHING FROM THE DEATHSPACE COULD TOUCH HER. SHE'S GRIEVING, YOU KNOW? LIKE A NORMAL PERSON.
BUT DIANA IS...WEIRD, ADDICTED, DISTANT. IF THE DEATHSPACE COULD *TOUCH* HER...THEN MAYBE NO ONE WOULD *NOTICE*.
THANKS FOR THE RIDE, BY THE WAY.
INDIGO SEEMED LIKE HE DIDN'T LOVE THE IDEA OF ME COMING HERE.
I DON'T BLAME HIM, DIANA'S A LOOSE CANNON. SHE'S AS FAR FROM KAREN AS YOU CAN GET.
10
KNOCK KNOCK
OH, HEY.
WE'VE MET, RIGHT?
YEAH, I WORKED WITH YOUR MOM. LONG AFTER YOUR DAD PASSED.
MAY WE COME IN?

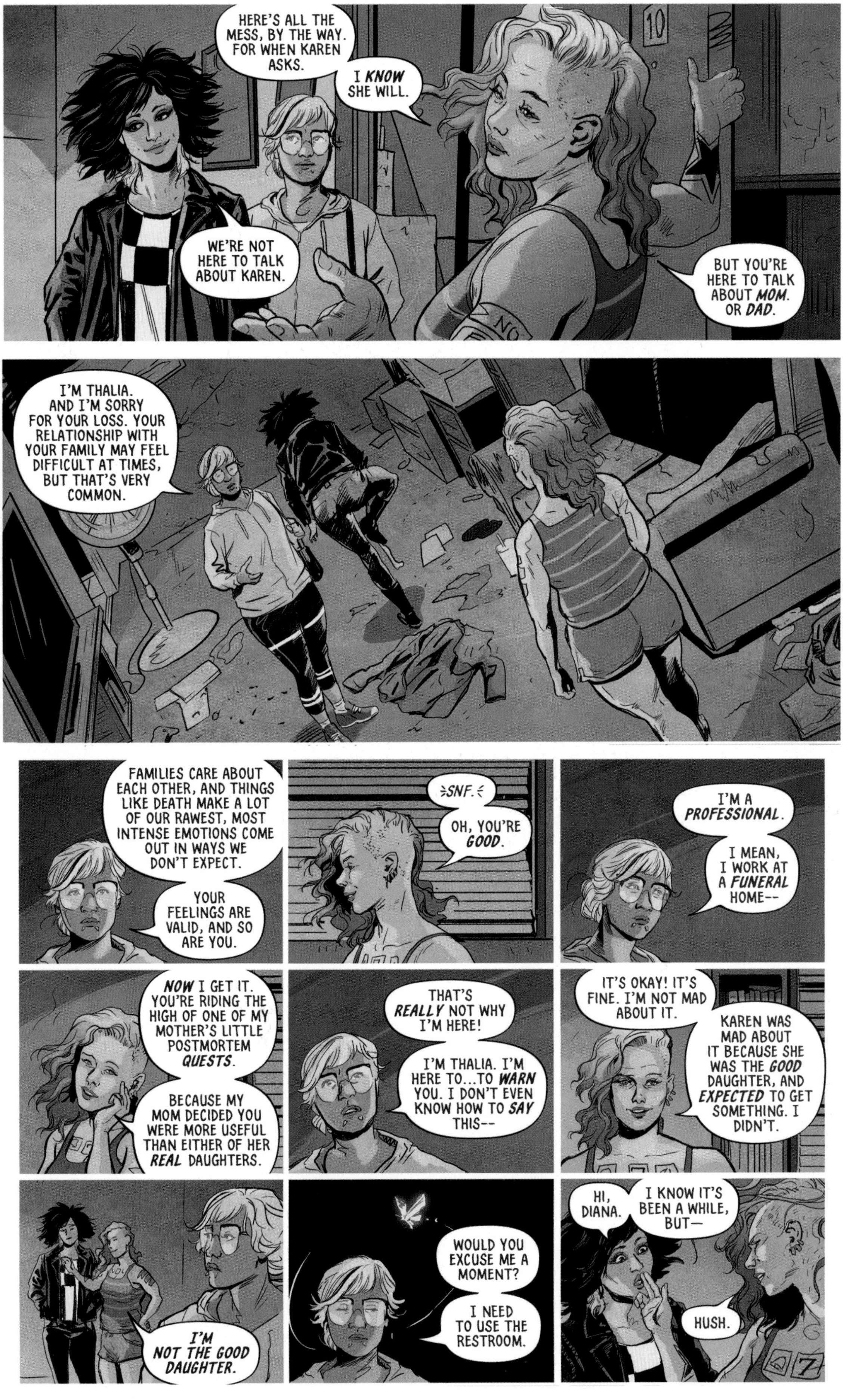

HERE'S ALL THE MESS, BY THE WAY. FOR WHEN KAREN ASKS.
I KNOW SHE WILL.
WE'RE NOT HERE TO TALK ABOUT KAREN.
BUT YOU'RE HERE TO TALK ABOUT MOM. OR DAD.
I'M THALIA. AND I'M SORRY FOR YOUR LOSS. YOUR RELATIONSHIP WITH YOUR FAMILY MAY FEEL DIFFICULT AT TIMES, BUT THAT'S VERY COMMON.
FAMILIES CARE ABOUT EACH OTHER, AND THINGS LIKE DEATH MAKE A LOT OF OUR RAWEST, MOST INTENSE EMOTIONS COME OUT IN WAYS WE DON'T EXPECT.
YOUR FEELINGS ARE VALID, AND SO ARE YOU.
SNF.
OH, YOU'RE GOOD.
I'M A PROFESSIONAL.
I MEAN, I WORK AT A FUNERAL HOME--
NOW I GET IT. YOU'RE RIDING THE HIGH OF ONE OF MY MOTHER'S LITTLE POSTMORTEM QUESTS.
BECAUSE MY MOM DECIDED YOU WERE MORE USEFUL THAN EITHER OF HER REAL DAUGHTERS.
THAT'S REALLY NOT WHY I'M HERE!
I'M THALIA. I'M HERE TO...TO WARN YOU. I DON'T EVEN KNOW HOW TO SAY THIS--
IT'S OKAY! IT'S FINE. I'M NOT MAD ABOUT IT.
KAREN WAS MAD ABOUT IT BECAUSE SHE WAS THE GOOD DAUGHTER, AND EXPECTED TO GET SOMETHING. I DIDN'T.
I'M NOT THE GOOD DAUGHTER.
WOULD YOU EXCUSE ME A MOMENT?
I NEED TO USE THE RESTROOM.
HI, DIANA.
I KNOW IT'S BEEN A WHILE, BUT—
HUSH.

JUST *IN CASE.*

JUST IN CASE I REALLY HAVE TO GO IN THERE AFTER MERCY.

JUST IN CASE I REALLY *AM* DYING.

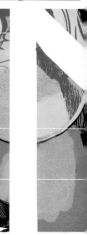

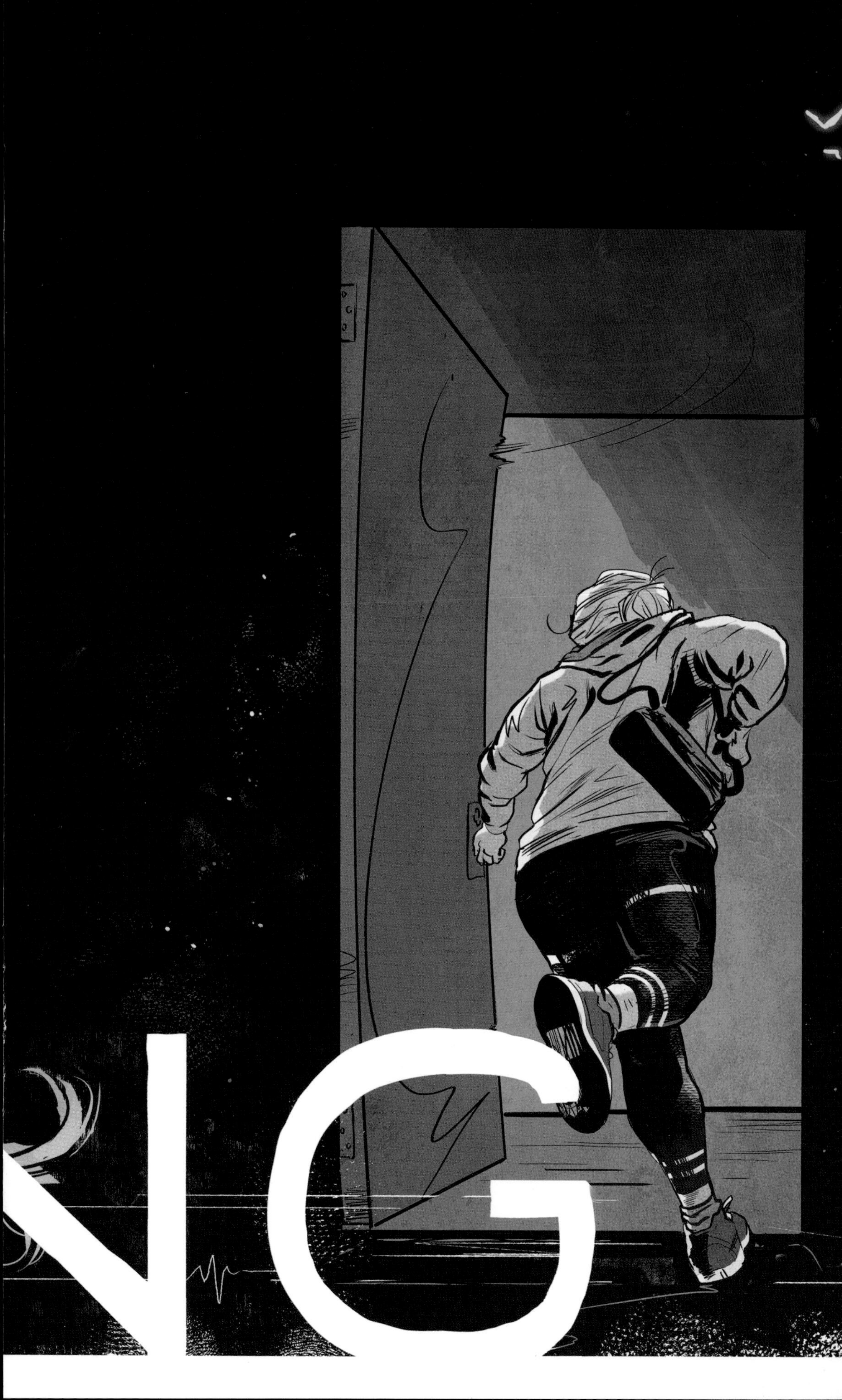
NG

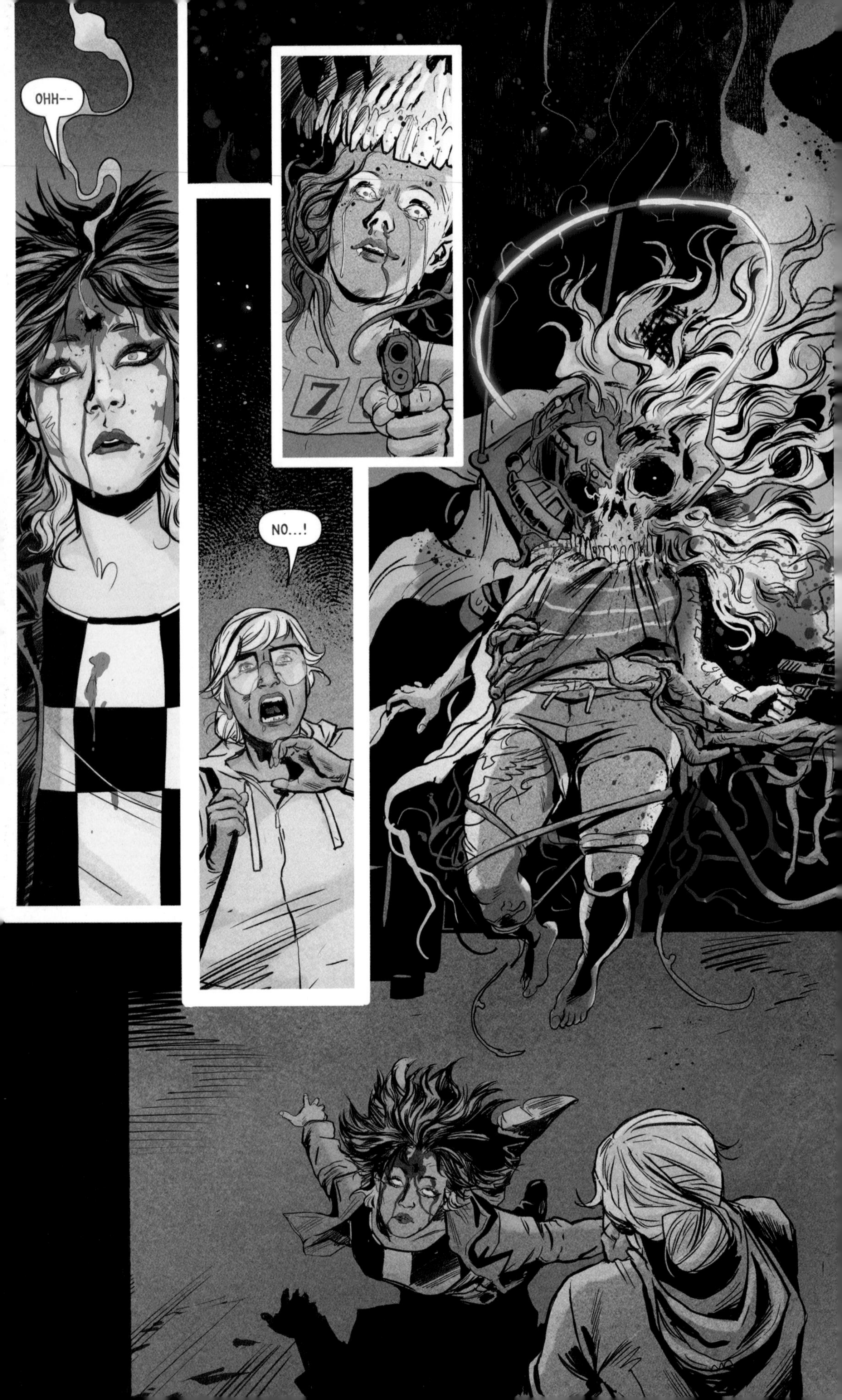
OHH--
NO...!

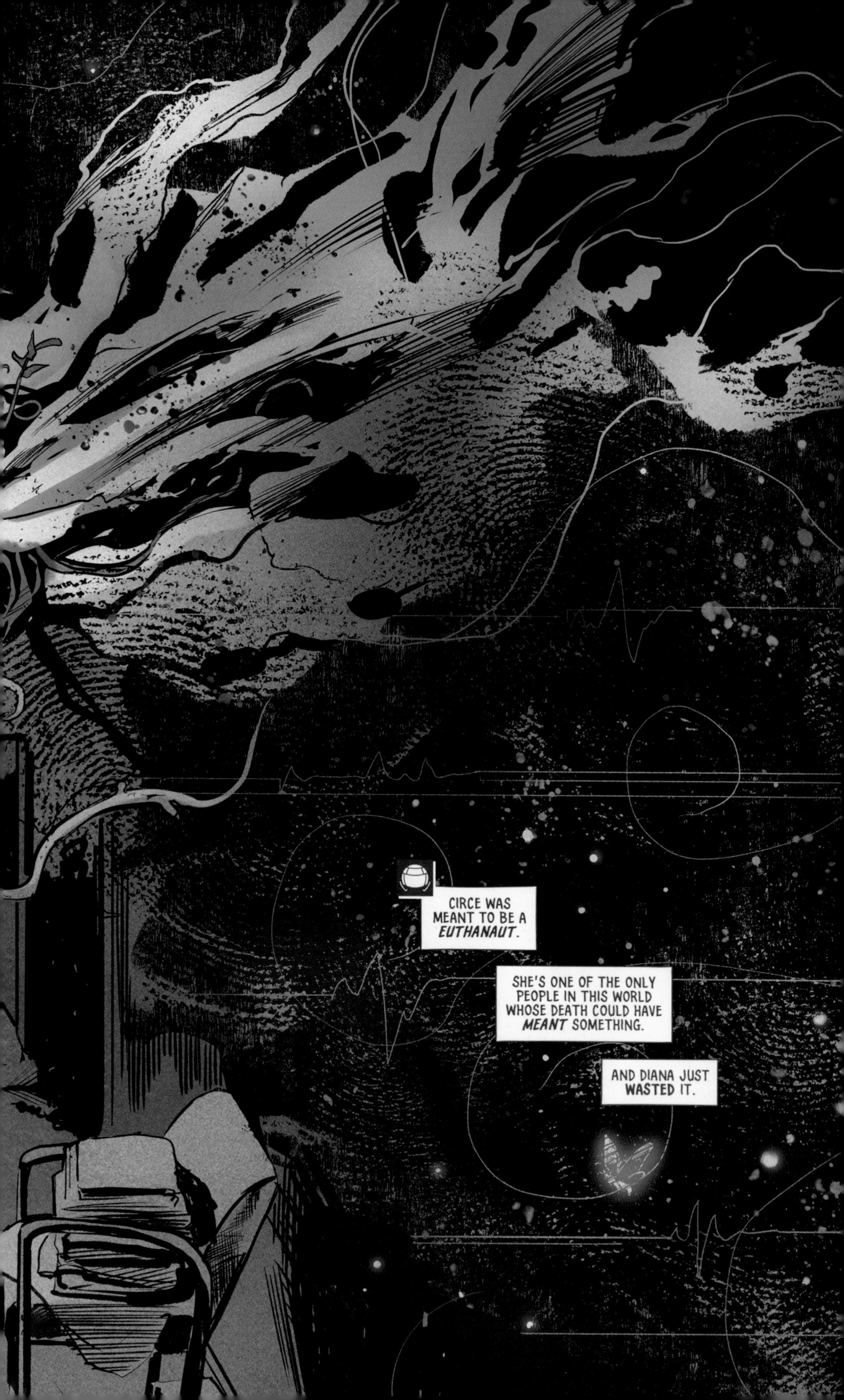
CIRCE WAS MEANT TO BE A *EUTHANAUT*.
SHE'S ONE OF THE ONLY PEOPLE IN THIS WORLD WHOSE DEATH COULD HAVE *MEANT* SOMETHING.
AND DIANA JUST **WASTED** IT.

"IF THIS GOES BADLY, THIS MIGHT BE MY FINAL TRANSMISSION."

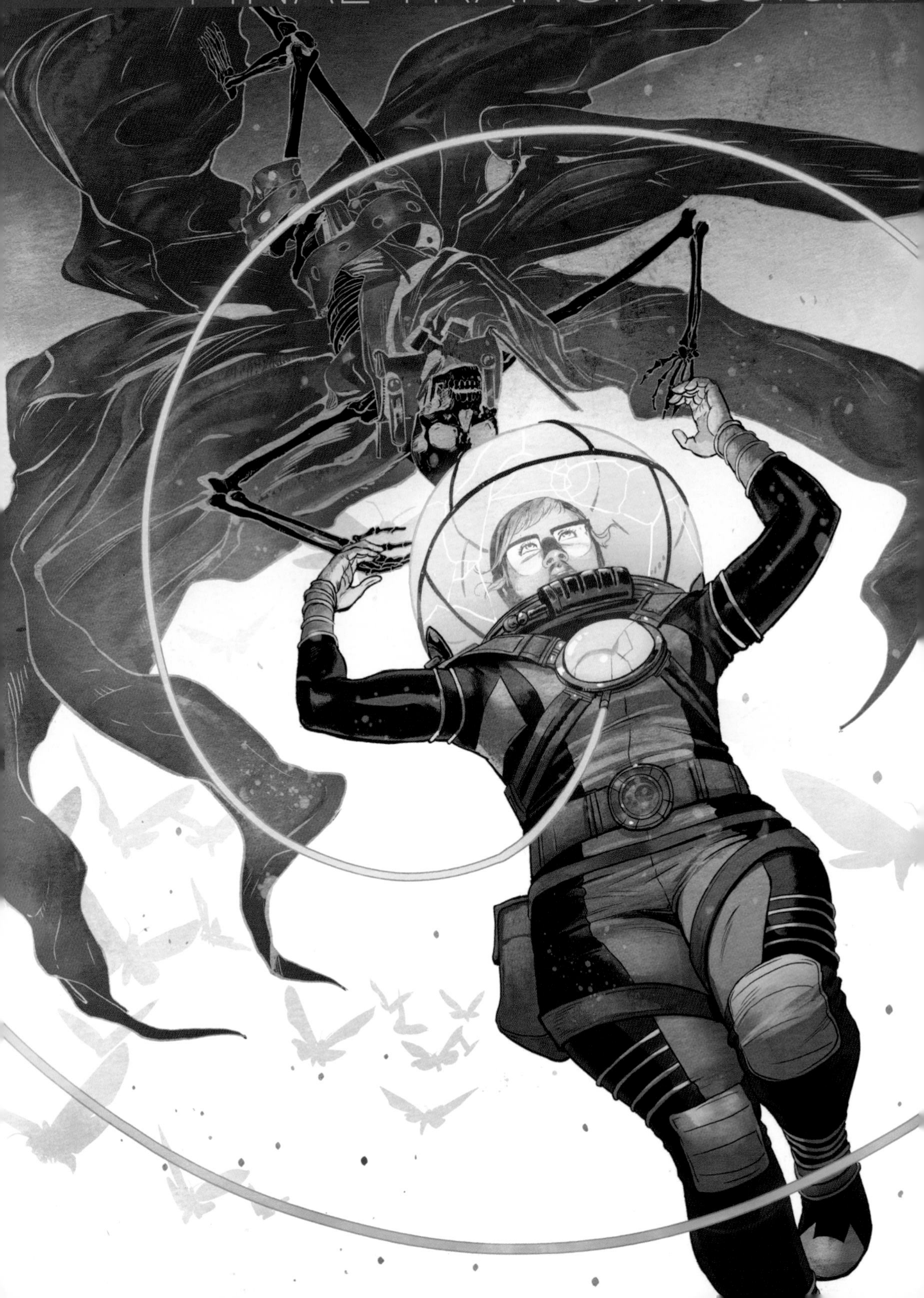

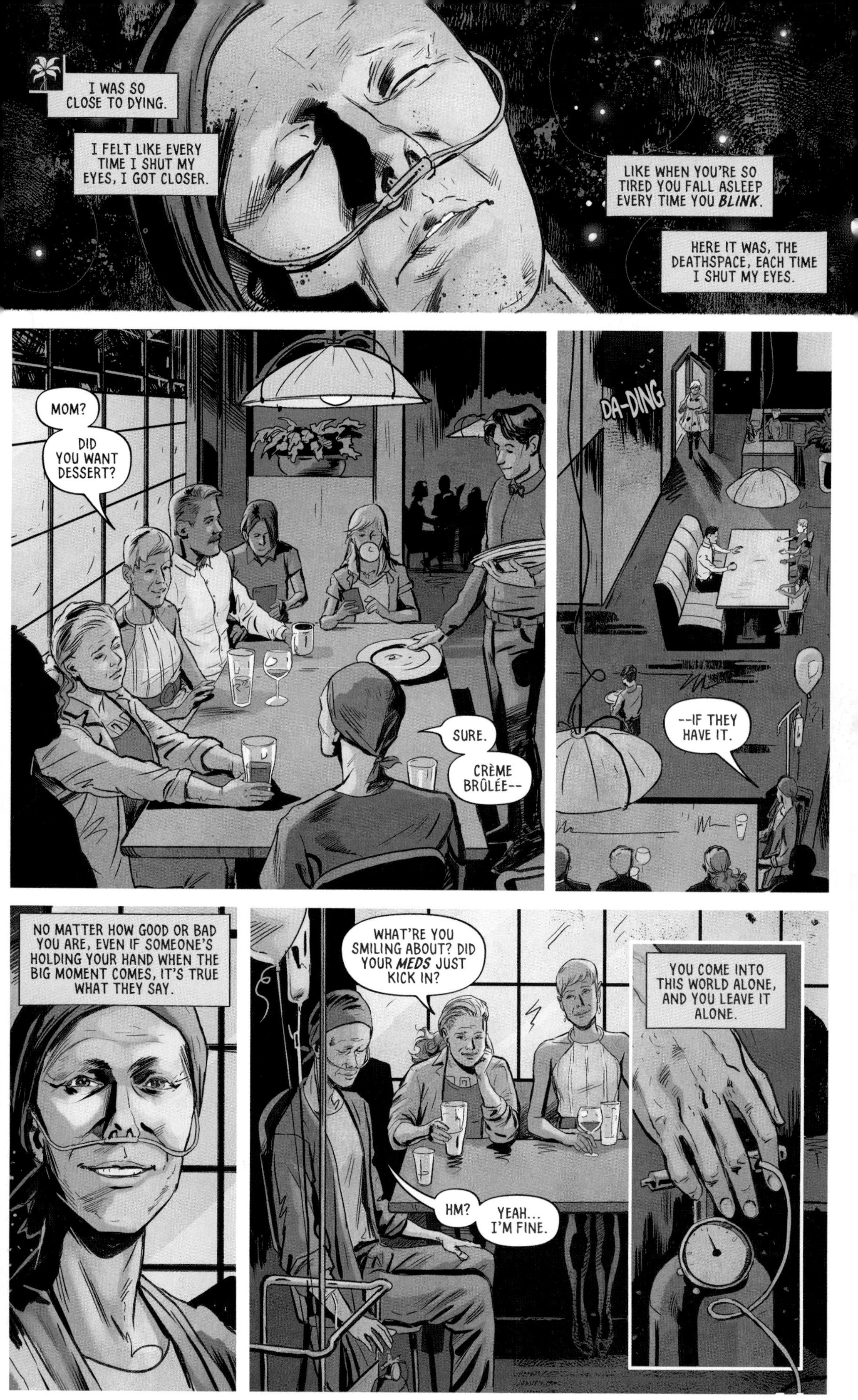
I WAS SO CLOSE TO DYING.
I FELT LIKE EVERY TIME I SHUT MY EYES, I GOT CLOSER.
LIKE WHEN YOU'RE SO TIRED YOU FALL ASLEEP EVERY TIME YOU *BLINK*.
HERE IT WAS, THE DEATHSPACE, EACH TIME I SHUT MY EYES.
MOM?
DID YOU WANT DESSERT?
SURE.
CRÈME BRÛLÉE--
DA-DING
--IF THEY HAVE IT.
NO MATTER HOW GOOD OR BAD YOU ARE, EVEN IF SOMEONE'S HOLDING YOUR HAND WHEN THE BIG MOMENT COMES, IT'S TRUE WHAT THEY SAY.
WHAT'RE YOU SMILING ABOUT? DID YOUR *MEDS* JUST KICK IN?
HM?
YEAH... I'M FINE.
YOU COME INTO THIS WORLD ALONE, AND YOU LEAVE IT ALONE.

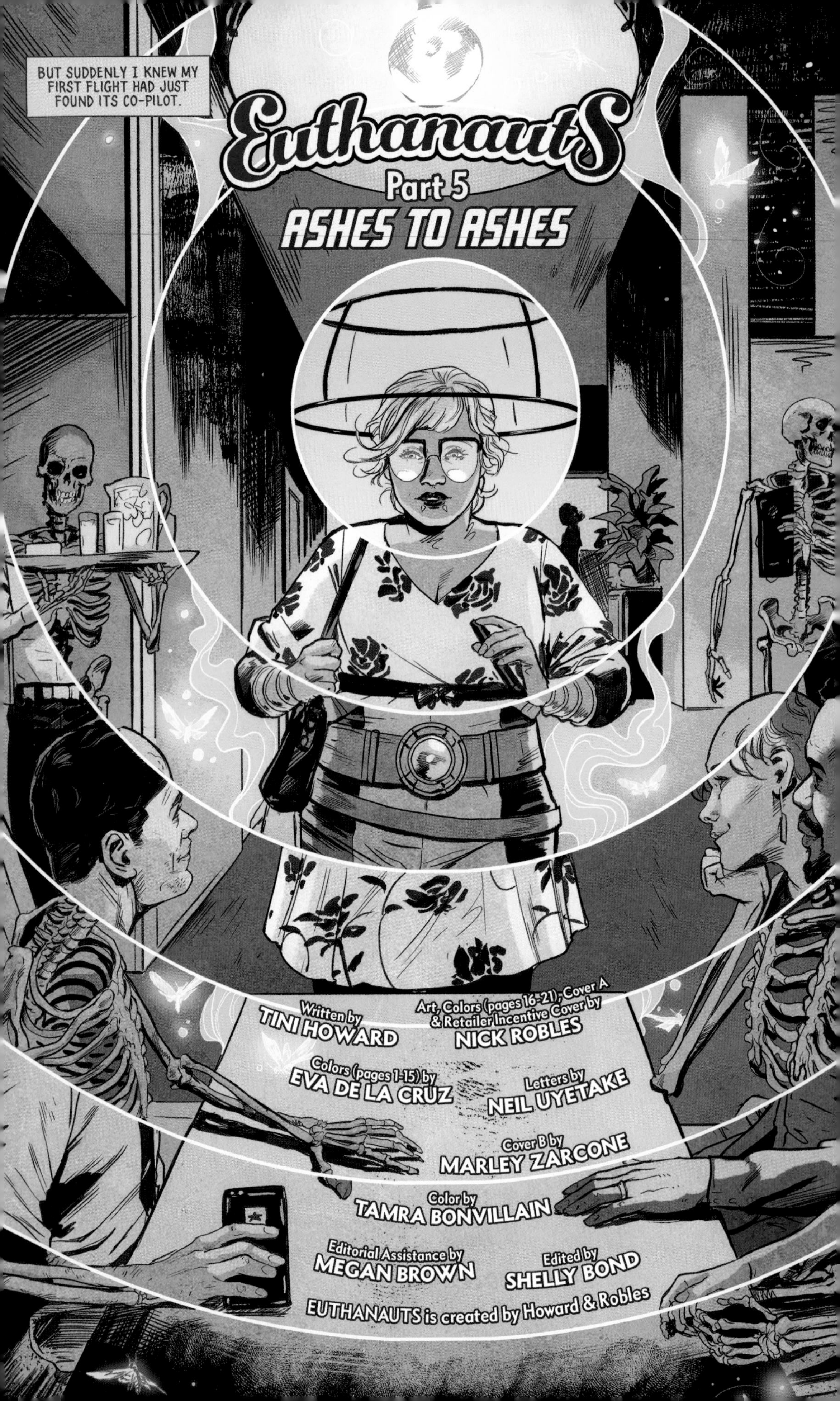
BUT SUDDENLY I KNEW MY FIRST FLIGHT HAD JUST FOUND ITS CO-PILOT.
EuthanautS
Part 5
ASHES TO ASHES
Written by TINI HOWARD
Art, Colors (pages 16-21), Cover A & Retailer Incentive Cover by NICK ROBLES
Colors (pages 1-15) by EVA DE LA CRUZ
Letters by NEIL UYETAKE
Cover B by MARLEY ZARCONE
Color by TAMRA BONVILLAIN
Editorial Assistance by MEGAN BROWN
Edited by SHELLY BOND
EUTHANAUTS is created by Howard & Robles

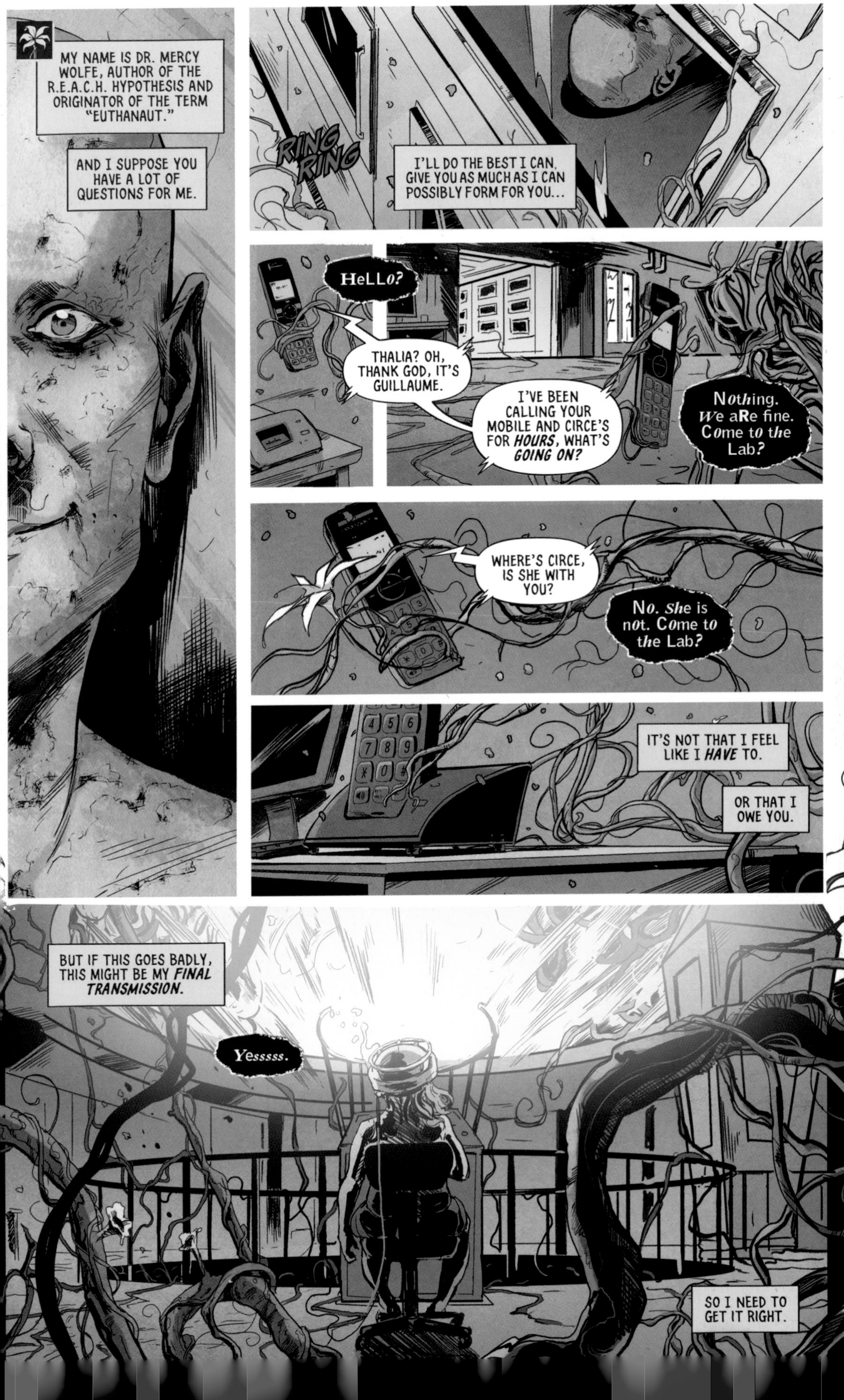
MY NAME IS DR. MERCY WOLFE, AUTHOR OF THE R.E.A.C.H. HYPOTHESIS AND ORIGINATOR OF THE TERM "EUTHANAUT."
AND I SUPPOSE YOU HAVE A LOT OF QUESTIONS FOR ME.
RING RING
I'LL DO THE BEST I CAN, GIVE YOU AS MUCH AS I CAN POSSIBLY FORM FOR YOU...
HeLLo?
THALIA? OH, THANK GOD, IT'S GUILLAUME.
I'VE BEEN CALLING YOUR MOBILE AND CIRCE'S FOR HOURS, WHAT'S GOING ON?
Nothing. We aRe fine. Come to the Lab?
WHERE'S CIRCE, IS SHE WITH YOU?
No. She is not. Come to the Lab?
IT'S NOT THAT I FEEL LIKE I HAVE TO.
OR THAT I OWE YOU.
BUT IF THIS GOES BADLY, THIS MIGHT BE MY FINAL TRANSMISSION.
Yesssss.
SO I NEED TO GET IT RIGHT.

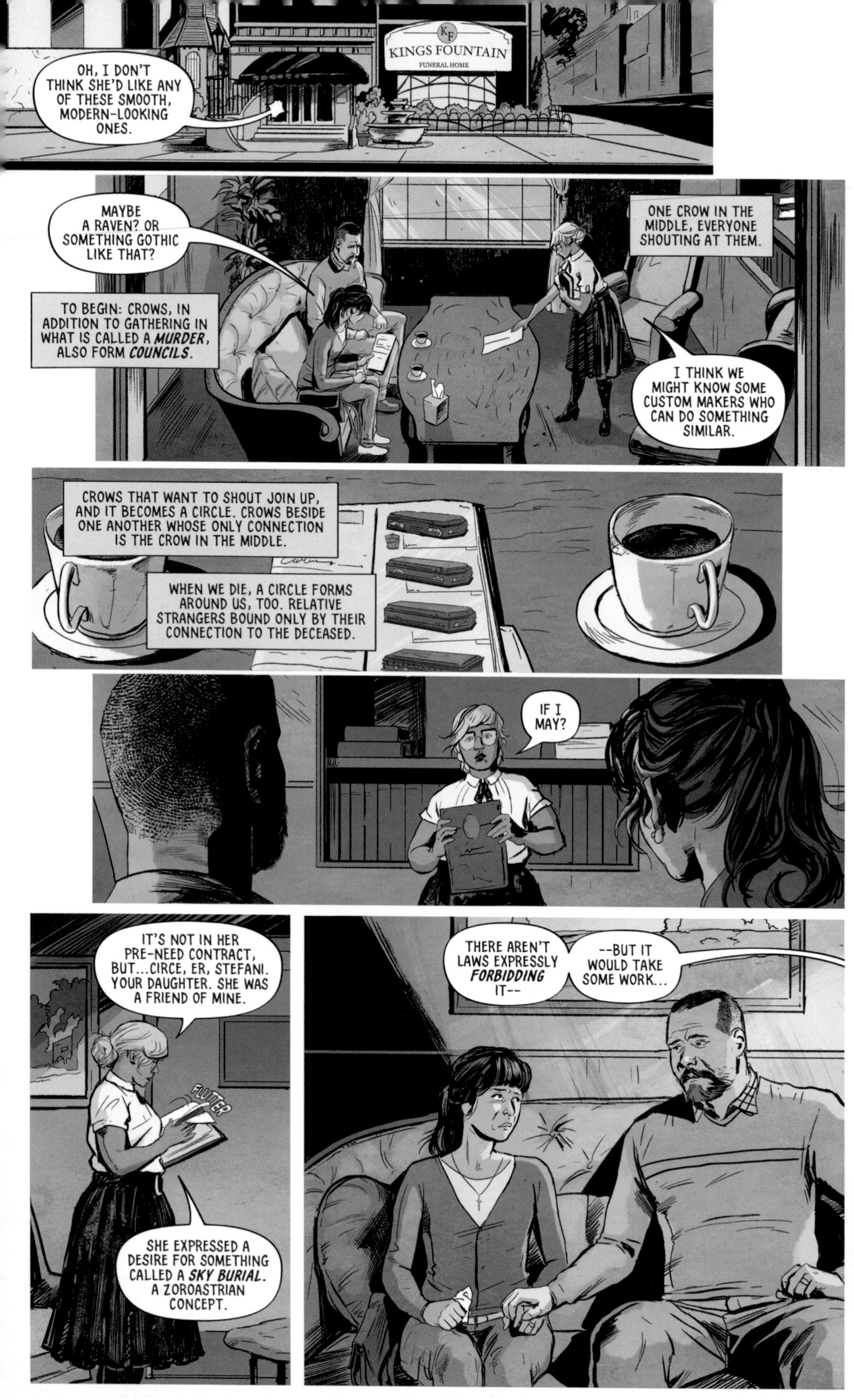
KF
KINGS FOUNTAIN
FUNERAL HOME
OH, I DON'T THINK SHE'D LIKE ANY OF THESE SMOOTH, MODERN-LOOKING ONES.
MAYBE A RAVEN? OR SOMETHING GOTHIC LIKE THAT?
TO BEGIN: CROWS, IN ADDITION TO GATHERING IN WHAT IS CALLED A *MURDER*, ALSO FORM *COUNCILS*.
ONE CROW IN THE MIDDLE, EVERYONE SHOUTING AT THEM.
I THINK WE MIGHT KNOW SOME CUSTOM MAKERS WHO CAN DO SOMETHING SIMILAR.
CROWS THAT WANT TO SHOUT JOIN UP, AND IT BECOMES A CIRCLE. CROWS BESIDE ONE ANOTHER WHOSE ONLY CONNECTION IS THE CROW IN THE MIDDLE.
WHEN WE DIE, A CIRCLE FORMS AROUND US, TOO. RELATIVE STRANGERS BOUND ONLY BY THEIR CONNECTION TO THE DECEASED.
IF I MAY?
IT'S NOT IN HER PRE-NEED CONTRACT, BUT...CIRCE, ER, STEFANI. YOUR DAUGHTER. SHE WAS A FRIEND OF MINE.
FLUTTER
SHE EXPRESSED A DESIRE FOR SOMETHING CALLED A *SKY BURIAL*. A ZOROASTRIAN CONCEPT.
THERE AREN'T LAWS EXPRESSLY *FORBIDDING* IT--
--BUT IT WOULD TAKE SOME WORK...

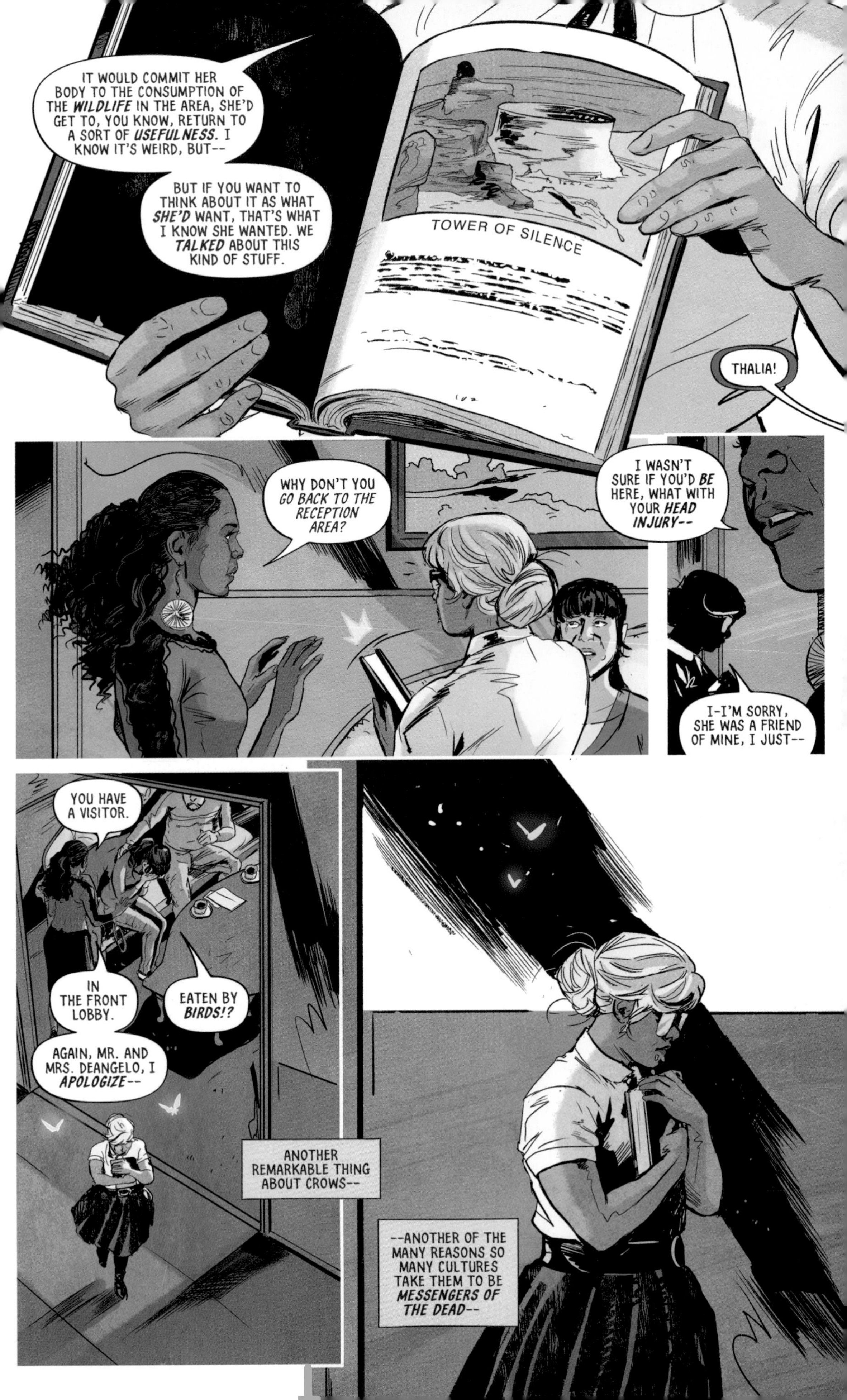
IT WOULD COMMIT HER BODY TO THE CONSUMPTION OF THE WILDLIFE IN THE AREA, SHE'D GET TO, YOU KNOW, RETURN TO A SORT OF USEFULNESS. I KNOW IT'S WEIRD, BUT--
BUT IF YOU WANT TO THINK ABOUT IT AS WHAT SHE'D WANT, THAT'S WHAT I KNOW SHE WANTED. WE TALKED ABOUT THIS KIND OF STUFF.
TOWER OF SILENCE
THALIA!
WHY DON'T YOU GO BACK TO THE RECEPTION AREA?
I WASN'T SURE IF YOU'D BE HERE, WHAT WITH YOUR HEAD INJURY--
I-I'M SORRY, SHE WAS A FRIEND OF MINE, I JUST--
YOU HAVE A VISITOR.
IN THE FRONT LOBBY.
EATEN BY BIRDS!?
AGAIN, MR. AND MRS. DEANGELO, I APOLOGIZE--
ANOTHER REMARKABLE THING ABOUT CROWS--
--ANOTHER OF THE MANY REASONS SO MANY CULTURES TAKE THEM TO BE MESSENGERS OF THE DEAD--

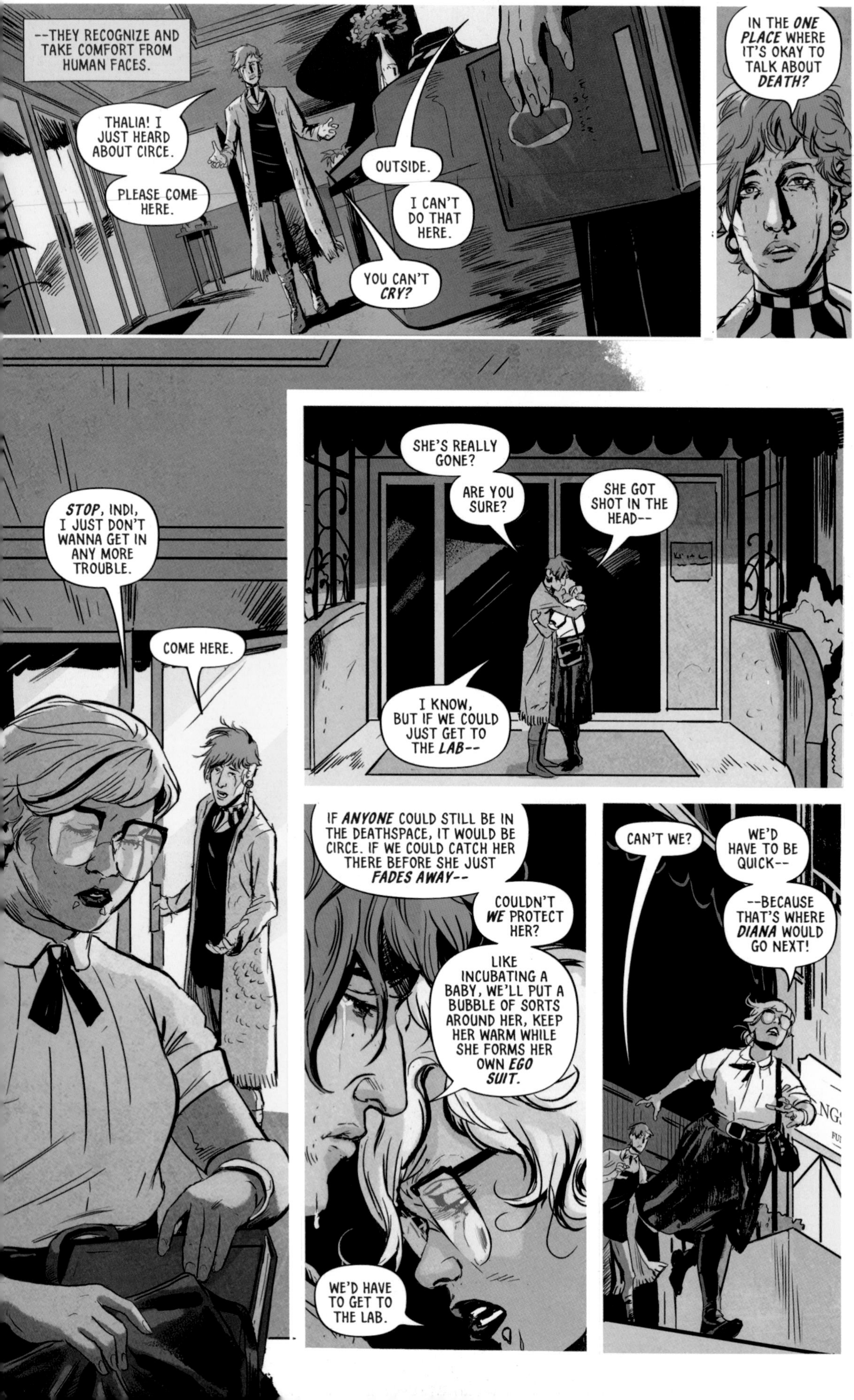
--THEY RECOGNIZE AND TAKE COMFORT FROM HUMAN FACES.
THALIA! I JUST HEARD ABOUT CIRCE.
PLEASE COME HERE.
OUTSIDE.
I CAN'T DO THAT HERE.
YOU CAN'T CRY?
IN THE ONE PLACE WHERE IT'S OKAY TO TALK ABOUT DEATH?
STOP, INDI, I JUST DON'T WANNA GET IN ANY MORE TROUBLE.
COME HERE.
SHE'S REALLY GONE?
ARE YOU SURE?
SHE GOT SHOT IN THE HEAD--
I KNOW, BUT IF WE COULD JUST GET TO THE LAB--
IF ANYONE COULD STILL BE IN THE DEATHSPACE, IT WOULD BE CIRCE. IF WE COULD CATCH HER THERE BEFORE SHE JUST FADES AWAY--
COULDN'T WE PROTECT HER?
LIKE INCUBATING A BABY, WE'LL PUT A BUBBLE OF SORTS AROUND HER, KEEP HER WARM WHILE SHE FORMS HER OWN EGO SUIT.
WE'D HAVE TO GET TO THE LAB.
CAN'T WE?
WE'D HAVE TO BE QUICK--
--BECAUSE THAT'S WHERE DIANA WOULD GO NEXT!

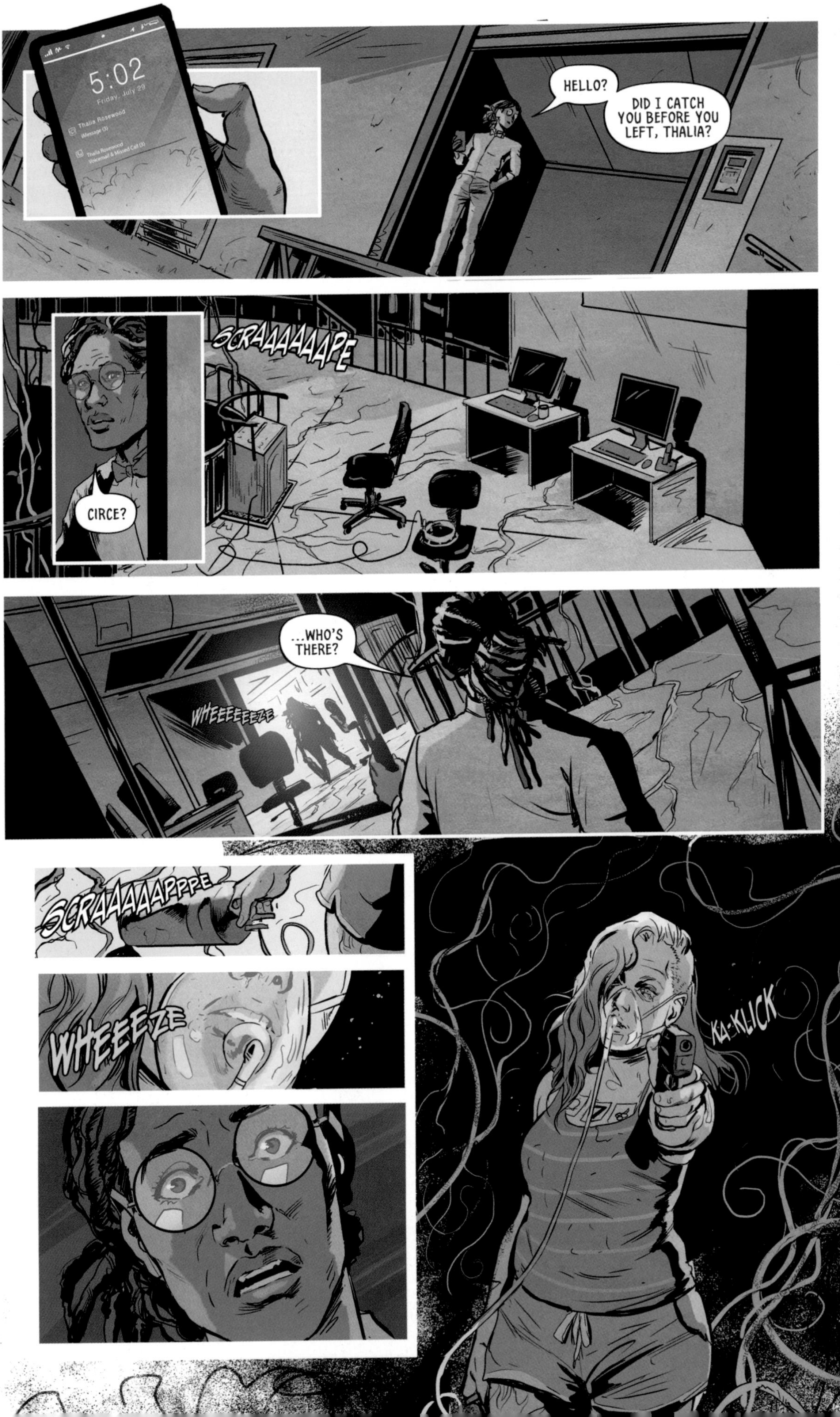
5:02
Friday, July 29
Thalia Rosewood
iMessage (3)
Thalia Rosewood
Voicemail & Missed Call (3)
HELLO?
DID I CATCH YOU BEFORE YOU LEFT, THALIA?
SCRAAAAAAPE
CIRCE?
...WHO'S THERE?
WHEEEEEEZE
SCRAAAAAPPPE
WHEEEZE
KA-KLICK

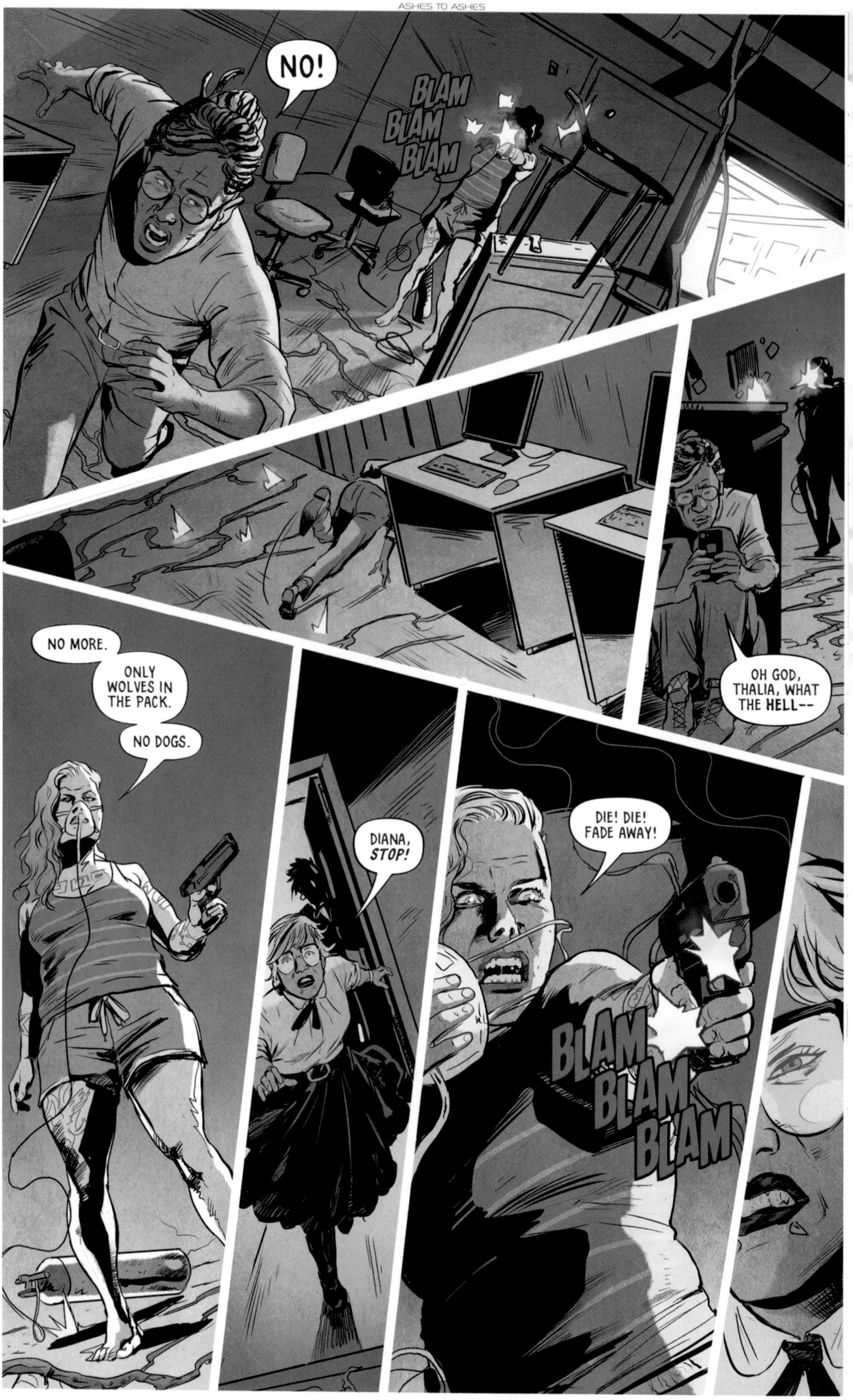
NO!
BLAM BLAM BLAM
OH GOD, THALIA, WHAT THE HELL--
NO MORE.
ONLY WOLVES IN THE PACK.
NO DOGS.
DIANA, STOP!
DIE! DIE! FADE AWAY!
BLAM BLAM BLAM

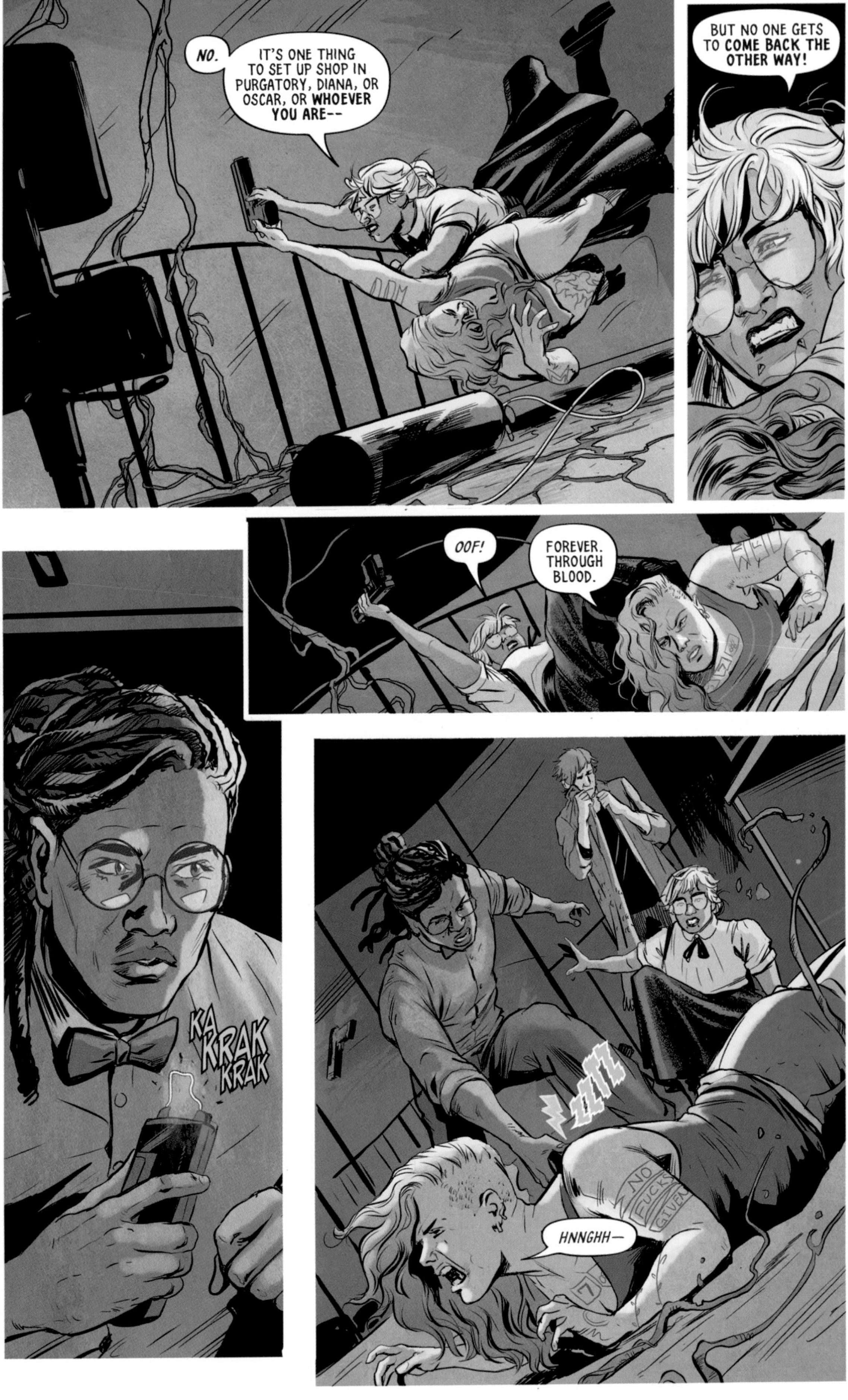
NO.
IT'S ONE THING TO SET UP SHOP IN PURGATORY, DIANA, OR OSCAR, OR **WHOEVER YOU ARE--**
BUT NO ONE GETS TO **COME BACK THE OTHER WAY!**
OOF!
FOREVER. THROUGH BLOOD.
KA KRAK KRAK
ZZZZ
HNNGHH—
NO FUCKS GIVEN

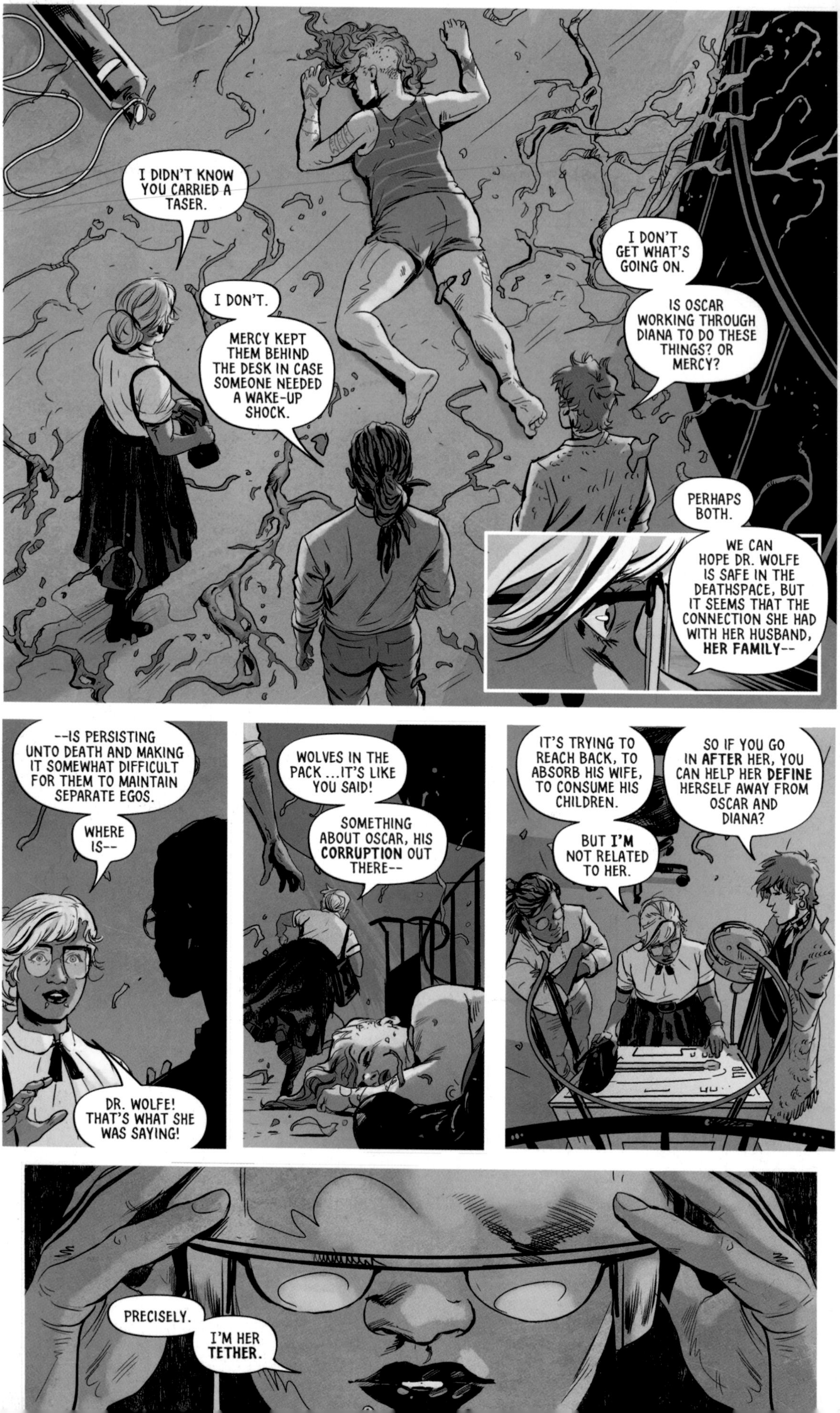
I DIDN'T KNOW YOU CARRIED A TASER.
I DON'T.
MERCY KEPT THEM BEHIND THE DESK IN CASE SOMEONE NEEDED A WAKE-UP SHOCK.
I DON'T GET WHAT'S GOING ON.
IS OSCAR WORKING THROUGH DIANA TO DO THESE THINGS? OR MERCY?
PERHAPS BOTH.
WE CAN HOPE DR. WOLFE IS SAFE IN THE DEATHSPACE, BUT IT SEEMS THAT THE CONNECTION SHE HAD WITH HER HUSBAND, **HER FAMILY**--
--IS PERSISTING UNTO DEATH AND MAKING IT SOMEWHAT DIFFICULT FOR THEM TO MAINTAIN SEPARATE EGOS.
WHERE IS--
DR. WOLFE! THAT'S WHAT SHE WAS SAYING!
WOLVES IN THE PACK ...IT'S LIKE YOU SAID!
SOMETHING ABOUT OSCAR, HIS **CORRUPTION** OUT THERE--
IT'S TRYING TO REACH BACK, TO ABSORB HIS WIFE, TO CONSUME HIS CHILDREN.
SO IF YOU GO IN **AFTER** HER, YOU CAN HELP HER **DEFINE** HERSELF AWAY FROM OSCAR AND DIANA?
BUT **I'M** NOT RELATED TO HER.
PRECISELY.
I'M HER **TETHER**.

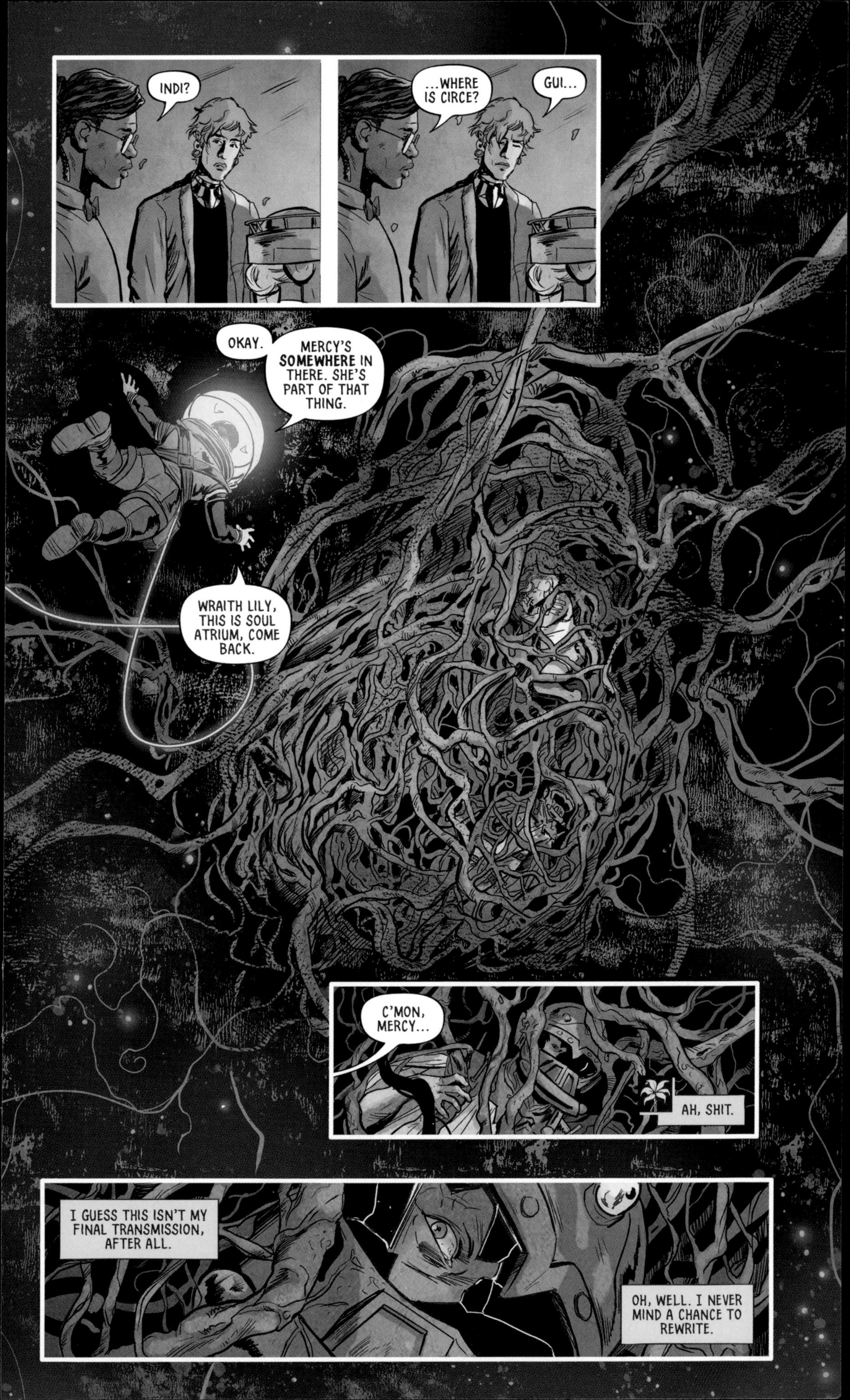
INDI?
...WHERE IS CIRCE?
GUI...
OKAY.
MERCY'S **SOMEWHERE** IN THERE. SHE'S PART OF THAT THING.
WRAITH LILY, THIS IS SOUL ATRIUM, COME BACK.
C'MON, MERCY...
AH, SHIT.
I GUESS THIS ISN'T MY FINAL TRANSMISSION, AFTER ALL.
OH, WELL. I NEVER MIND A CHANCE TO REWRITE.

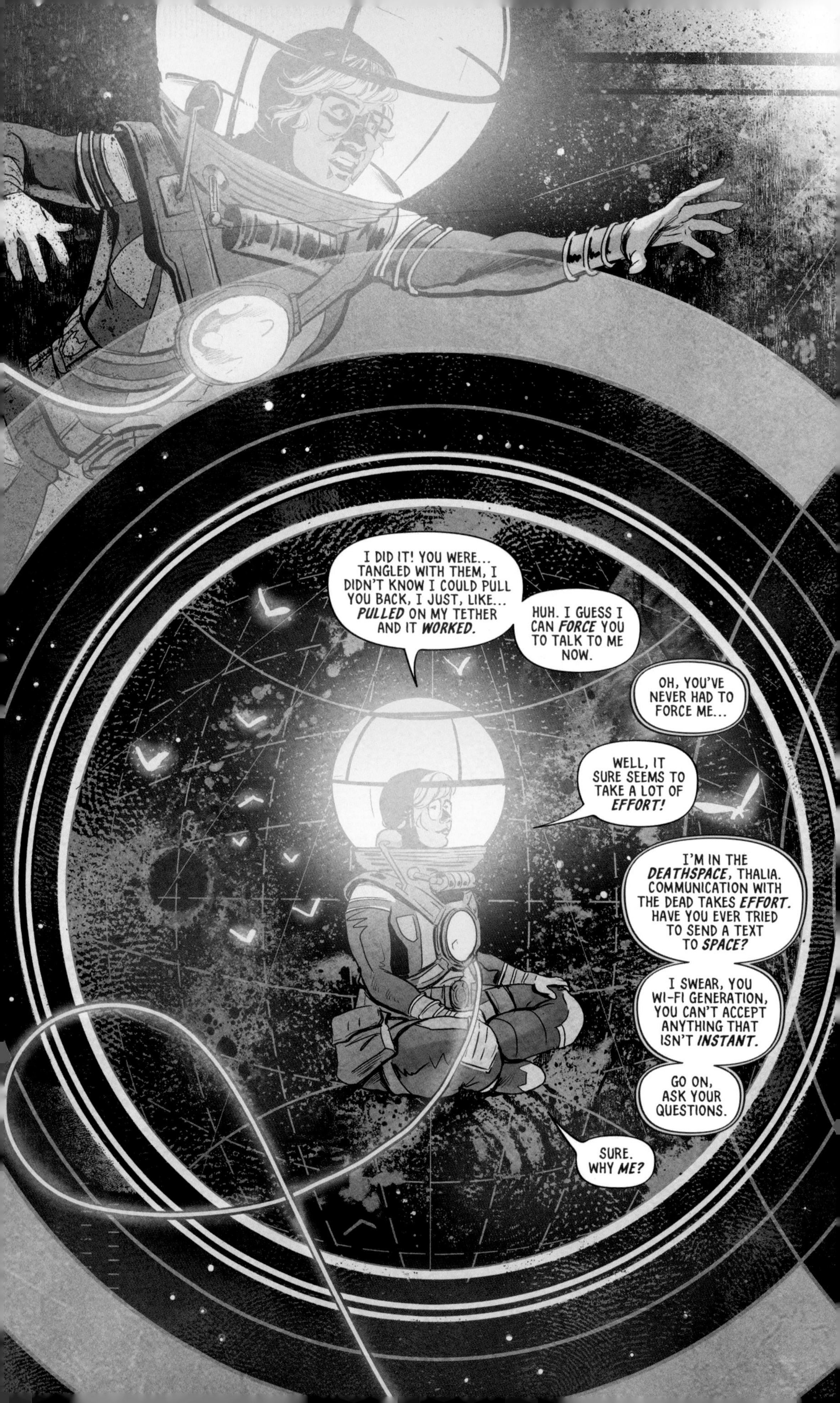
I DID IT! YOU WERE... TANGLED WITH THEM, I DIDN'T KNOW I COULD PULL YOU BACK, I JUST, LIKE... PULLED ON MY TETHER AND IT WORKED.
HUH. I GUESS I CAN FORCE YOU TO TALK TO ME NOW.
OH, YOU'VE NEVER HAD TO FORCE ME...
WELL, IT SURE SEEMS TO TAKE A LOT OF EFFORT!
I'M IN THE DEATHSPACE, THALIA. COMMUNICATION WITH THE DEAD TAKES EFFORT. HAVE YOU EVER TRIED TO SEND A TEXT TO SPACE?
I SWEAR, YOU WI-FI GENERATION, YOU CAN'T ACCEPT ANYTHING THAT ISN'T INSTANT.
GO ON, ASK YOUR QUESTIONS.
SURE. WHY ME?

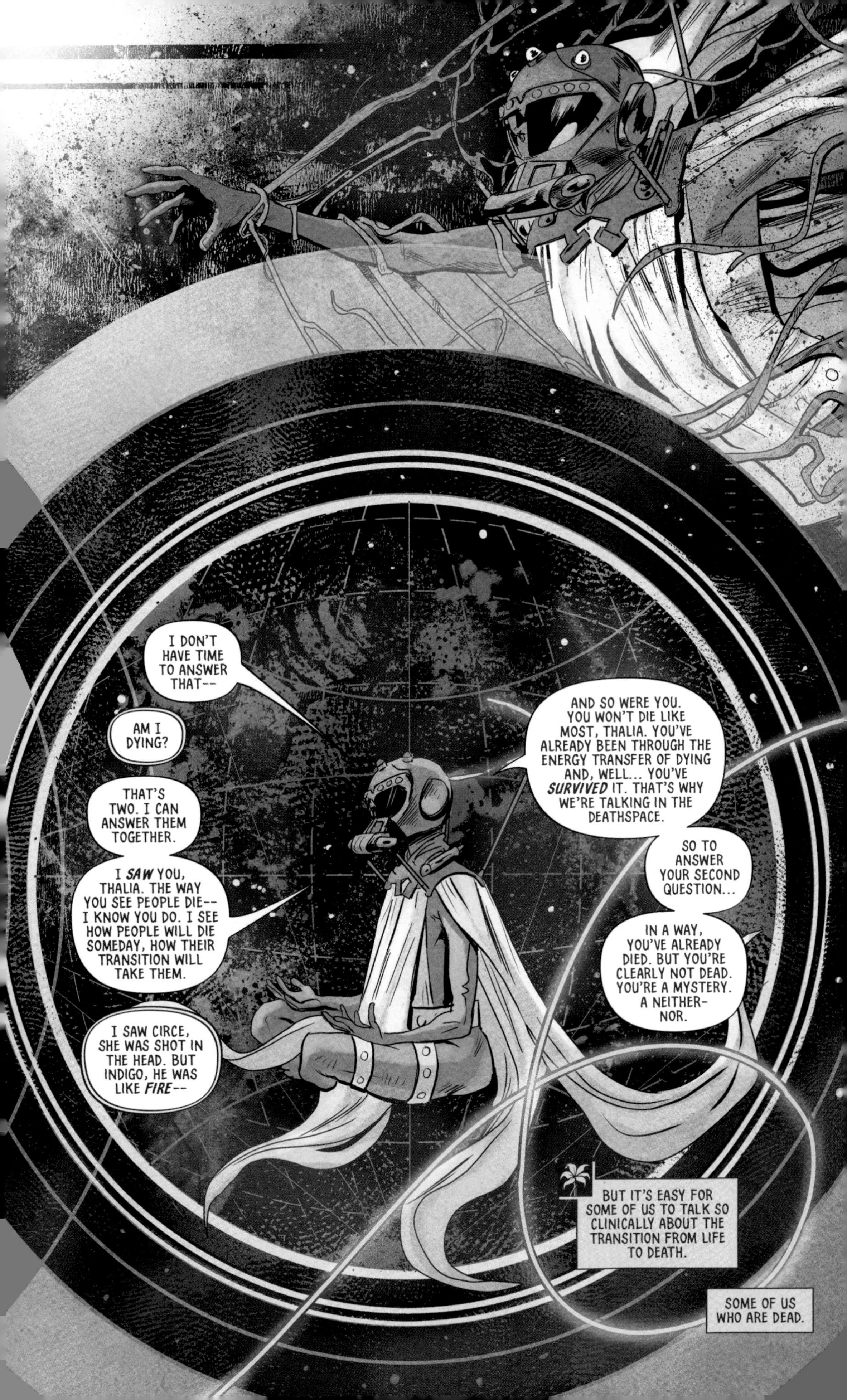
AM I DYING?
I DON'T HAVE TIME TO ANSWER THAT--
THAT'S TWO. I CAN ANSWER THEM TOGETHER.
I SAW YOU, THALIA. THE WAY YOU SEE PEOPLE DIE-- I KNOW YOU DO. I SEE HOW PEOPLE WILL DIE SOMEDAY, HOW THEIR TRANSITION WILL TAKE THEM.
I SAW CIRCE, SHE WAS SHOT IN THE HEAD. BUT INDIGO, HE WAS LIKE FIRE--
AND SO WERE YOU. YOU WON'T DIE LIKE MOST, THALIA. YOU'VE ALREADY BEEN THROUGH THE ENERGY TRANSFER OF DYING AND, WELL... YOU'VE SURVIVED IT. THAT'S WHY WE'RE TALKING IN THE DEATHSPACE.
SO TO ANSWER YOUR SECOND QUESTION...
IN A WAY, YOU'VE ALREADY DIED. BUT YOU'RE CLEARLY NOT DEAD. YOU'RE A MYSTERY. A NEITHER-NOR.
BUT IT'S EASY FOR SOME OF US TO TALK SO CLINICALLY ABOUT THE TRANSITION FROM LIFE TO DEATH.
SOME OF US WHO ARE DEAD.

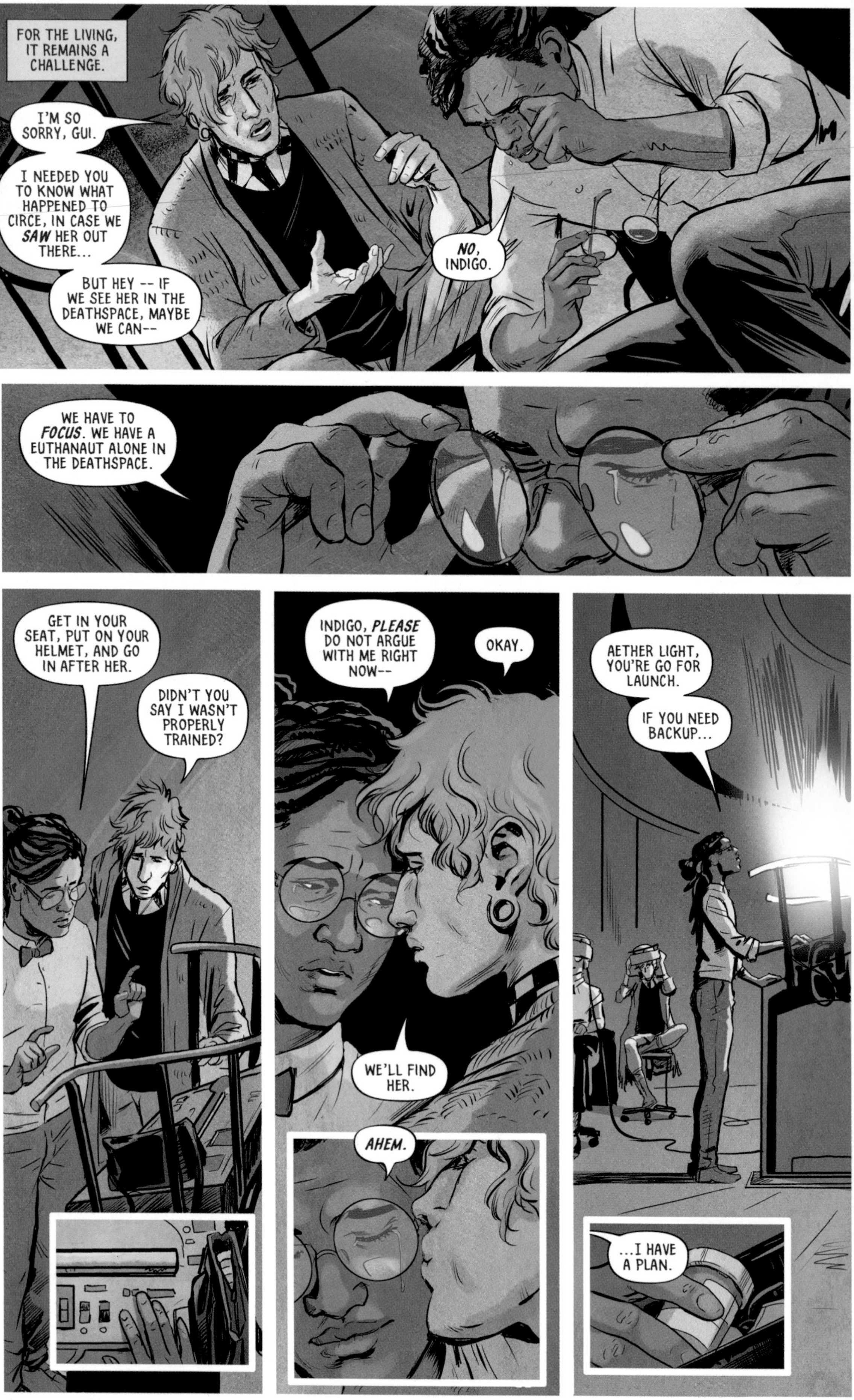
FOR THE LIVING, IT REMAINS A CHALLENGE.
I'M SO SORRY, GUI.
I NEEDED YOU TO KNOW WHAT HAPPENED TO CIRCE, IN CASE WE SAW HER OUT THERE...
BUT HEY -- IF WE SEE HER IN THE DEATHSPACE, MAYBE WE CAN--
NO, INDIGO.
WE HAVE TO FOCUS. WE HAVE A EUTHANAUT ALONE IN THE DEATHSPACE.
GET IN YOUR SEAT, PUT ON YOUR HELMET, AND GO IN AFTER HER.
DIDN'T YOU SAY I WASN'T PROPERLY TRAINED?
INDIGO, PLEASE DO NOT ARGUE WITH ME RIGHT NOW--
OKAY.
WE'LL FIND HER.
AHEM.
AETHER LIGHT, YOU'RE GO FOR LAUNCH.
IF YOU NEED BACKUP...
...I HAVE A PLAN.

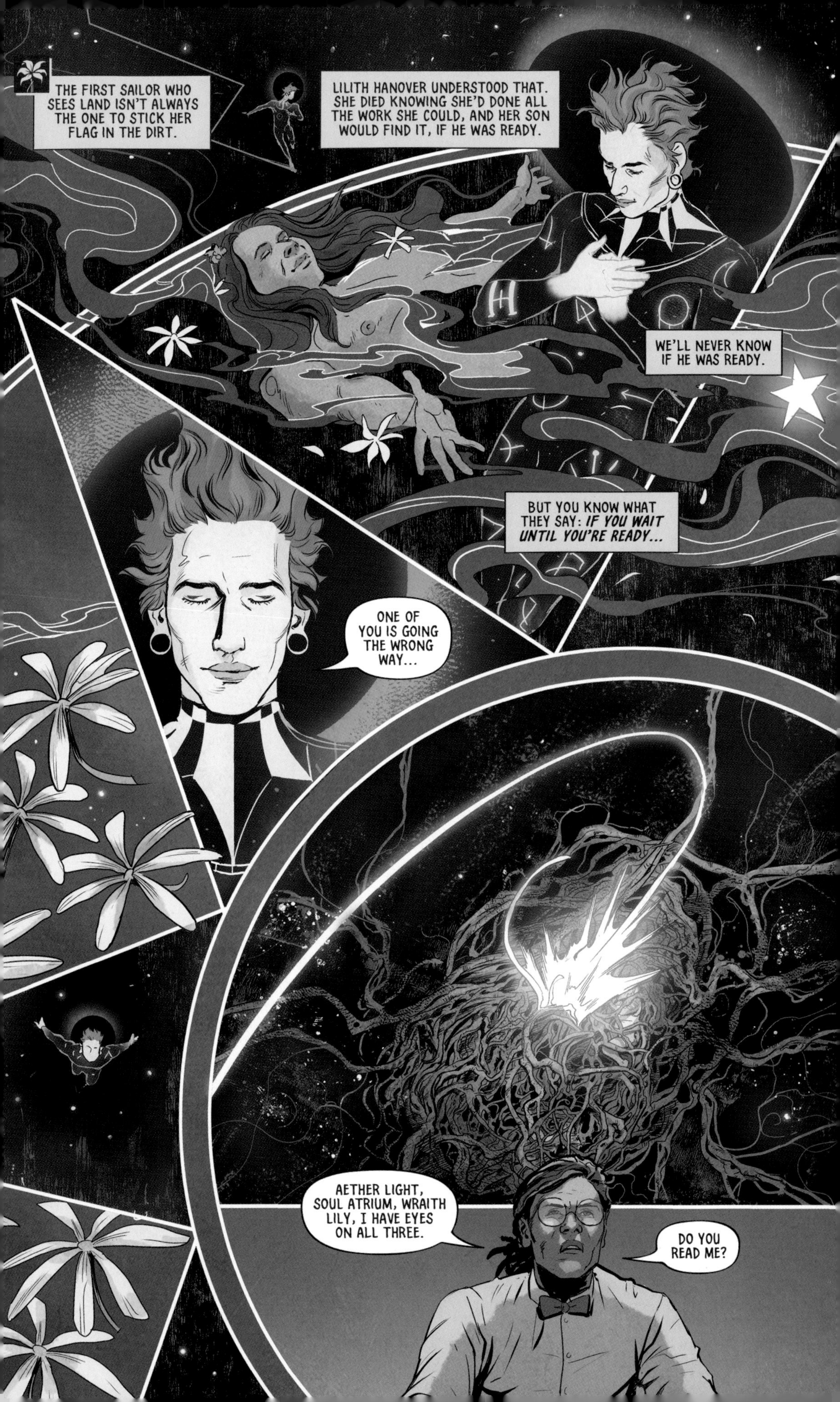
THE FIRST SAILOR WHO SEES LAND ISN'T ALWAYS THE ONE TO STICK HER FLAG IN THE DIRT.
LILITH HANOVER UNDERSTOOD THAT. SHE DIED KNOWING SHE'D DONE ALL THE WORK SHE COULD, AND HER SON WOULD FIND IT, IF HE WAS READY.
WE'LL NEVER KNOW IF HE WAS READY.
BUT YOU KNOW WHAT THEY SAY: *IF YOU WAIT UNTIL YOU'RE READY...*
ONE OF YOU IS GOING THE WRONG WAY...
AETHER LIGHT, SOUL ATRIUM, WRAITH LILY, I HAVE EYES ON ALL THREE.
DO YOU READ ME?

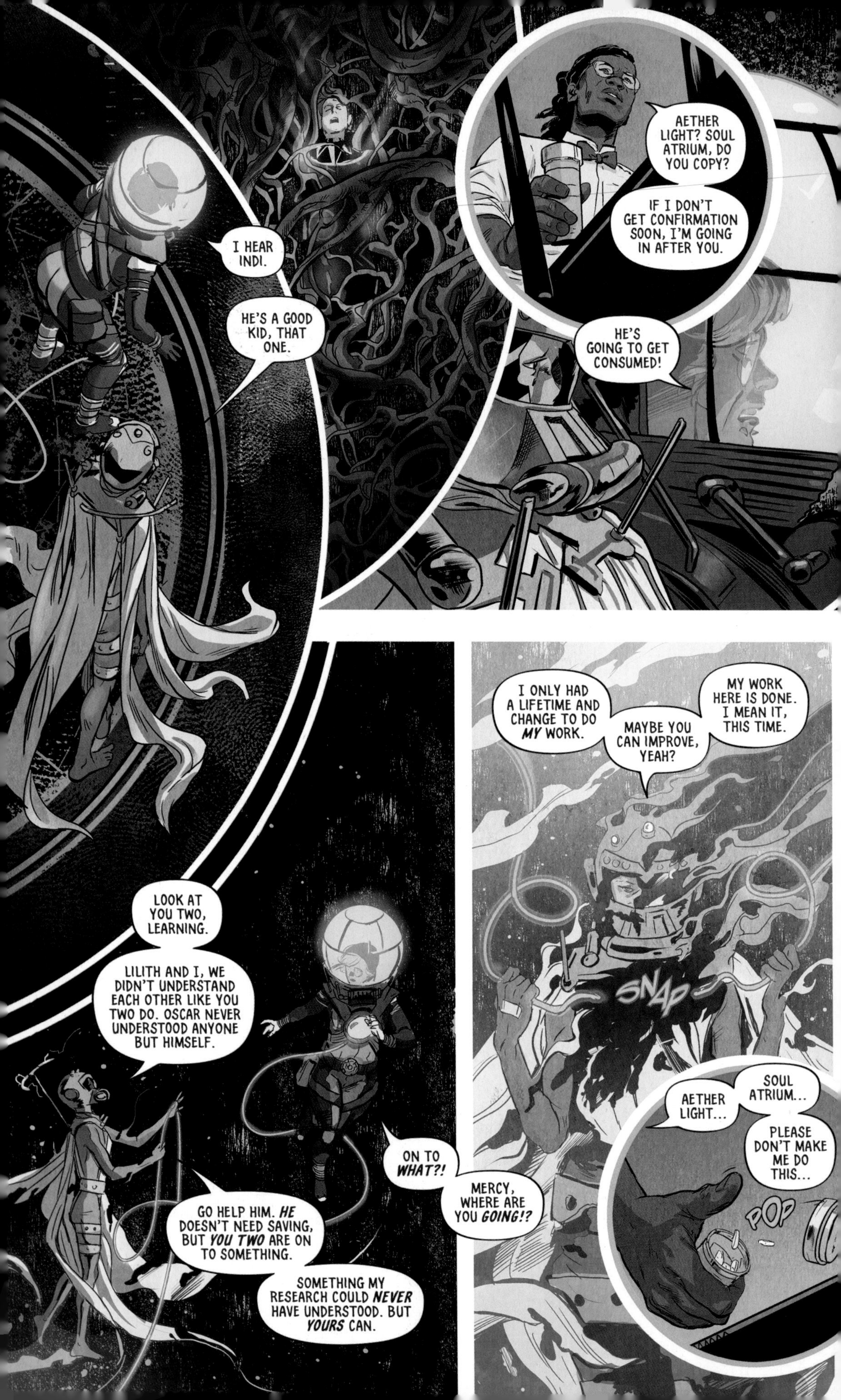

I HEAR INDI.
HE'S A GOOD KID, THAT ONE.
AETHER LIGHT? SOUL ATRIUM, DO YOU COPY?
IF I DON'T GET CONFIRMATION SOON, I'M GOING IN AFTER YOU.
HE'S GOING TO GET CONSUMED!
LOOK AT YOU TWO, LEARNING.
LILITH AND I, WE DIDN'T UNDERSTAND EACH OTHER LIKE YOU TWO DO. OSCAR NEVER UNDERSTOOD ANYONE BUT HIMSELF.
GO HELP HIM. *HE* DOESN'T NEED SAVING, BUT *YOU TWO* ARE ON TO SOMETHING.
SOMETHING MY RESEARCH COULD *NEVER* HAVE UNDERSTOOD. BUT *YOURS* CAN.
ON TO *WHAT?!*
MERCY, WHERE ARE YOU *GOING!?*
I ONLY HAD A LIFETIME AND CHANGE TO DO *MY* WORK.
MAYBE YOU CAN IMPROVE, YEAH?
MY WORK HERE IS DONE. I MEAN IT, THIS TIME.
SNAP
AETHER LIGHT...
SOUL ATRIUM...
PLEASE DON'T MAKE ME DO THIS...
POP

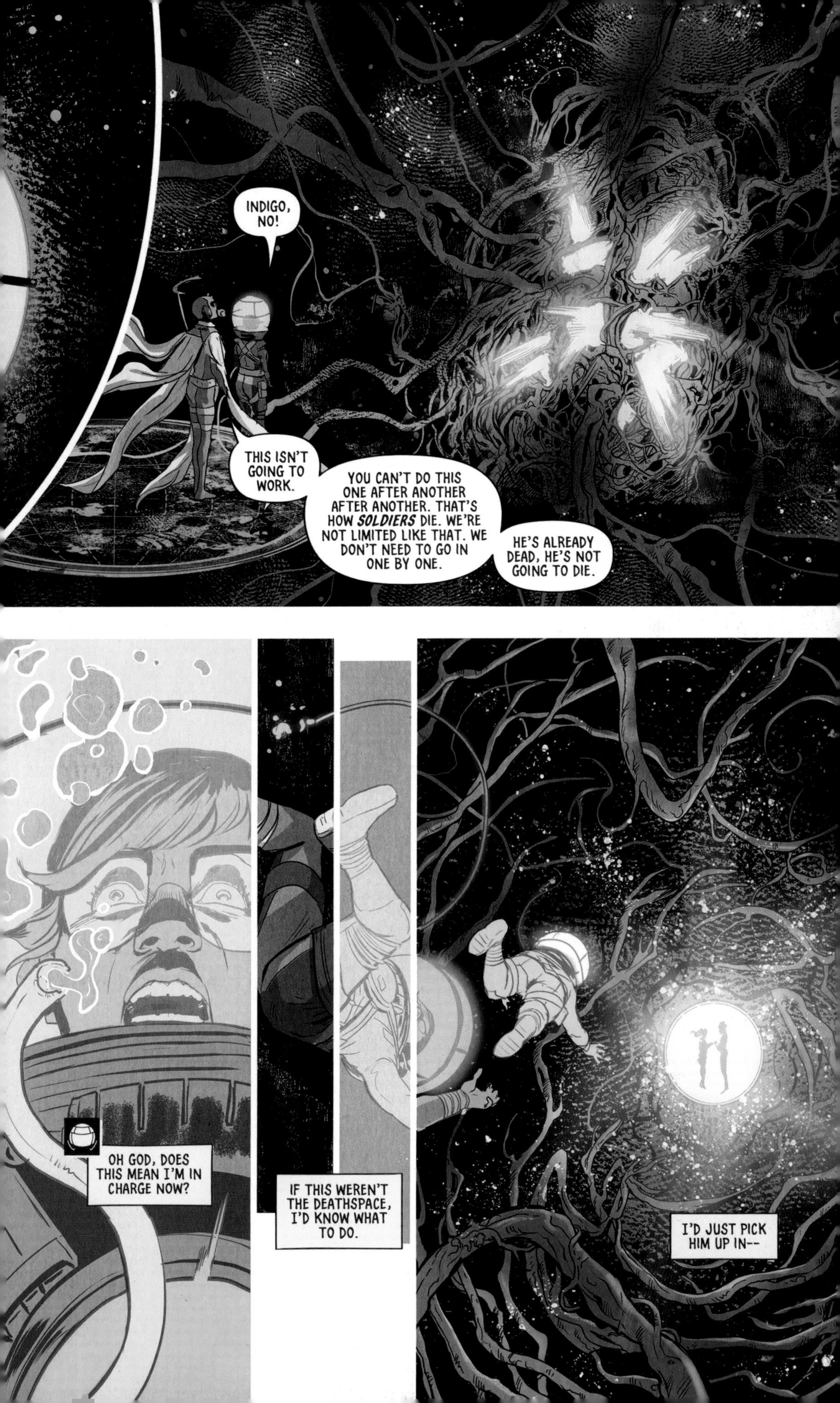
INDIGO, NO!
THIS ISN'T GOING TO WORK.
YOU CAN'T DO THIS ONE AFTER ANOTHER AFTER ANOTHER. THAT'S HOW *SOLDIERS* DIE. WE'RE NOT LIMITED LIKE THAT. WE DON'T NEED TO GO IN ONE BY ONE.
HE'S ALREADY DEAD, HE'S NOT GOING TO DIE.
OH GOD, DOES THIS MEAN I'M IN CHARGE NOW?
IF THIS WEREN'T THE DEATHSPACE, I'D KNOW WHAT TO DO.
I'D JUST PICK HIM UP IN--

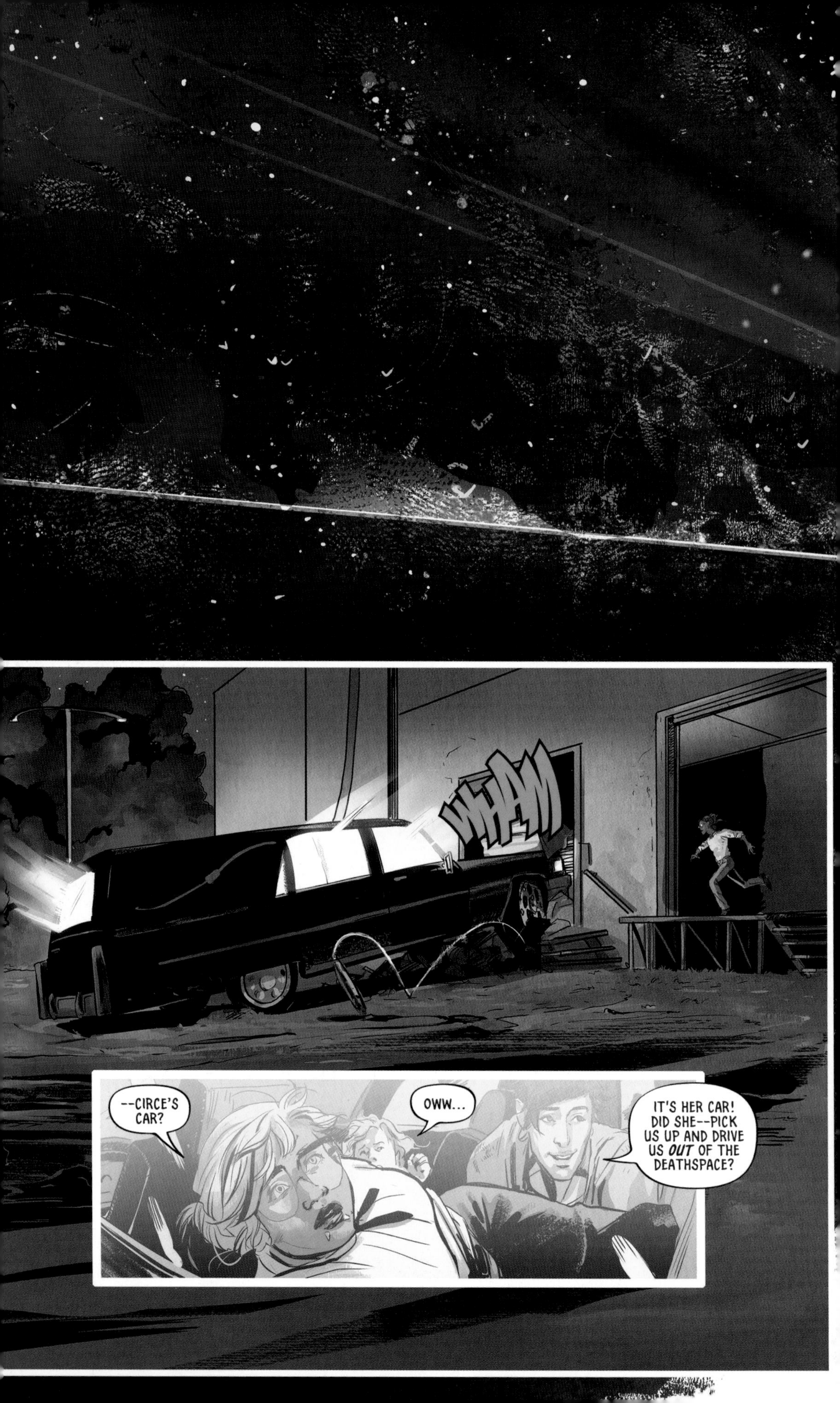
WHAM
--CIRCE'S CAR?
OWW...
IT'S HER CAR! DID SHE--PICK US UP AND DRIVE US OUT OF THE DEATHSPACE?

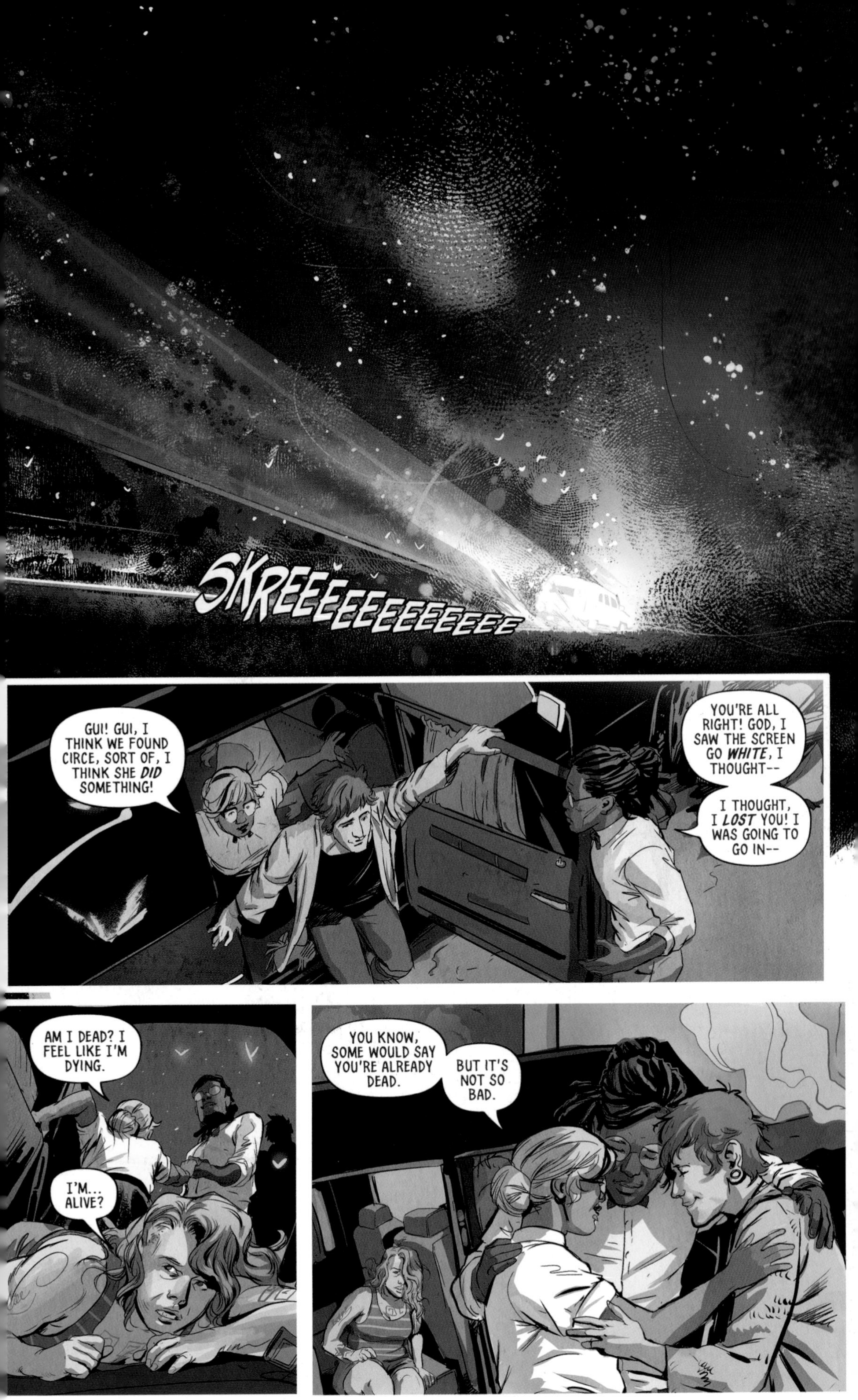
SKREEEEEEEEEEEEEE
GUI! GUI, I THINK WE FOUND CIRCE, SORT OF, I THINK SHE *DID* SOMETHING!
YOU'RE ALL RIGHT! GOD, I SAW THE SCREEN GO *WHITE*, I THOUGHT--
I THOUGHT, I *LOST* YOU! I WAS GOING TO GO IN--
AM I DEAD? I FEEL LIKE I'M DYING.
I'M... ALIVE?
YOU KNOW, SOME WOULD SAY YOU'RE ALREADY DEAD.
BUT IT'S NOT SO BAD.

MERCY WOLFE
1956-2018

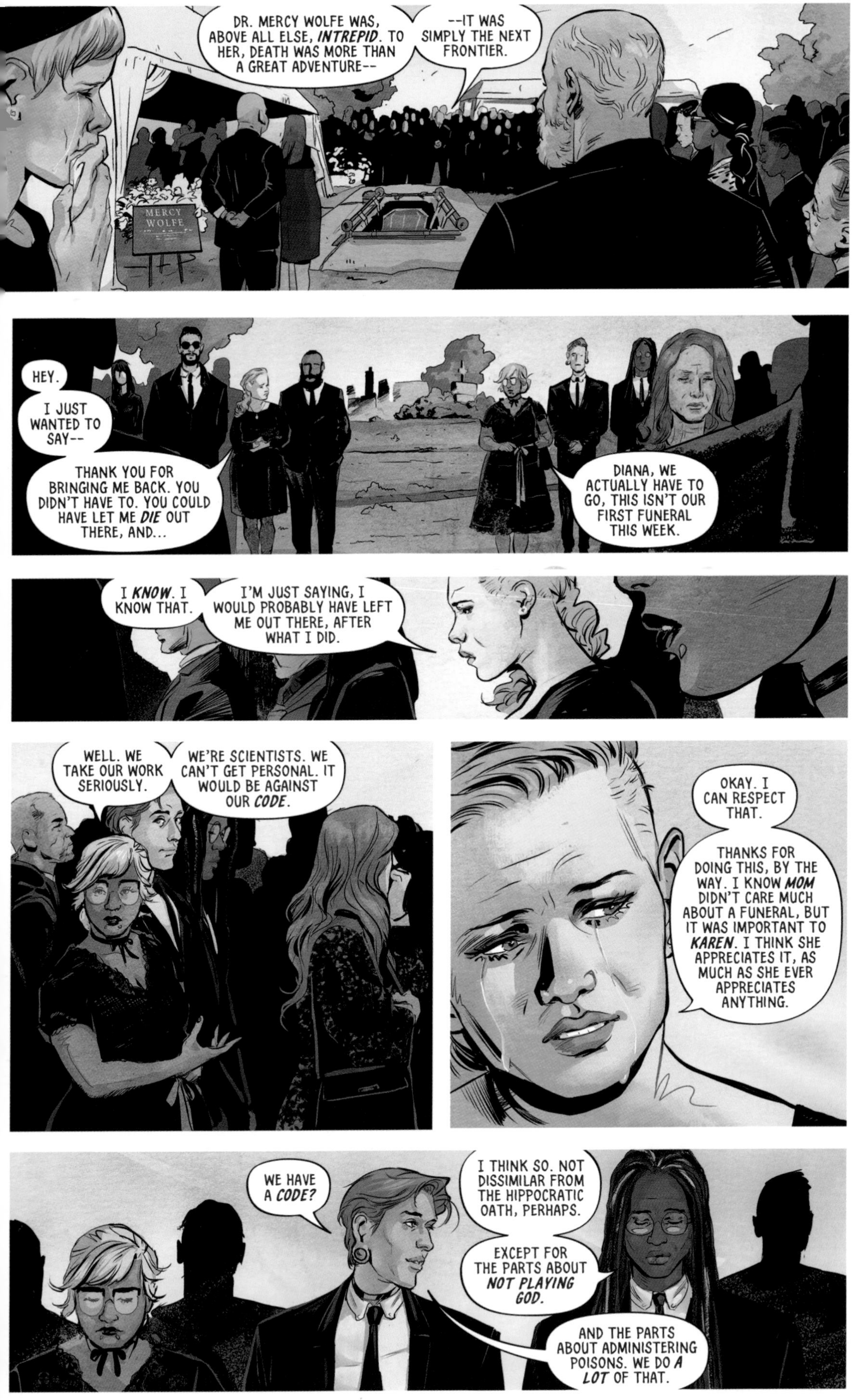

DR. MERCY WOLFE WAS, ABOVE ALL ELSE, INTREPID. TO HER, DEATH WAS MORE THAN A GREAT ADVENTURE--
--IT WAS SIMPLY THE NEXT FRONTIER.
MERCY WOLFE
HEY.
I JUST WANTED TO SAY--
THANK YOU FOR BRINGING ME BACK. YOU DIDN'T HAVE TO. YOU COULD HAVE LET ME DIE OUT THERE, AND...
DIANA, WE ACTUALLY HAVE TO GO, THIS ISN'T OUR FIRST FUNERAL THIS WEEK.
I KNOW. I KNOW THAT.
I'M JUST SAYING, I WOULD PROBABLY HAVE LEFT ME OUT THERE, AFTER WHAT I DID.
WELL. WE TAKE OUR WORK SERIOUSLY.
WE'RE SCIENTISTS. WE CAN'T GET PERSONAL. IT WOULD BE AGAINST OUR CODE.
OKAY. I CAN RESPECT THAT.
THANKS FOR DOING THIS, BY THE WAY. I KNOW MOM DIDN'T CARE MUCH ABOUT A FUNERAL, BUT IT WAS IMPORTANT TO KAREN. I THINK SHE APPRECIATES IT, AS MUCH AS SHE EVER APPRECIATES ANYTHING.
WE HAVE A CODE?
I THINK SO. NOT DISSIMILAR FROM THE HIPPOCRATIC OATH, PERHAPS.
EXCEPT FOR THE PARTS ABOUT NOT PLAYING GOD.
AND THE PARTS ABOUT ADMINISTERING POISONS. WE DO A LOT OF THAT.

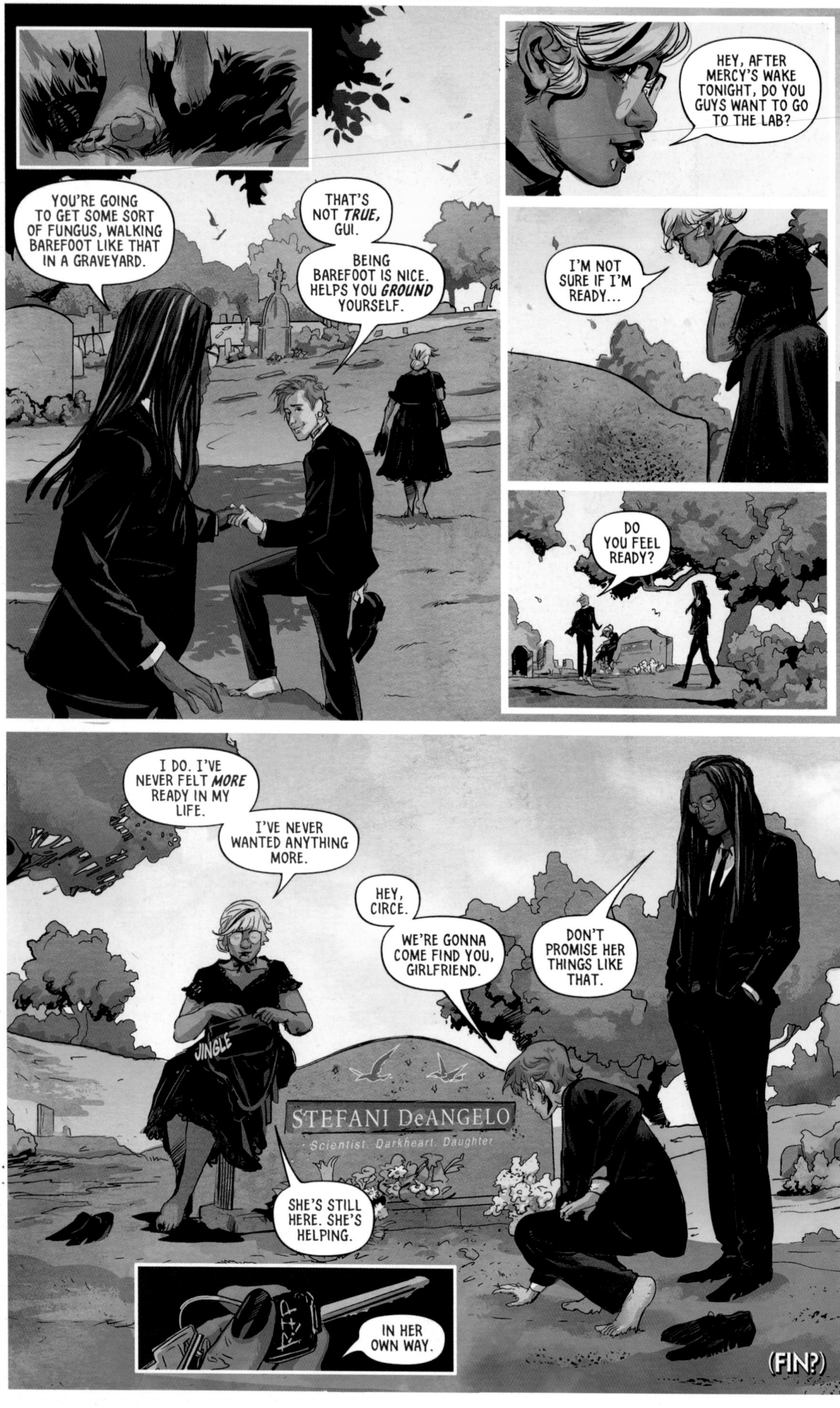

HEY, AFTER MERCY'S WAKE TONIGHT, DO YOU GUYS WANT TO GO TO THE LAB?
YOU'RE GOING TO GET SOME SORT OF FUNGUS, WALKING BAREFOOT LIKE THAT IN A GRAVEYARD.
THAT'S NOT *TRUE,* GUI.
BEING BAREFOOT IS NICE. HELPS YOU *GROUND* YOURSELF.
I'M NOT SURE IF I'M READY...
DO YOU FEEL READY?
I DO. I'VE NEVER FELT *MORE* READY IN MY LIFE.
I'VE NEVER WANTED ANYTHING MORE.
HEY, CIRCE.
WE'RE GONNA COME FIND YOU, GIRLFRIEND.
DON'T PROMISE HER THINGS LIKE THAT.
JINGLE
STEFANI DeANGELO
Scientist. Darkheart. Daughter
SHE'S STILL HERE. SHE'S HELPING.
R.I.P
IN HER OWN WAY.
(FIN?)

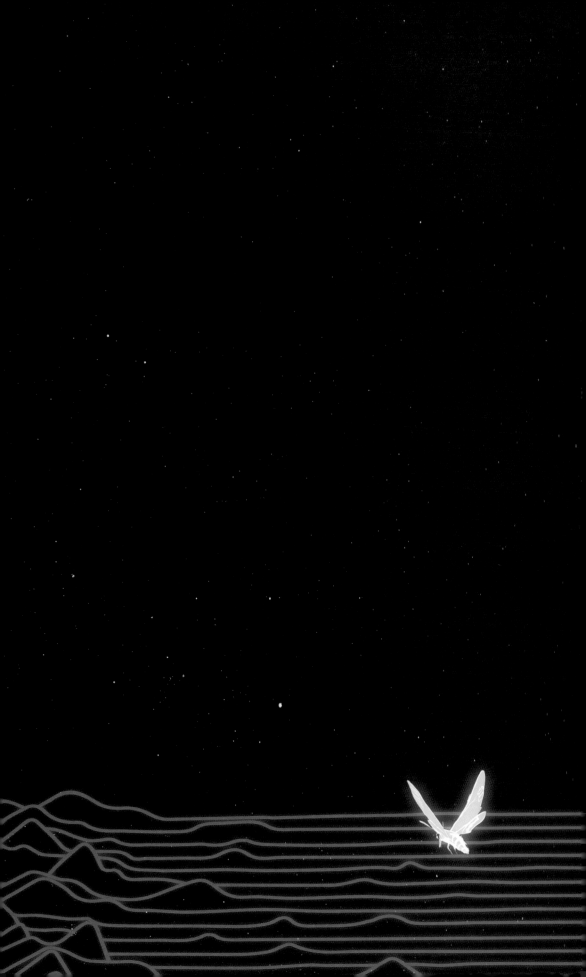

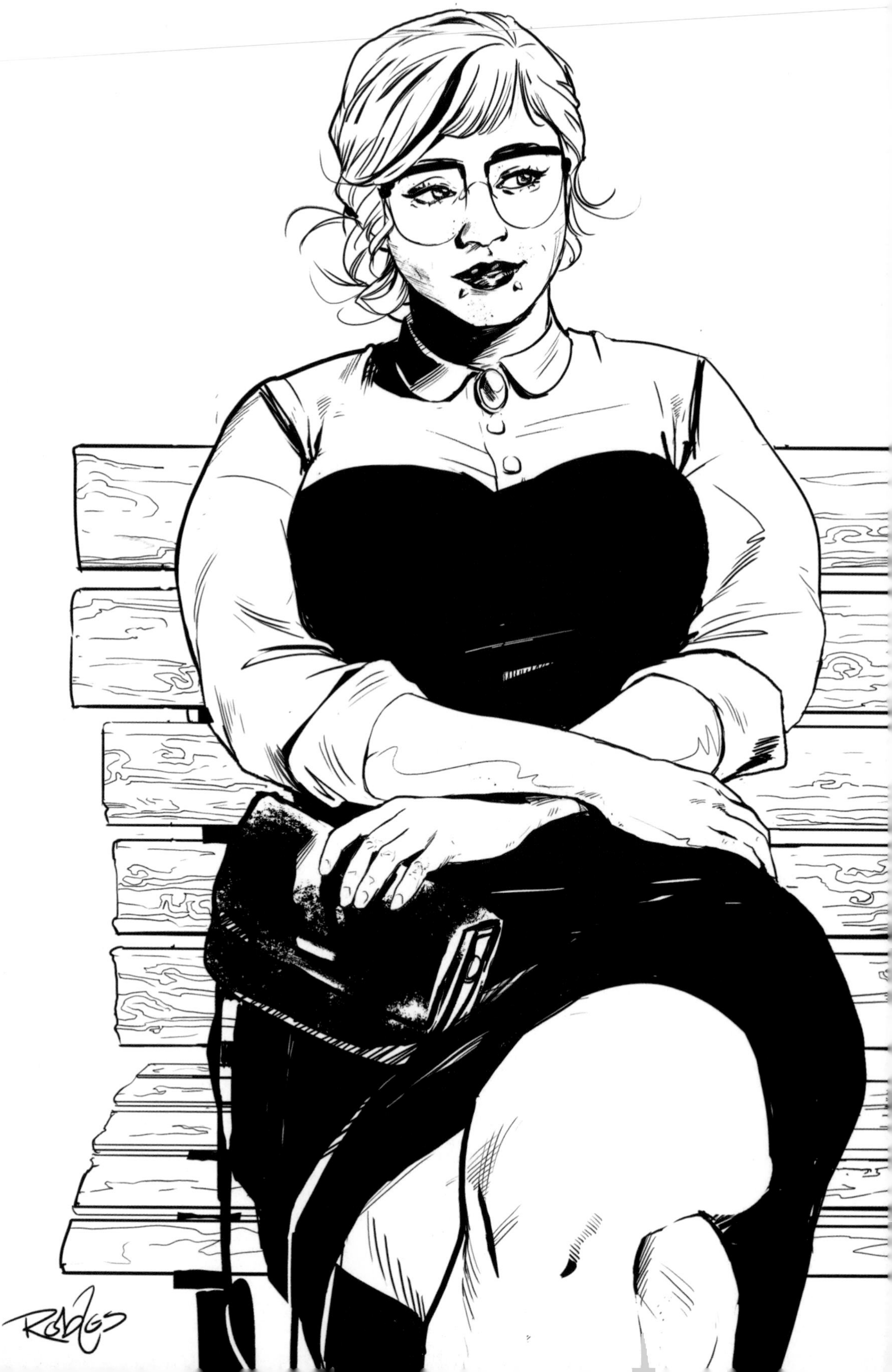

EUTHANAUTS #1 variant cover by MARK BUCKINGHAM & EVA de la CRUZ

EUTHANAUTS #2 variant cover by CAITLIN YARSKY

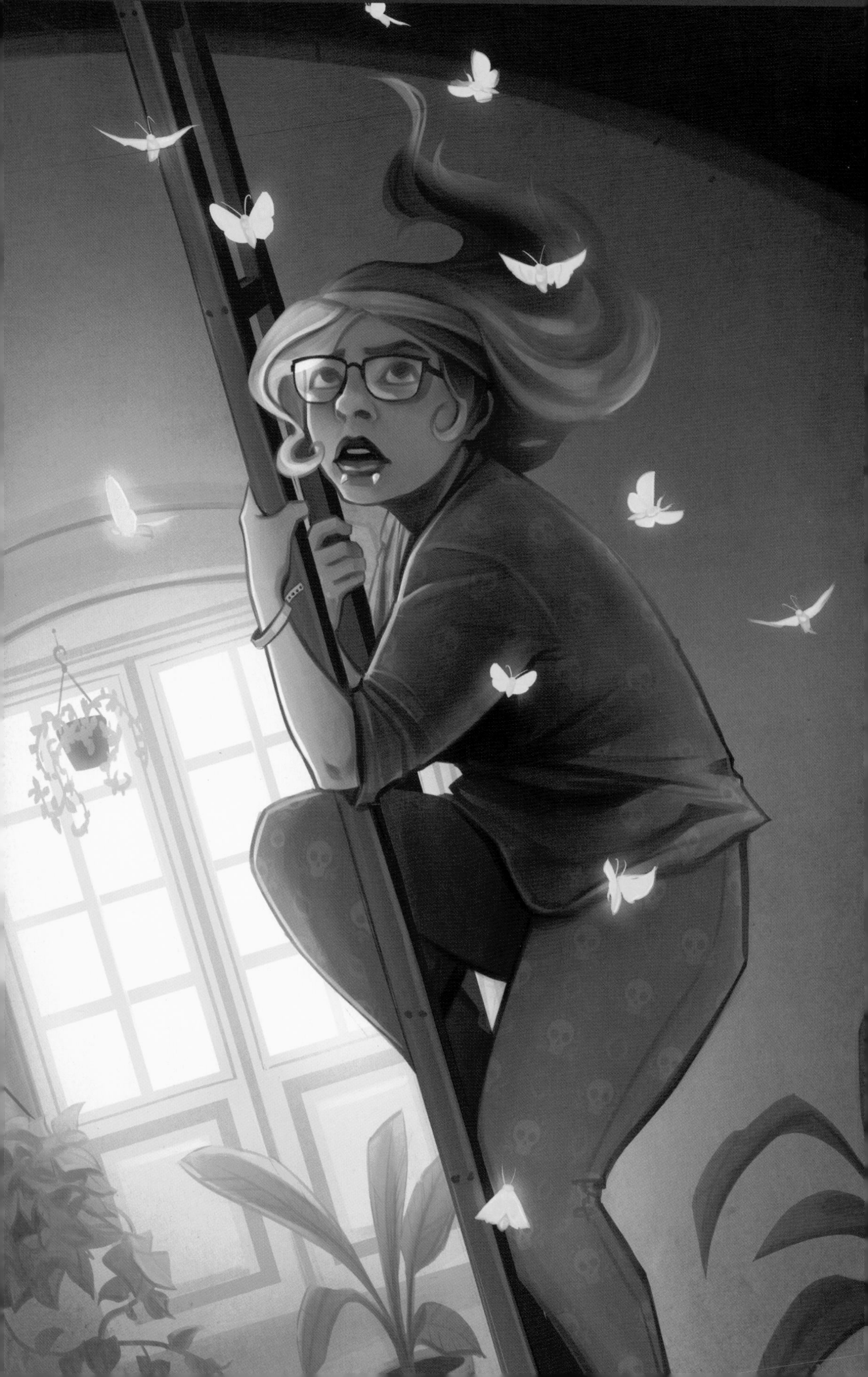

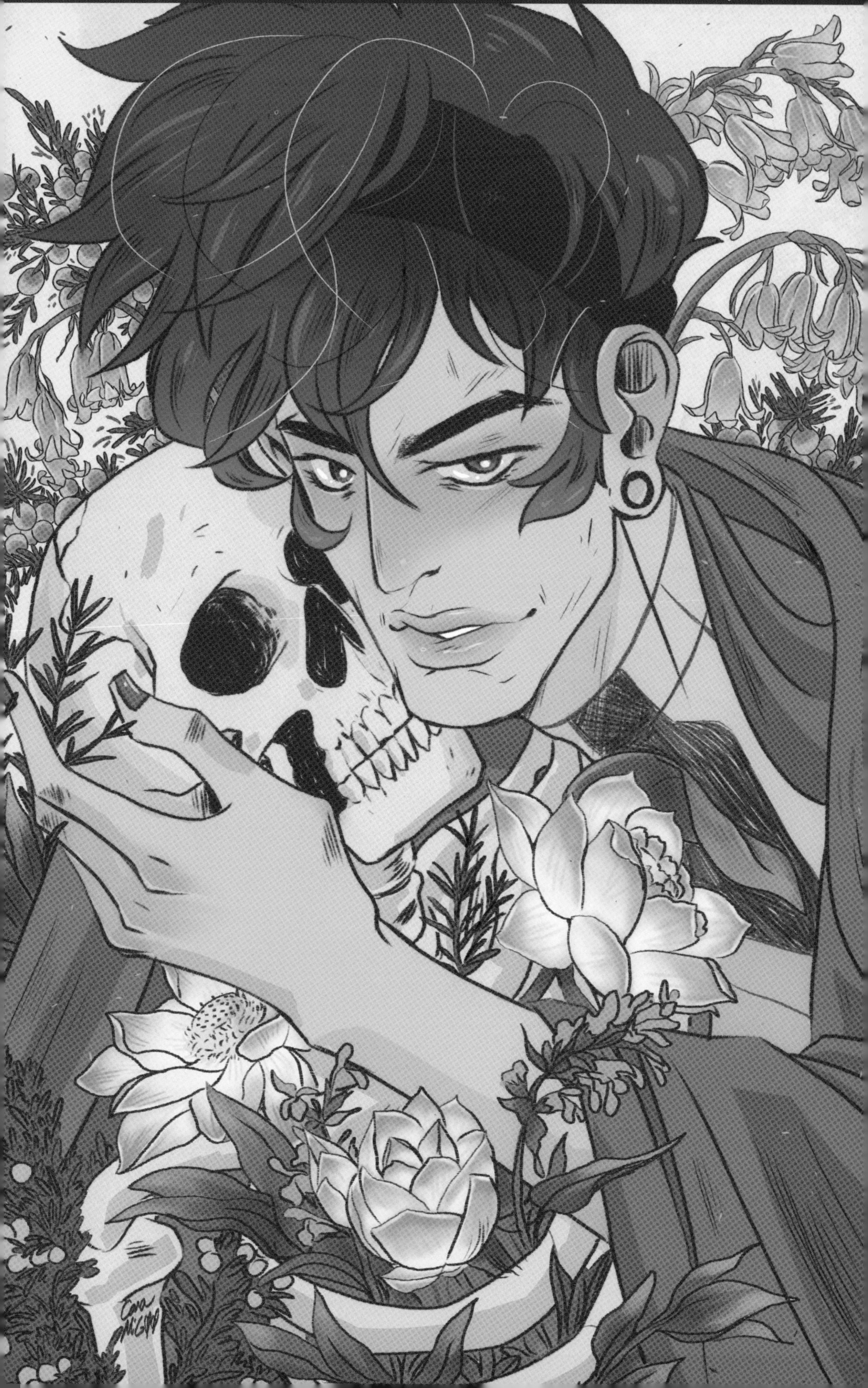

EUTHANAUTS #3 variant cover by CARA McGEE

EUTHANAUTS #4 variant cover by KATIE SKELLY

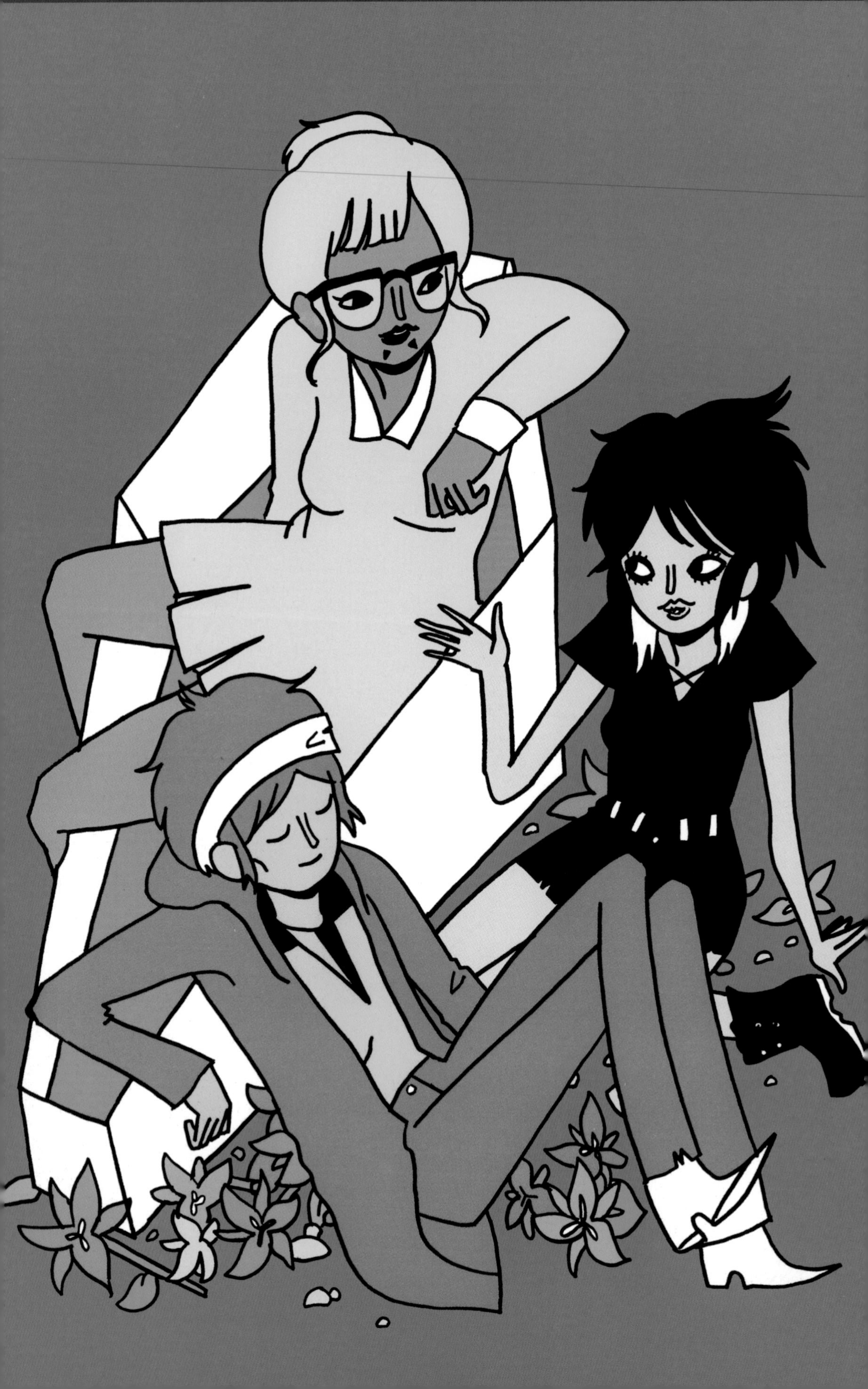

EUTHANAUTS #5 variant cover by MARLEY ZARCONE & TAMRA BONVILLAIN

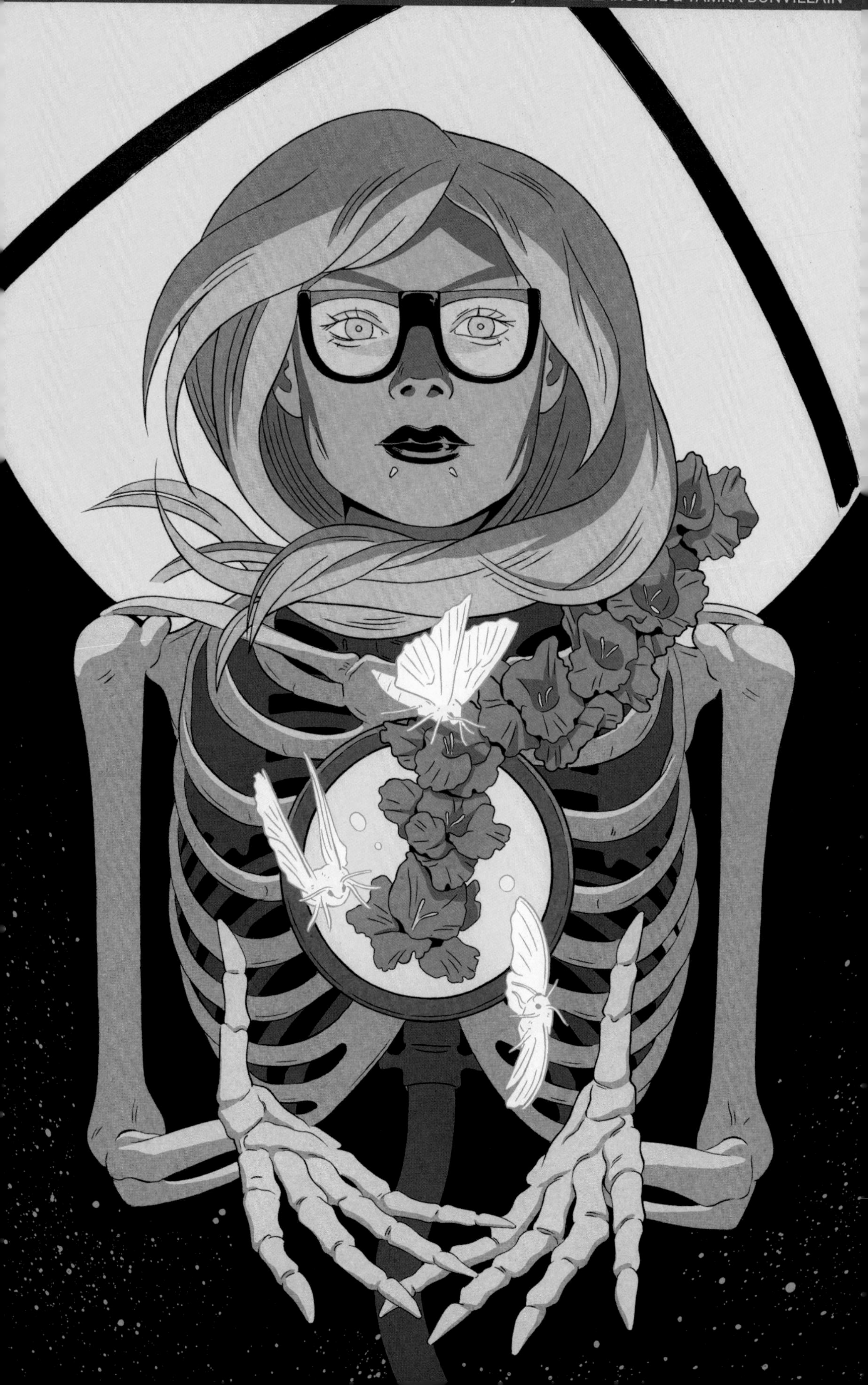

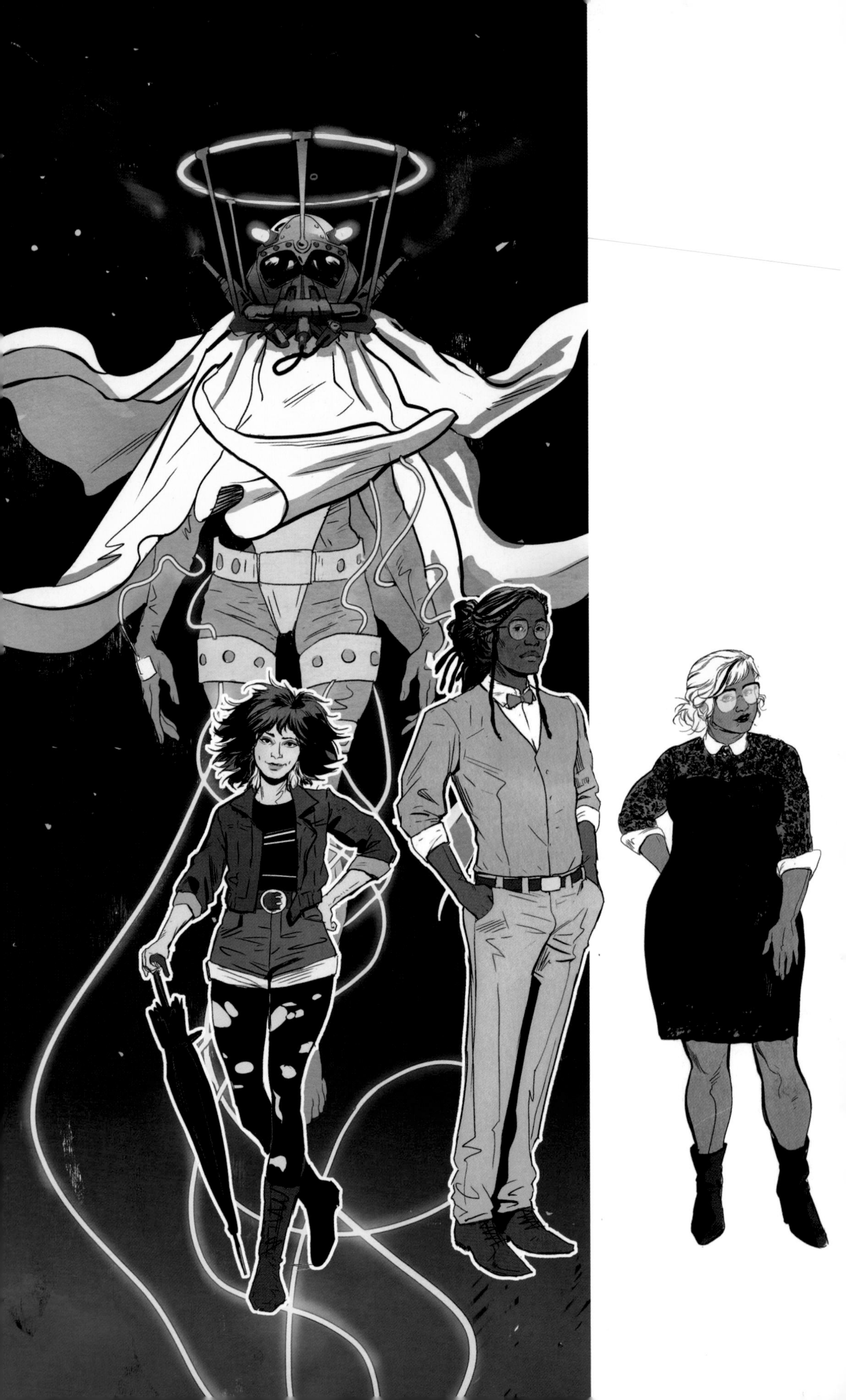

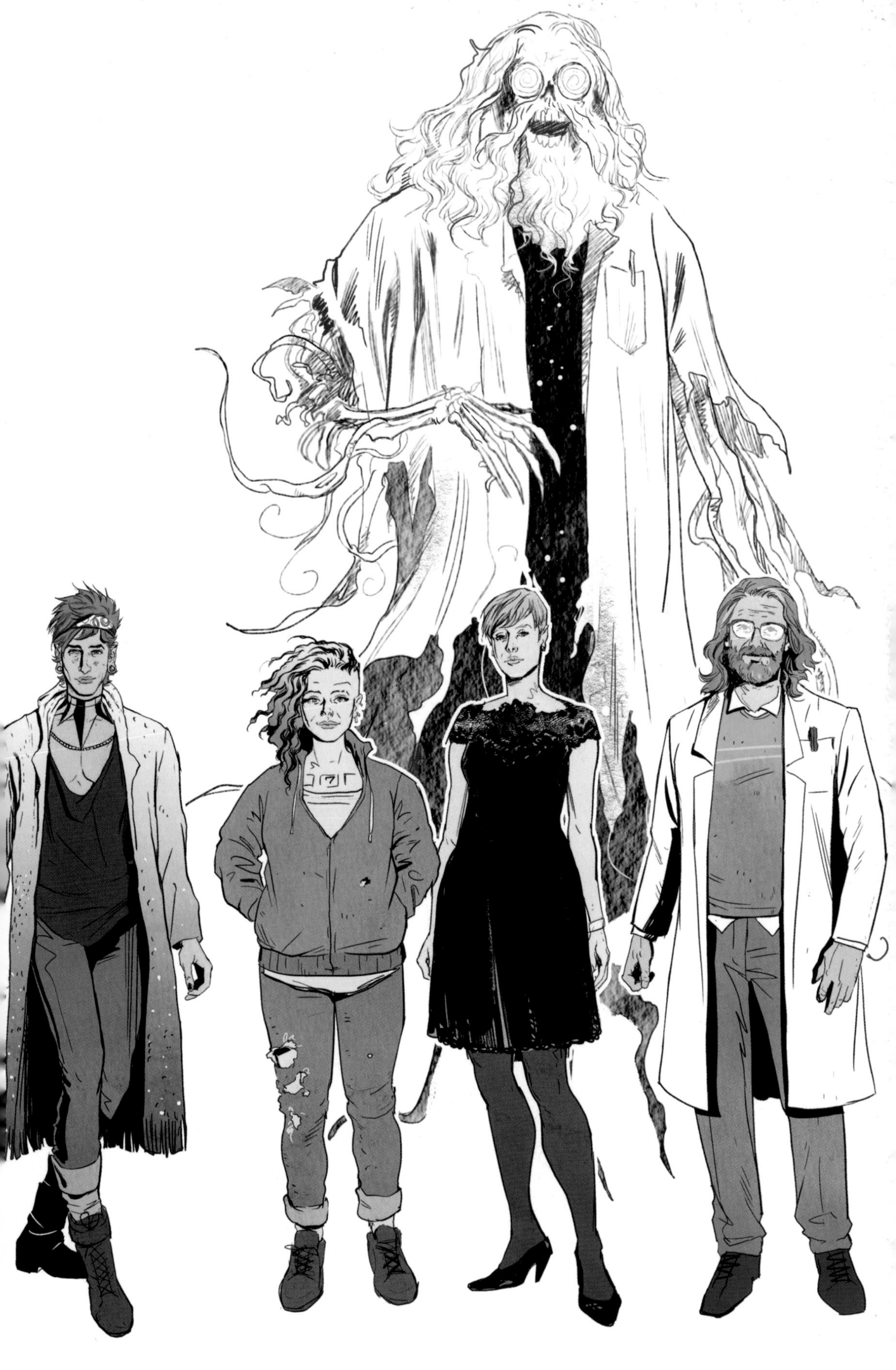

TINI HOWARD

is the writer of EUTHANAUTS, ASSASSINISTAS and GHOST-WALK WITH ME. She is a writer and witch who lives in the Carolina wetlands with her partner and their two sons, who are cats. In addition to her work at BLACK CROWN HQ, she writes *Rick and Morty*, *Hack/Slash:Resurrection* and *Captain America* among others. @TiniHoward

NICK ROBLES

is the artist of EUTHANAUTS. He's worked with BOOM!, IDW, Dark Horse and Vault. A freelance artist from southern Louisiana, he is self-taught and works with digital tools and programs as his main medium. Nick has dabbled in the arts as far back as he can remember — whether it be drawing, music or writing — and he can't see the dabbling going away any time soon. @ArtofNickRobles

EVA DE LA CRUZ

is the colorist on EUTHANAUTS. She has been collaborating with 2000AD and Vertigo/DC Comics for more than a decade.

ADITYA BIDIKAR

is BLACK CROWN's esteemed house letterer and the recipient of Broken Frontier's 2017 Best Letterer Award. He designed the fonts and lettered the first two issues of EUTHANAUTS. Based in India, Adi also letters *Motor Crush* and *Grafity's Wall*. @adityab adityab.net.

NEIL UYETAKE

is the letterer of EUTHANAUTS issues 3, 4 and 5.

MEGAN BROWN

is an Assistant Editor and BLACK CROWN's San Diego connection. When she's not racking up a tab at the Black Crown Pub, you can find her at one of the coffee shops around town, perfecting the art of being a struggling writer. @megan_mb

CHASE MAROTZ

is the Associate Editor of BLACK CROWN.
A self-proclaimed "Johnny-on-the-spot," he provides much-needed eyes, ears, hands and feet between the Los Angeles-based BCHQ and the IDW mothership in San Diego. @thrillothechase

SHELLY BOND

is the editor and curator of BLACK CROWN. Driven to edit + curate comic books, crush deadlines and innovate for over a quarter-century, Bond lives in Los Angeles with husband Philip, son Spencer, five guitars and a drum kit. @sxbond @blackcrownhq and blackcrown.pub

"...a truly brilliant, cohesive, curated line of creator-owned comics that will pick up the comics industry, shake it up, and spit it out."
— Comicosity

kid lobotomy · black crown quarterly · assassinistas · punks not dead · euthanauts · house amok · lodger
@blackcrownhq   blackcrown.pub

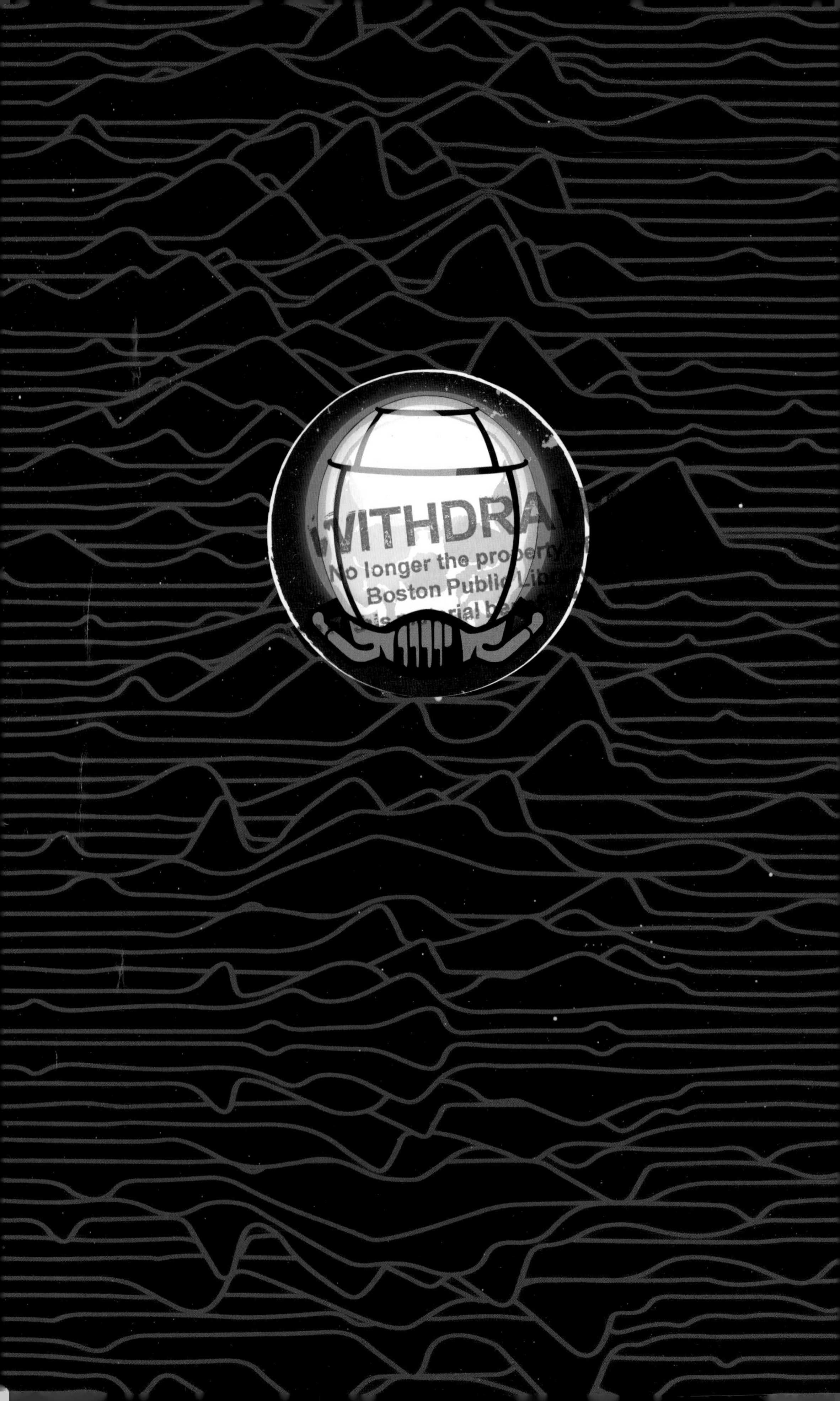